THE DRAWINGS OF FRANK LLOYD WRIGHT

the drawings of

Frank Lloyd Wright

ARTHUR DREXLER

PUBLISHED FOR THE MUSEUM OF MODERN ART BY HORIZON PRESS, NEW YORK

The drawings included in this book were first selected for an exhibition of original Frank Lloyd Wright drawings held at The Museum of Modern Art, New York, from March 14 to May 6, 1962. The preliminary selection of drawings was made at Taliesin, Wisconsin, by Arthur Drexler, Director, and Wilder Green, Assistant Director, of the Museum's Department of Architecture and Design. Wilder Green made the final selection for the exhibition and designed the installation; the final selection of material for the book was made by the author.

On behalf of the Museum I wish to thank Mrs. Frank Lloyd Wright, President of The Frank Lloyd Wright Foundation, for placing at our disposal the Foundation's archive of drawings. Without Mrs. Wright's generous assistance, patience, and sympathy, neither the exhibition nor this book would have been possible.

We are grateful to the many members of The Frank Lloyd Wright Foundation and the Taliesin Associated Architects who have given so generously of their time and knowledge. I wish particularly to thank Mr. William Wesley Peters, Chief Architect of the Taliesin Associated Architects; Mr. Eugene Masselink, Secretary to The Frank Lloyd Wright Foundation; and Mr. Jack Howe of the Taliesin Associated Architects, for their assistance and advice.

Mr. and Mrs. David Wheatley and Mr. John Amarantides have cataloged many of the drawings in the Foundation's archives, and were especially helpful in organizing material for selection.

Mr. George Barrows, of the Museum's Department of Architecture and Design, has photographed for purposes of record all the drawings included in this book, and has rendered assistance in every phase of the work.

I wish to thank Mr. Philip C. Johnson for his timely generosity which has enabled the Museum to undertake the restoration of certain drawings most urgently in need of repair.

—A.D.

Library of Congress Catalog Card Number 62-11236
© 1962 The Frank Lloyd Wright Foundation
Printed in the United States of America

ISBN: 0-8180-0019-8

CONTENTS

The Taliesin archives hold an estimated 8,000 drawings. Most of them are of technical or historic interest, and they provide the specialist with an invaluable record of Frank Lloyd Wright's work. They comprise a history of ideas still new, still relevant, and often untried. But there are several hundred drawings that are more than a record: they are beautiful drawings of great buildings. Their quality comes through to us from pages sometimes so faded and torn that they have acquired, like Japanese paintings, an exotic fragility Wright himself knew how to savor.

Frank Lloyd Wright's published drawings are part of every architect's education. They have long since entered the life and colored the history of architecture wherever it is understood as an art, as will no doubt those of his drawings that are published here for the first time. But however beautiful the drawings may be in themselves, they cannot be separated from the thought and feeling that made them so; indeed, the drawings sometimes tell us more about Wright's thought than is apparent in the finished buildings. They are the pure reflection of an attitude irreconcilably opposed to that manifested by the recent history of modern architecture. It is worth considering what Wright's drawings mean not only in relation to his own work but to some aspects of architecture as it is practiced now.

From the late 'twenties until the mid-fifties most architects have preferred to think of their work as the result of rational decisions. The plan, for instance, has been considered the primary instrument by which architectural spaces are to be organized: by implication the ideal building could be deduced in its entirety from its plan alone. Embarrassed by whatever cannot be attributed to pragmatic requirements, and intimidated by the rigors of the plan as an abstract discipline (increasingly a discipline of structural details), architects have tried to persuade themselves that their favorite forms are the inevitable result of an almost scientific analysis of practical problems. Most often they have worked from plan to elevation and then, in order to see what their buildings look like, have made perspective drawings or highly detailed scale models. Few architects now rely on perspective drawings for any purpose more serious than to sell the building to the client, which is serious enough, and few architects have the time or the inclination to draw. Those who do find drawings valuable for presentation to the client, or for publication, most often obtain the services of a professional draftsman who "renders" the building in any one of several popular styles.

The advantage of the model is that it can be photographed with a startling realism that no drawing can match, and that it offers architects and clients alike the chance to study a design in three dimensions and from all possible angles. But the scale model does not yield such an advantage without imposing some subtle restrictions of its own. For the architect, fidelity to an original vision gradually shifts away from capturing the elusive life of a sketch, and becomes instead a matter of holding fast to the requirements of the model. Like the industrial artifacts it imitates, the model is valued according to its impersonal precision. A kind of success is achieved when the real building seems itself to be a model, made at giant scale and carried bodily to the site.

Whatever may be the present reaction to it, such architecture is not easily dismissed. Its practitioners are not, as Wright sometimes seemed to be saying, necessarily insincere or perverse. There is a sense in which an architecture related to product design does indeed exalt the society that produces it. Architecture as "the will of an epoch" evolves, at its best, from the acceptance of what is considered always and universally good, as well as from the acceptance of those bizarre aspects of a commercial culture for which architecture is not an end in itself but is merely a commodity; a product among products. The techniques of design will thus be found "realistically" adapted to the problem—as the problem has been stated. Whether it is possible to enhance the product by forcing the development of more varied forms (without re-examining the idea of architecture in technology) is not yet proved, but the outcome is not hard to imagine.

Over and against this recent history the long career of Frank Lloyd Wright has been a continuous protest. Not that his work could conceivably be described as a negation: it is rather an affirmation of all things human, of whatever makes up life; if it is also a protest it is a protest against the fragmentation of life into all-consuming obsessions. It is a protest against death. To the public both Wright and his work have often seemed only a more interesting version of whatever is "modern" and, therefore, beyond comprehension. Wright's place as the greatest architect America has yet produced is obvious enough; he was also one of the most original architects in all history. But his buildings have simultaneously attracted and annoyed the very architects he might best have influenced. No single approach to Wright's work will suffice: he is vast, complex, simple and subtle, and deceptive. He protested the imitation of effects he had invented when the principle, as he thought, was ignored or misunderstood. He spoke willingly of his principles and hardly at all of his practice. That is one reason his drawings are valuable beyond their intrinsic beauty: they are a clue to the processes of his thought.

Wright has written of his preference for first visualizing a building in its entirety before beginning to sketch it out. His capacity to do so may account for the compelling clarity of the drawings, but it also makes us tend to think of them as the last phase in the development of an idea. The contrary is true. Wright's drawings were very much part of the day to day process of design. This fact is revealed not only by the preliminary sketches for perspective drawings that are now famous, but by rough sketches of elevations and plans, and by certain unpublished perspective studies which for various reasons were not carried through to completion. Often these rough sketches show the building as if it were not quite in focus. On some of them Wright has indicated modifications of mass and profile. Revisions to the plans would then be made on the basis of these studies, and the work would be carried forward by the self-balancing interaction of perspective and plan. More than the finished drawings, the rough sketches offer to the student of Wright's work a most encouraging lesson. Masterpieces, even Wright's masterpieces, are not always born entire and perfect. The capacity to nourish inspiration with hard work was a part of his strength Wright seldom cared to communicate to the public, much less to his fellow architects.

Except for preliminary sketches or notations of ideas, most of Wright's detailed perspective views were developed by mechanical projection. In this method the plan of a building is first drawn at the angle from which the building is to be shown. A "horizon line" terminated by "vanishing points" is then established, and on it the position of various parts of the building is accurately projected from the plan. Though it must be augmented by intuitive corrections, this laborious process ensures that a building be represented in its true proportions. The draftsman is discouraged from those distortions of perspective that suggest a building is much larger or longer or higher than it really is.

That Wright's drawings should be free of such defects is remarkable only because certain forms characteristic of his work, most notably the extended horizontal masses and bold cantilevers, invite exaggeration. So far from exaggerating, however, the drawings sometimes portray the reality of the buildings with greater truthfulness than could later be achieved by even the most skillful and sympathetic photographer. Wright has pointed out that the horizontal plane best conveys the quality of depth, of physical extension through and around space. In a photograph these horizontal planes may be obscured by the aggressive prominence of some singular detail, more interesting to the photographer than to the architect. A walk through Wright's buildings, especially if one has first known them only in their reduction to photographs, reveals a disciplined hierarchy of incident that is always surprising and is in fact the "truth" of his architecture. The drawings, like metaphors reconstructed from another language, transmit the truth of architectural form by accepting the different truth of the pictorial image.

Colored pencils were Wright's favorite media, and he has written engagingly about the pleasures he derived from spreading out on his worktable the full spectrum of colors. Usually the drawing would be blocked out with light pencil lines, and sky, trees and ground would then be filled in with the appropriate shades. Only infrequently would the building itself be given any very pronounced color; a copper roof, perhaps, or blue shadows on a glass wall, or details of ornament might be so treated, but most often ordinary black lead pencil, in line and pale grey shading, would define the architecture. Although even the freest elevation studies and plans are often highly colored (the plans in particular taking on a decorative intricacy), Wright's preference for color by no means excluded other treatments. A drawing might consist entirely of brown ink outlines with no color or shading of any sort. Or the brown ink outline might be combined with colored pencils to add depth and contrast to their usually pale tones. Drawings of the prairie houses often include not only ink and colored pencils but also brown ink washes, green, blue and yellow watercolor washes, and sometimes a layer of white paint ranging from thin transparency to an opaque, chalk-like texture. The prairie house drawings, however, are to some extent uncharacteristic. In many of them the emphasis on heavy line is such that they take on the character of a leaded glass window, with a variety of contrasts Wright seems to have sought only infrequently. His range of color includes earth tones as well as the primary hues, but all of these colors are in a value range so closely related that adjacent pale green and pale yellow areas, for example, blend into a silvery shimmer when seen at a distance. This closeness of value, despite differences of hue, accounts for the great difficulty of preserving the identity of color areas when the drawings are photographed in black and white. It also unifies the different kinds of line that so often appear in one drawing, and it lends a delicacy that belies the sometimes almost brutal strength of the architecture.

The colored drawing on tracing paper might be preceded by several preparatory sketches in black pencil alone. From these or from the colored original, also on tracing paper, duplicates similar to blueprints would often be run off on a machine. These prints, with black or dark brown lines on a greyish-white background, could then be hand-colored. The result is an "edition" of a drawing in which the color differs slightly from print to print, and by means of which it was possible to study different color effects on what was essentially the same drawing.

Characteristically Wright drew his buildings as they would be seen by an observer of normal height standing at ground level. In at least one surviving series he studied effects of mass and detail with consecutive drawings in which the point of view is slowly shifted to one side, a few degrees at a time (plates 128, 129, 130). For presentation to a client the customary front and rear ground-level views at a 45 degree angle would usually suffice to explain a building's size and character, but in many cases he chose to place the observer some distance above the building. Wright's preference for steep hillsides and other sites of marked irregularity added to the difficulty of conveying the true size of a building with any single view. Aerial perspectives present views seldom possible in reality, but because they summarize in a single image the overall relationship of parts, they make the perspectives at ground-level more easily understood.

When the design of a building was pronouncedly frontal, Wright preferred to turn the facade at an angle close to the picture plane: the observer is left in no doubt that he is looking at the main, and probably the entrance, elevation. Buildings composed of numerous extended wings, or L-shaped plans, or intricate intersections and varying heights, are most often shown at what appears to be a 45 degree angle, giving nearly equal importance to each side.

A distinguishing and persistent characteristic of Wright's drawings is the placement of a building at the extreme top or bottom of the sheet. The amount of paper left blank is sometimes due merely to the drawing having been left untrimmed, but usually the unfilled area is part of the composition. It is intended to suggest a space between the observer and the building. Thus buildings that are seen from below are most often placed at the top of a sheet, and when details of the landscape are omitted the presence of a vast and empty surface of paper suffices to convey distance. The quantity of paper sometimes used in this way has meant that reproducing the full sheet, in magazines and books, diminishes the size of the building so much that all detail is lost. Wright himself never hesitated to trim these drawings of excessive blank paper, and many of them bear trim marks approved by him. But the quality of many of the originals can only be preserved by maintaining a certain spaciousness of background when they are reproduced.

Placement on a page was of course often determined by a building's shape and the complexity of its massing. The main intersection in a composition involving two or more distinct masses usually falls on or near the center of the drawing. This is an observation which must immediately be qualified: it is perhaps arbitrary to assume that a particular intersection can be described as the main one because of its proximity to center. Nevertheless, in the most characteristic of the long, horizontal compositions a vertical line drawn through the center of the picture will more often than not fall directly on an intersection of masses that seems to mark the building's center of gravity; an area of maximum density, so to speak, holding the composition at rest. An exception, or one class of exceptions, is provided by those similarly long horizontal pictures in which a building is turned away from the observer and is placed to one side.

The eye travels across these pictures in a rhythm established by vertical lines made by features of the architecture. It is a rhythm inaugurated and often concluded by a vertical mass at the extreme right or left of the picture, usually a tree trunk augmented by a single horizontal branch, and almost never a person or an architectural feature. Frequently these elements frame the end of the building and even hide part of it. They establish the foreground plane closest to the observer, setting up a tension that pulls the eye backward and forward in the implied space between tree and building, insisting that the building is not an isolated form.

Enough of the natural setting is shown to establish both the scale of a building and its distance from the observer. The building is always surrounded by space. But drawings of interiors, because by implication the walls extend beyond the limits of the picture to envelop the observer, present a more difficult problem. Perhaps Wright's most interesting interior studies are those in which first one and then another balance of light and dark, of accent and ornament, is explored from the same point of view; instructive examples are two studies of the interior of Unity Church (33, 34). Often such drawings are combined with cross-sections and cutaway views, so that their usefulness as information takes precedence over their quality as drawings. Only the rougher sketches, perhaps because of their vagueness, succeed in suggesting the quality of Wright's kind of interior. As if in recognition of the inherent limitations of the problem, Wright seems in his later work to have devoted less effort to rendering interiors.

The quality of depth is further increased by a device that recalls such Japanese printmakers as Hiroshige. It consists of treating the sky as a finite element of the composition. The sky is given a top and sides. Its limits are emphatically defined by a heavily drawn outline, while its Japanese flavor is heightened by finely drawn horizontal lines which fill the area and grow darker as they near the top. When Wright used blue pencil for the sky, as he nearly always did, the darker blue lines at the top immediately recall similar effects in Hiroshige's *Fifty-three Stations of the Tokaido Road*. This effect so pleased Wright that he employed it throughout his life. The most diverse architectural conceptions are presented to us sandwiched between protecting layers of foliage and a supporting layer of sky. Trees in the foreground and sometimes even part of the building are made to extend beyond the rectangular backdrop, thereby enhancing the effect of cut-out layers representing degrees of distance, like the stage flats of painted foliage and painted hills used in a ballet. A remarkable example is the set of drawings of the 1925 project for a spiral building on Sugar Loaf Mountain, in Maryland (112, 113).

A related device frequently employed by Wright to establish depth is a line drawn around the entire picture. This frame is usually broken; that is to say, it may begin at the lower left hand corner of the page, make its way almost around the drawing and suddenly stop, leaving a gap of several inches. Details of the landscape pour through this gap (181) and sometimes run off the edge of the page. There is perhaps more than a purely graphic consideration involved in this scheme. The drawings seem to affirm in every possible way Wright's insistence on breaking through constraints. That buildings should not be like boxes, but should open themselves to the landscape by unfolding and extending their walls and roofs, is of course the transformation in our way of looking at architecture that Wright brought about. In the drawings he seems to be further demonstrating the satisfactions of demolishing the box by setting up a containing frame for the purpose of breaking through it.

Wright preferred to indicate depth by establishing fixed, separate planes, but transitions from one plane to the next are avoided. The range of graphic techniques used to suggest depth is in fact relatively limited. Despite the great variety of line weights and accents, buildings are drawn with an almost uniform crispness. The distribution of emphasis is seemingly regular. There are no atmospheric renditions of air, by means of which the distant might be blurred and the near made sharp. Strong contrasts of foreground and background occur often enough, but they are contrasts between a building and its natural setting rather than between parts of the building itself. On this regular rendition of architectural forms depends much of the pictorial unity the drawings achieve; and the fact that they really are unified makes Wright's rough rendering of landscape-in-layers all the more satisfying.

Landscape is inextricably bound up with Wright's idea of architecture. Even the most extended buildings are normally shown from a distance great enough to encompass the entire structure and the land around it. Close-up or partial views are almost nonexistent in Wright's work. Certain buildings, however, either because of a particular feature, such as a completely enclosed courtyard, or buildings so extended that they are in fact an aggregate of separate buildings, might be shown as if the observer were placed in their midst. In this way the California ranch development projected for E. H. Doheny in 1921 yielded what is surely one of Wright's most beautiful images (68). We seem to be standing on a terrace suspended above and between other terraces. At the left and right solid masses of textured masonry beguile the eye over gardens, steps, and platforms into the middle-distance and finally into the hills beyond, the whole range of details and distances modulated with a pale and luminous delicacy. This is in fact a drawing of landscape—a landscape made and revealed by architecture. It is a lyric vision central to Wright's work, and nowhere more than in this drawing is it embodied with such gentle grace.

When a building was set on the crest of a hill, and was actually to be approached from below, Wright would only infrequently draw it just as it would be seen by someone standing at the bottom of the hill. More often the observer is suspended in mid-air, not directly in line with the main floor but slightly below it. A preliminary sketch of the great Kaufmann house, *Fallingwater*, shows the building as it would be seen from some distance and from a position below its site at the edge of a waterfall. The arrangement of cantilevered terraces is clear enough, but from this angle they tend to pull away from each other and the composition is somewhat disjointed (139). In the final presentation drawing the observer has been lifted into the air and the convergence of lines in perspective is less abrupt. Eye level is now just under the main floor (140). The underside of the lowest cantilevered terrace is still visible, providing the horizontal plane necessary to establish the size of the terrace, and the angle at which the house sits in relation to the waterfall is quite clear. In reality the building can be seen, with some effort, from the steeper angle chosen for the preliminary sketch. The very beautiful photograph that has become the standard and world-famous image was taken from an angle that combines advantages of both the preliminary and final drawings. It succeeds in presenting a unified image of the building although it mildly over-dramatizes an aspect Wright was content to leave to the imagination.

Other preliminary sketches of *Fallingwater* indicate the relation of overlapping terraces and intersecting parapets by showing them from above. One of these views, not previously published, is particularly successful in capturing the building's proportions and its relation to the site (137). Curiously, all of these preliminary studies have a buoyant, sparkling lightness of touch lost in the somewhat ponderous colored presentation rendering.

In the drawings of the great prairie houses made at the turn of the century, trees are heavily outlined with careful attention to details of branch, leaf, and blossom (35, 37), and sometimes a thick line is also used for the buildings. There is a quality in this slow-moving line that recalls the drawings in children's books, meant to be filled in with color. There is also a contrived intricacy that suggests both the illustrations of Kate Greenaway and the elaborate Celtic turns of much Art Nouveau graphic design. It is a quality marginal to Wright's architecture. Set among trees in this style, his buildings seem at first sight but little removed from the conventions of the day; a more careful study separates them from their ingratiating borders of foliage and discloses their often monumental scale. Nevertheless, some of these early drawings, executed by Marion Mahony, are among the most beautiful and convincingly unified to have come from Wright's studio.

As with most great draftsmen, Wright could set his style to a page by drawing a line across it. Conscious of the quality of line to an extraordinary degree, he could gauge with perfect accuracy just how much weight was needed to define the profile of a roof, or to pick out some detail worth more, in a drawing, than anyone else would have guessed. He varied line weights considerably without, so it seems, depending on any great range of hard or soft pencil leads, and he sometimes employed sharp points to terminate a line and lend it a kind of color. The dotted line was in fact of special interest to him, as it was centuries ago to Japanese painters, printmakers, and landscape gardeners who also observed its effect in nature; for Wright it became an element of his architecture as well.

When one considers how great was Wright's concern for the texture of a building, for the quality of materials and the feelings they elicit from us of weight, density, and permanence, it is surprising that he cared so little for the possibilities of sustained tonal development. But Wright was apparently uninterested in effects of chiarascuro; shadows play over walls and under eaves only as thin repeated lines, and in terms of line alone nearly every effect is obtained. What is missing is the continuous modulation of a surface, the suggestion of light moving across it. The limitation was deliberate; it was to some extent overcome in the studies of the Sugar Loaf Mountain project and the watercolor rendering of San Marcos-in-the-Desert, but never quite overcome in the drawings of the Guggenheim Museum. Here more than in any other building by Wright was a continuous, curved form that seemed to demand a sustained shading of its surface; instead the play of light is suggested by dots or lines (195, 196, 198) and even with a more deliberate effort at shading, the outline still predominates (197). Perhaps the closest Wright could bring himself to unbroken shading were the studies of ornament for the concrete block houses built in California during the 'twenties. In these drawings the small scale pattern is not so much picked out as smudged over a background otherwise crisp —but the pattern itself is comprised essentially of dots and lines.

Wright's sense of ornament was tied to the asymmetrical play of lines and shapes. The non-repetitive designs for windows, gates, and other accessories for the prairie houses were generated by the same sense of geometry as were the plans of the houses themselves. In this respect his ornament was, as Wright frequently explained, of the building and not on it. For architects today, Wright's ornament is more problematic than ever. From one point of view ornament that is truly *of* rather than *on*, in the sense of being applied, would thereby cease to be ornament, analogies with the iridescent encrustations of sea shells notwithstanding. In so many of his major buildings—perhaps in his greatest—Wright dispensed with all ornament whatsoever: *Fallingwater;* the administration building and laboratory tower for the Johnson's Wax Company; and any number of small houses come to mind. In those buildings a beautiful and interesting surface is simply the property of a particular stone or brick or wood; it is not an identifiable design dropped into the process by which materials were made or assembled. The point is perhaps not without interest because Wright's ornament, even though it has lacked admirers, was used by him in the classical way: to refresh the eye by increasing the range of dimensions a building might present, and by doing so to make the big look bigger and the small smaller. The geometry of pure square, circle, and triangle lends itself well enough to this purpose, however much it may lack grace and elegance — qualities not as negligible as might be supposed. But at its most engaging Wright's geometric ornament does indeed transform the materials of which it is made. The Young house project of 1928 (85) is an example of patterning that has come to alter not only the plan but the very manner in which building blocks are piled one above another. In this as in related projects a geometry of triangles informs the architecture and is seen even in stones and plants; and finally whole groups of buildings (90, 150, 177) participate in a magnificent universal triangulation.

Part of the beauty of Wright's work is the release it offers from the idea of perfection. His architecture, like life itself, renders perfection irrelevant. With every theme he explored Wright revealed a fresh realm of possibilities. For this reason it is helpful to study his drawings in a sequence at least approximating the order in which his ideas evolved. When he repeated and varied his themes it was to rediscover the universal in the particular, in the unique event. In Wright's architecture every event has significance but there is no final event, no perfect answer: history cannot come to an end. It was therefore possible for Wright to change without repudiating his earlier work. The composite image of Wright's architecture is like that produced by a kaleidoscope, in which elements appear and vanish, and reappear transformed; fresh juxtapositions surprise us. But no matter how often the ingredients shift into new patterns, they are after all bound together by a single process. Some of these patterns must seem to us more beautiful than others, but most beautiful of all is the process by which they are made.

—ARTHUR DREXLER

THE DRAWINGS

9505,01

1. DORMER WINDOW, CHAUNCEY L. WILLIAMS HOUSE, RIVER FOREST, ILLINOIS. 1895.

2. PROJECT: LUXFER PRISM COMPANY SKYSCRAPER. 1895.

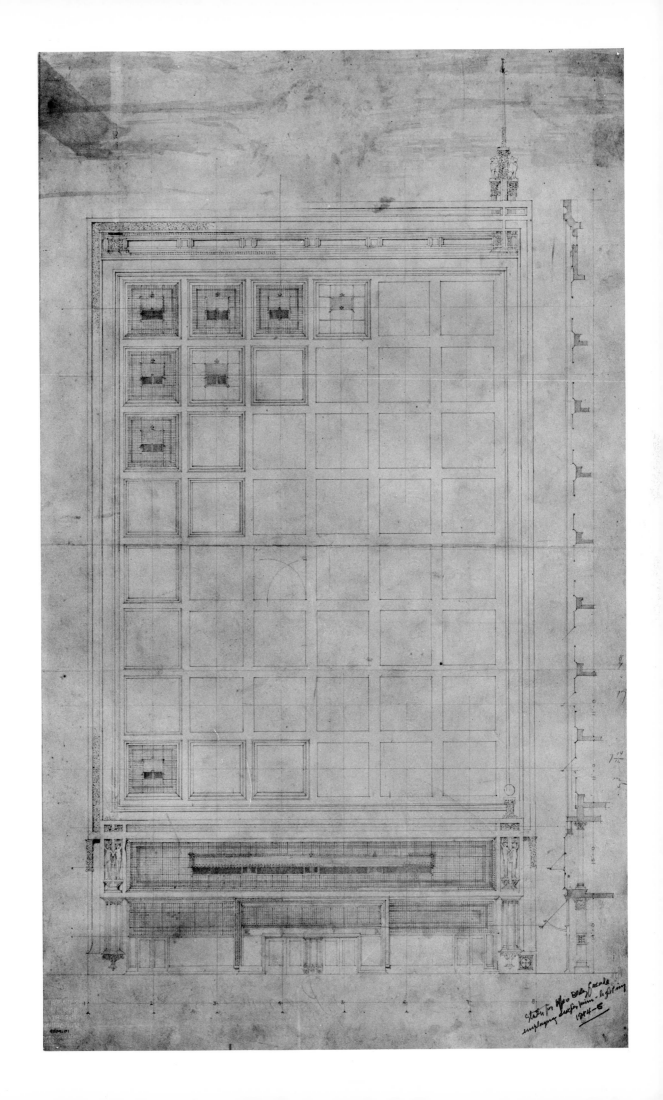

3. PROJECT: WOLF LAKE AMUSEMENT PARK, ILLINOIS. 1895.

4, 5. PROJECT: LEXINGTON TERRACE APARTMENTS, CHICAGO, ILLINOIS. 1901-09.

c. 1900 Lexington Terrace F.Ll.W.

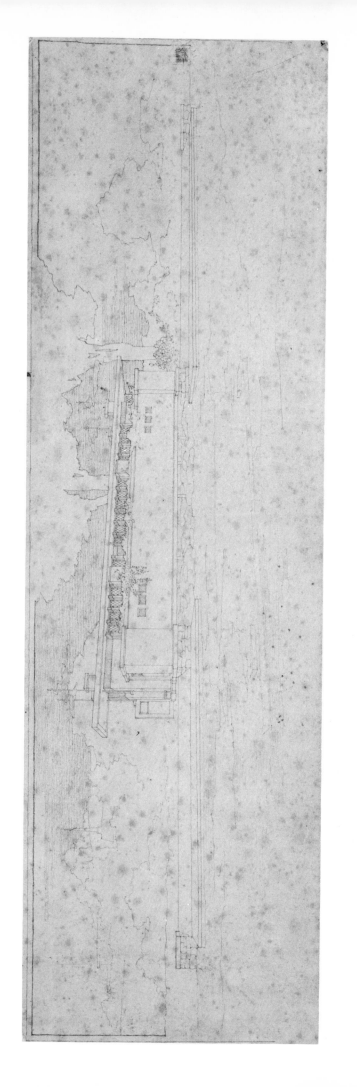

6. PROJECT: YAHARA BOAT CLUB, MADISON, WISCONSIN. 1902.

7. PROJECT: YAHARA BOAT CLUB, MADISON, WISCONSIN. 1902.

8. PROJECT: WALTER GERTS HOUSE, GLENCOE, ILLINOIS. 1906.

9, 10. FRANK LLOYD WRIGHT STUDIO, OAK PARK, ILLINOIS. 1895-1911.

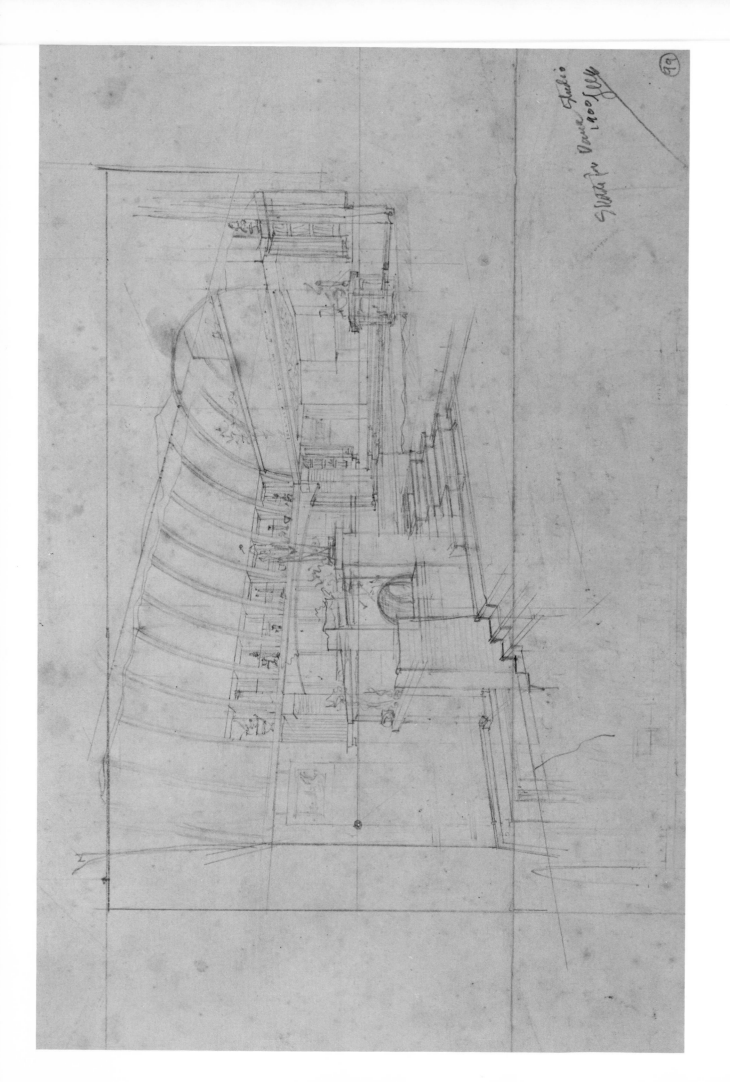

Susan Dana House

11, 12. SUSAN LAWRENCE DANA HOUSE, SPRINGFIELD, ILLINOIS. 1902-04.

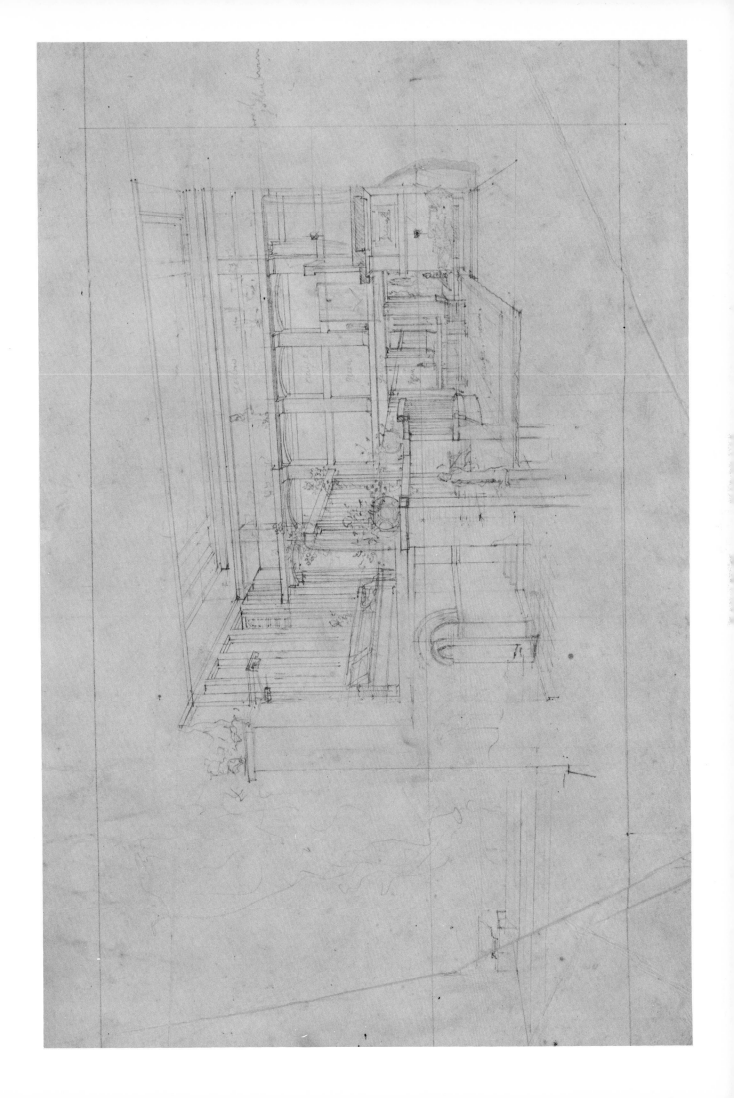

13. PROJECT: VICTOR METZGER HOUSE, ONTARIO, CANADA. 1901.

14. GEORGE MADISON MILLARD HOUSE, HIGHLAND PARK, ILLINOIS. 1906.

15. PROJECT: WOOD AND PLASTER HOUSE, HIGHLAND PARK, ILLINOIS. 1904.

16. WARD W. WILLITTS HOUSE, HIGHLAND PARK, ILLINOIS. 1902.

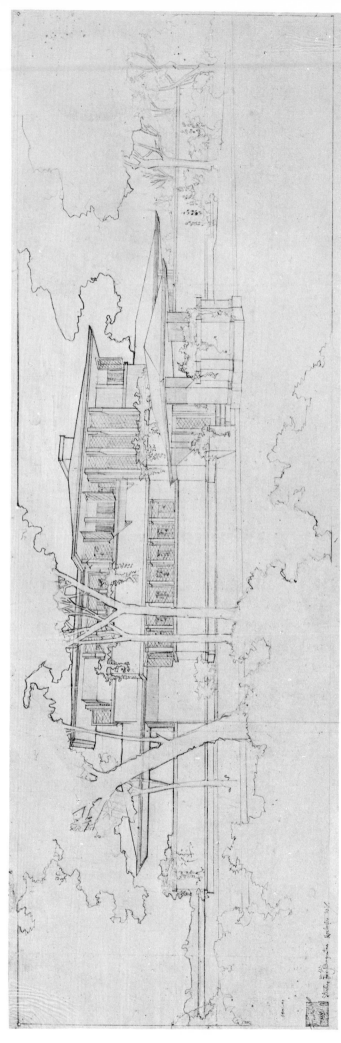

17. AVERY COONLEY HOUSE, RIVERSIDE, ILLINOIS. 1908-11.

18. E. E. BOYNTON HOUSE, ROCHESTER, NEW YORK. 1908.

19. PROJECT: WILLIAM NORMAN GUTHRIE HOUSE, SEWANEE, TENNESSEE. 1908.

20. C. THAXTER SHAW HOUSE, MONTREAL, CANADA. 1906.

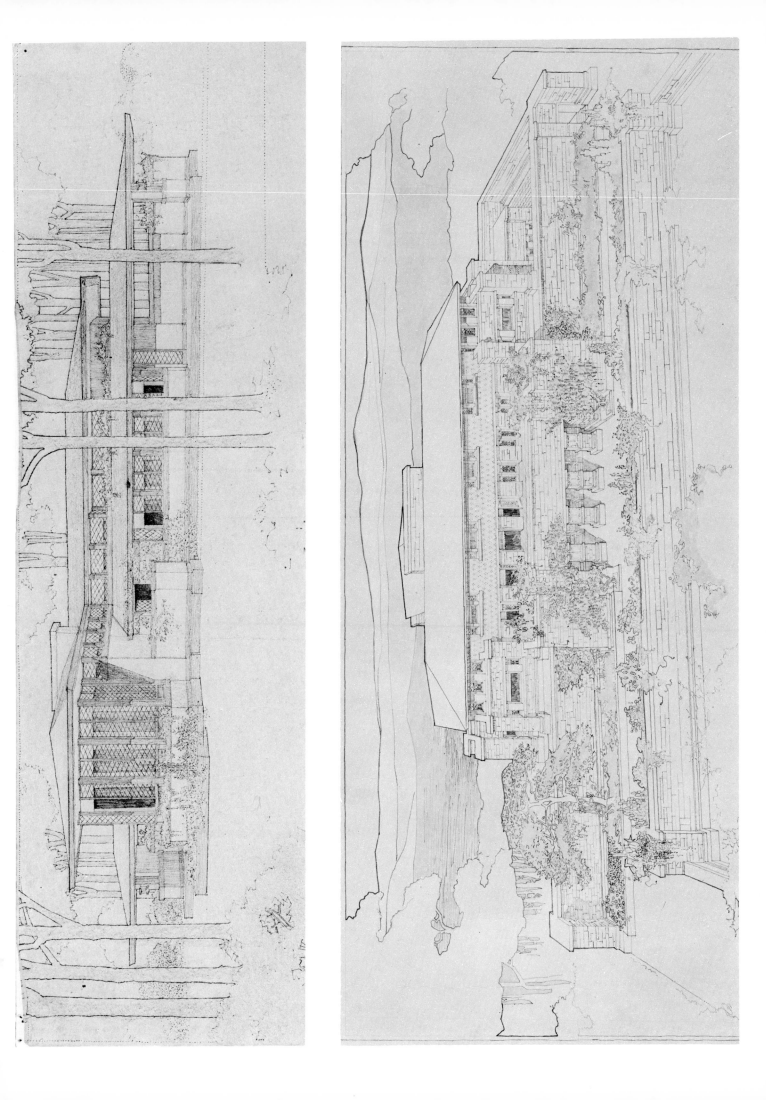

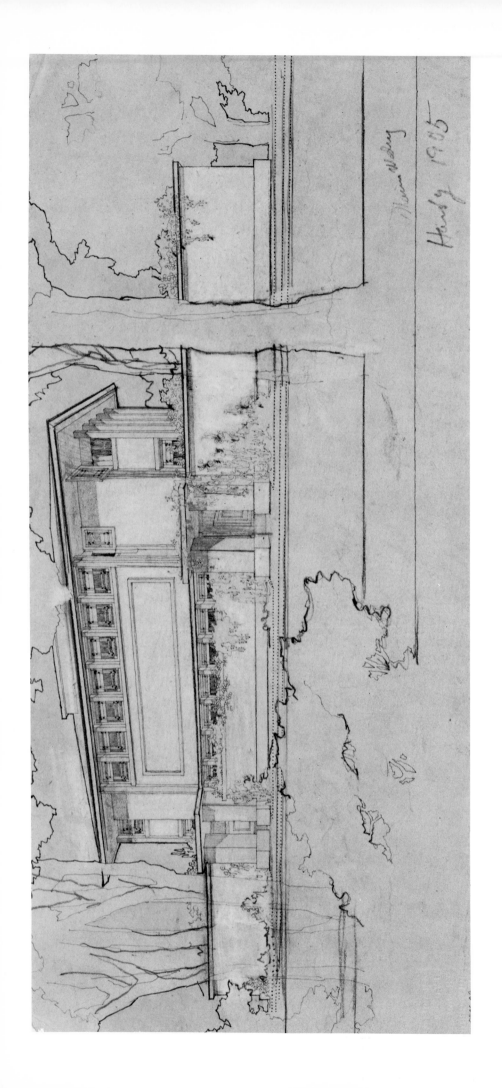

21, 22. THOMAS P. HARDY HOUSE, RACINE, WISCONSIN. 1905.

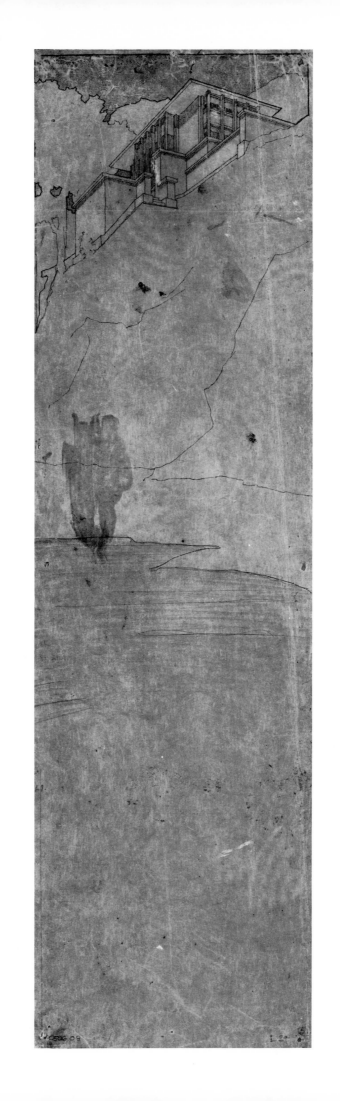

23, 24. LARKIN COMPANY ADMINISTRATION BUILDING, BUFFALO, NEW YORK. 1904.

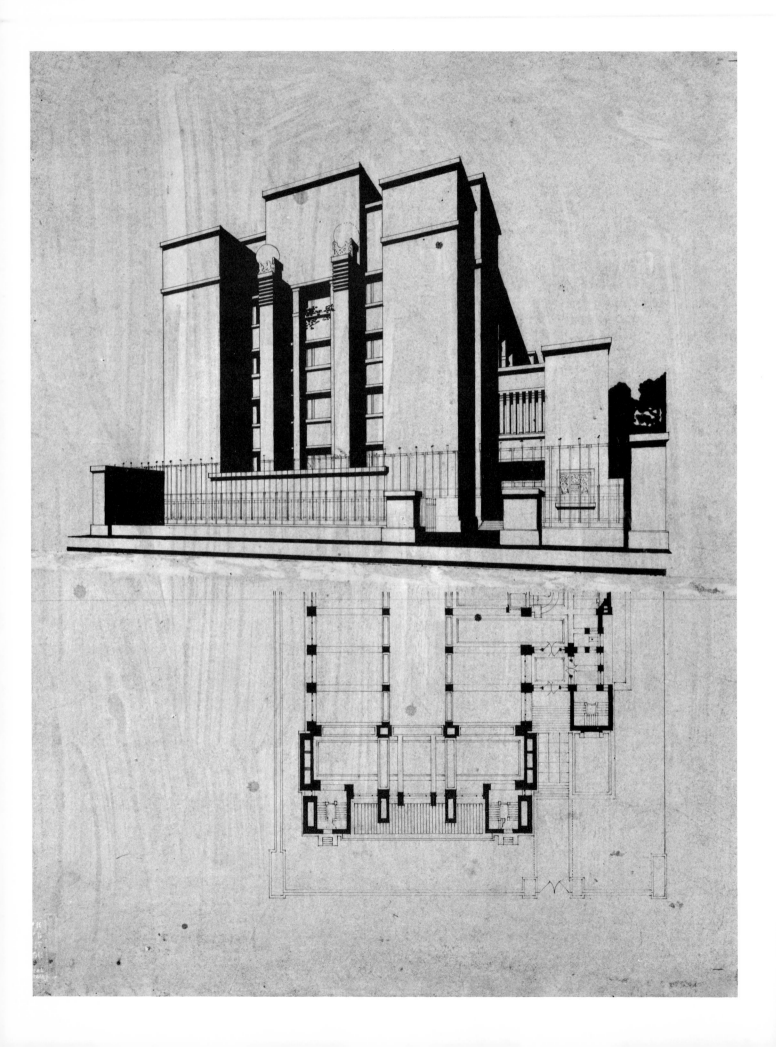

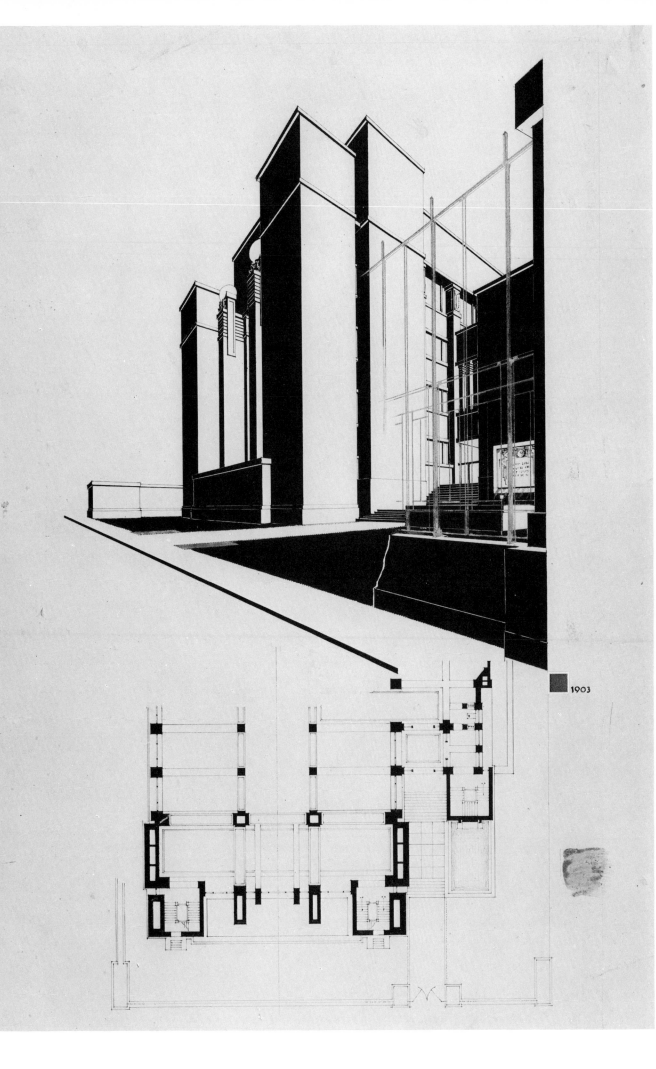

1903

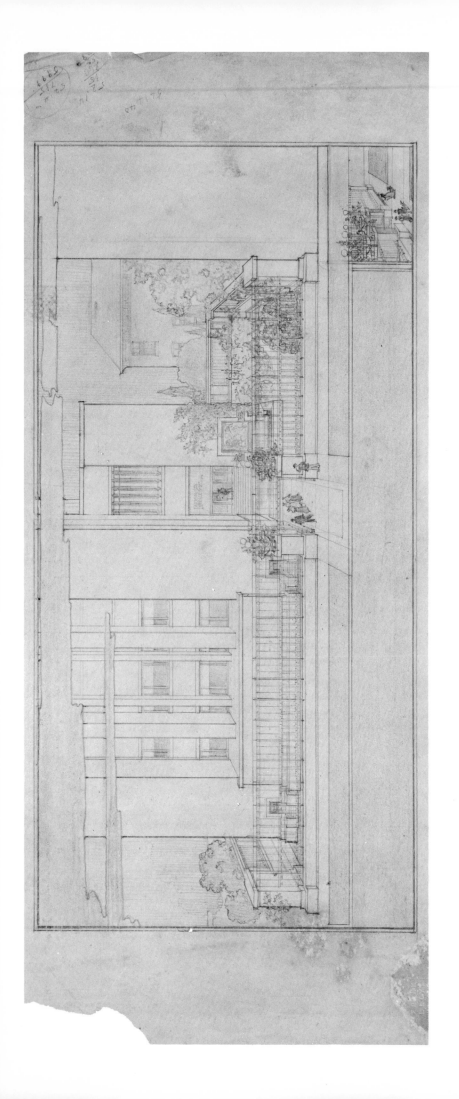

25. LARKIN COMPANY ADMINISTRATION BUILDING, BUFFALO, NEW YORK. 1904.

26. PROJECT: LARKIN COMPANY WORKERS' ROWHOUSES, BUFFALO, NEW YORK. 1904.

27. LARKIN COMPANY PAVILION, JAMESTOWN TERCENTENARY EXPOSITION, VIRGINIA. 1907.

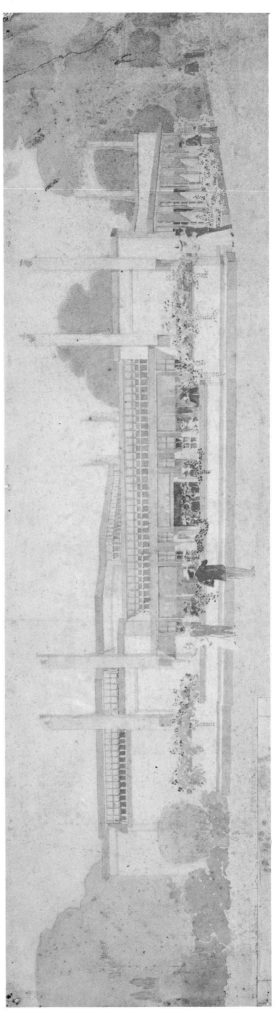

Grammar of 16.
Protestant

1903-05

28. LARKIN COMPANY ADMINISTRATION BUILDING, BUFFALO, NEW YORK. 1904.

29. FREDERICK C. ROBIE HOUSE, CHICAGO, ILLINOIS. 1909.

1906

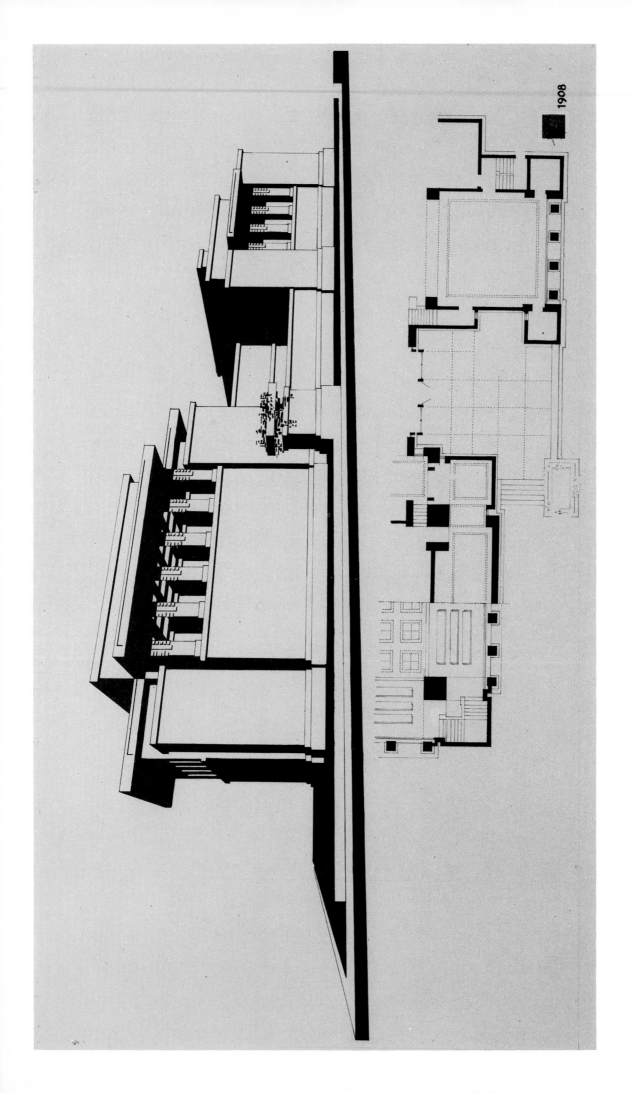

30, 31, 32. UNITY CHURCH AND PARISH HOUSE, OAK PARK, ILLINOIS. 1906.

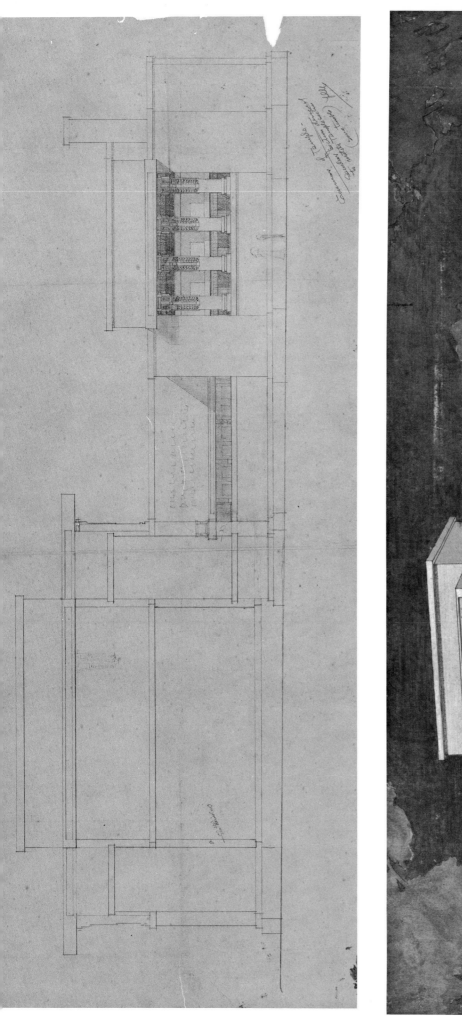

33. UNITY CHURCH, OAK PARK, ILLINOIS. 1906.

34. UNITY CHURCH, OAK PARK, ILLINOIS. 1906.

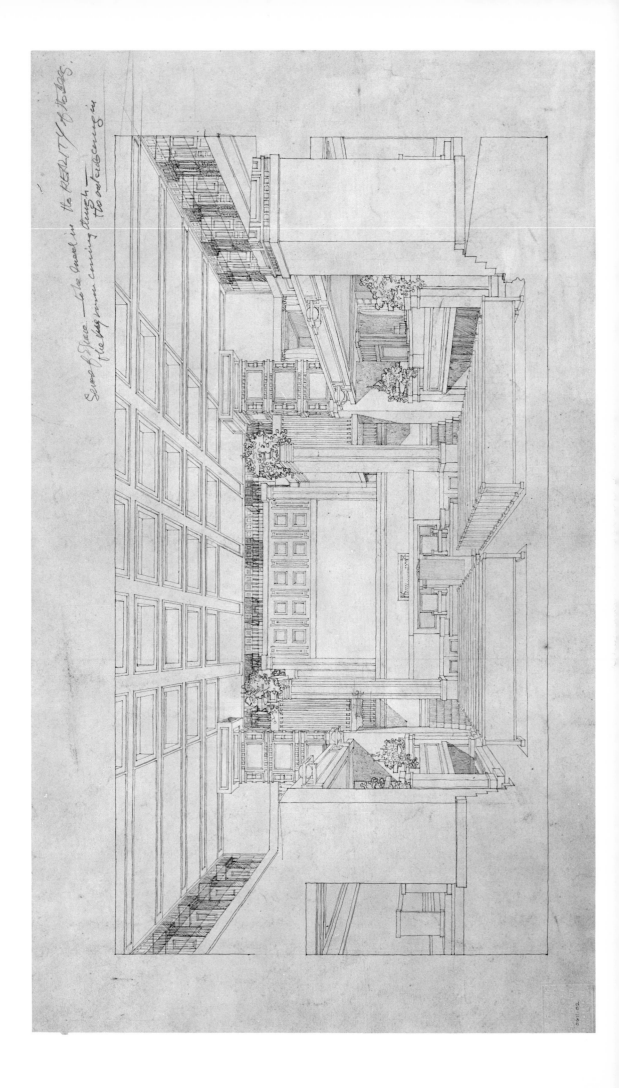

Sense of Space —to be had in the REALITY of the Edifice.

The layman coming through the vestibule comes in

35. K. C. DE RHODES HOUSE, SOUTH BEND, INDIANA. 1906.

36. RICHARD BOCK STUDIO HOUSE, MAYWOOD, ILLINOIS. 1906.

MRS GALE OAK PARK 1904
M.T.H.

37. MRS. THOMAS H. GALE HOUSE, OAK PARK, ILLINOIS. 1909.

38. PROJECT: FRANK LLOYD WRIGHT HOUSE AND STUDIO, VIALE VERDI, FIESOLE, ITALY. 1910.

39. PROJECT: EDWARD SCHROEDER HOUSE. MILWAUKEE, WISCONSIN. 1912.

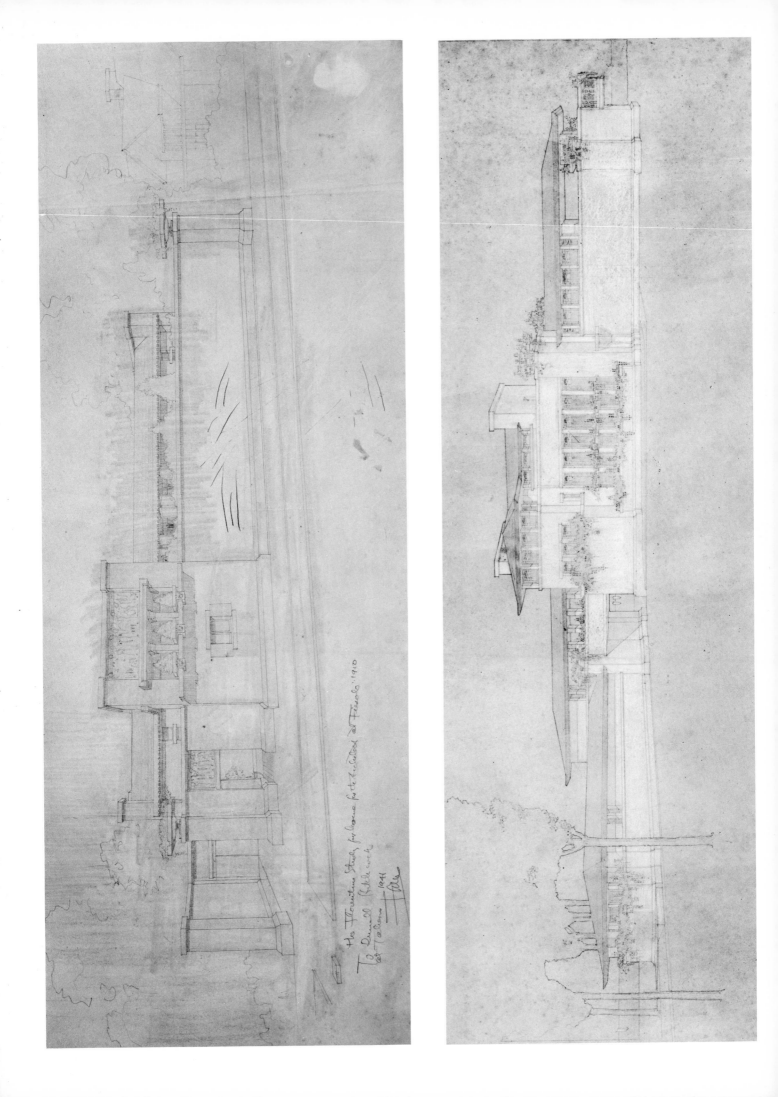

40. "TALIESIN", FRANK LLOYD WRIGHT HOUSE, STUDIO, AND FARM BUILDINGS, SPRING GREEN, WISCONSIN. 1911.

41. PROJECT: CARNEGIE LIBRARY, OTTOWA, CANADA. 1913.

42. BANFF NATIONAL PARK PAVILION, CANADA. 1911-12.

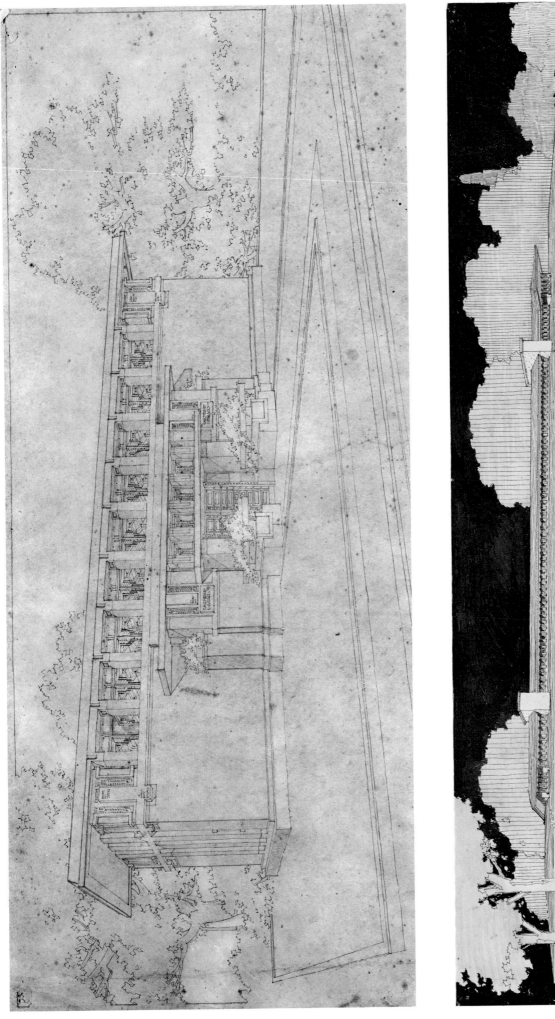

43. PROJECT: SHERMAN M. BOOTH HOUSE, GLENCOE, ILLINOIS. 1911.

44. BRIDGE, RAVINE BLUFFS DEVELOPMENT FOR SHERMAN M. BOOTH, GLENCOE, ILLINOIS. 1915.

45. PROJECT: PRESS BUILDING (SAN FRANCISCO CALL) SAN FRANCISCO, CALIFORNIA. 1912.

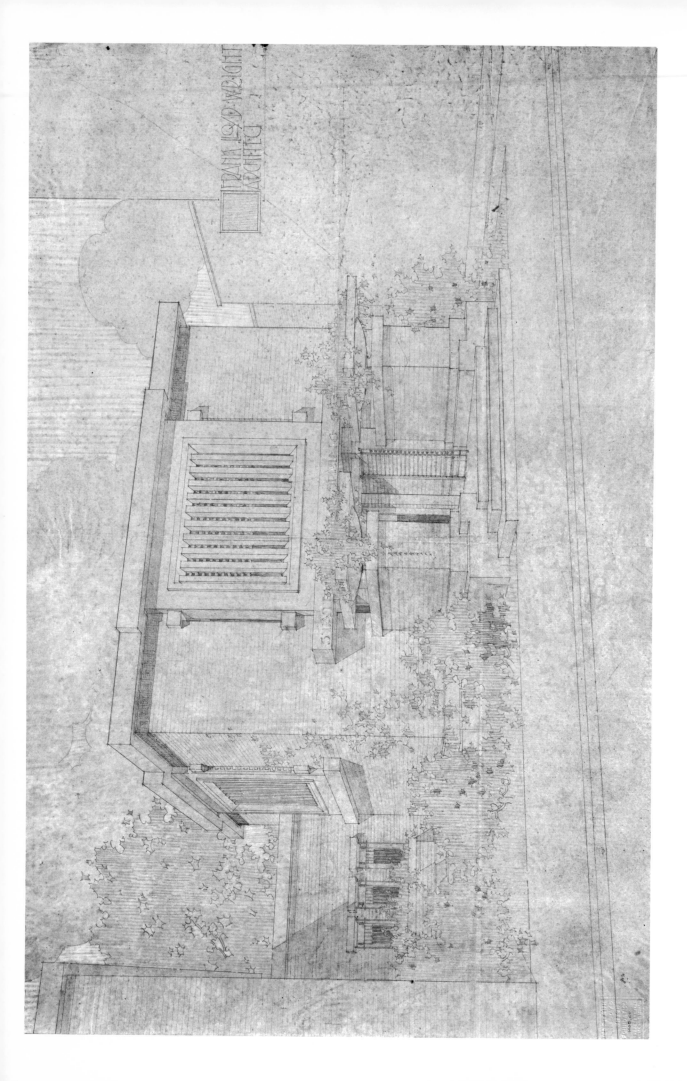

46. PROJECT: STATE BANK, SPRING GREEN, WISCONSIN. 1914.

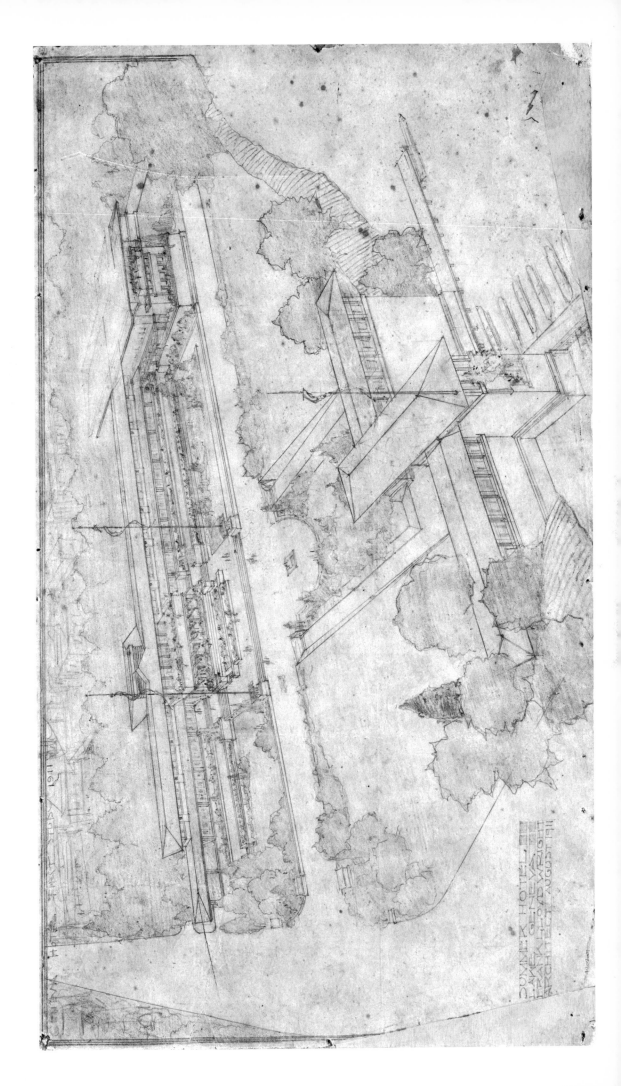

47. LAKE GENEVA INN (NOW GENEVA HOTEL), LAKE GENEVA, WISCONSIN. 1912.

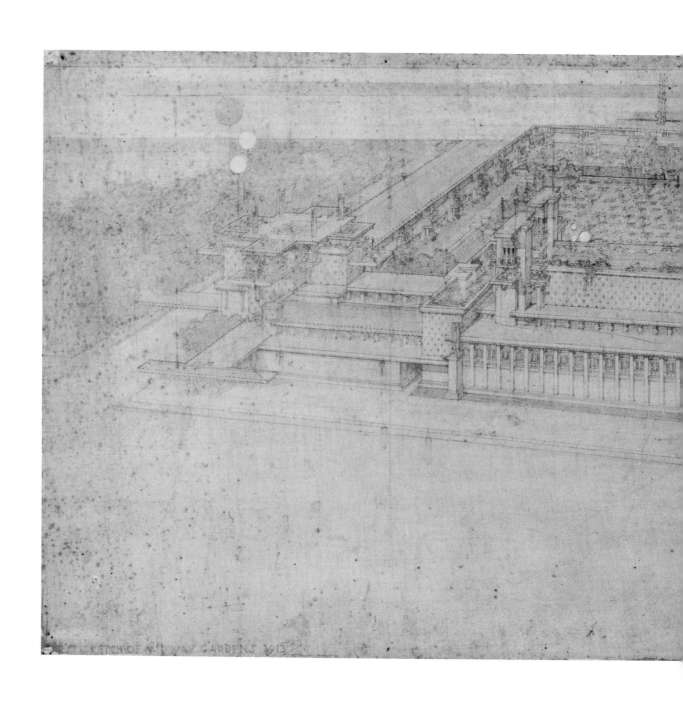

48. MIDWAY GARDENS, CHICAGO, ILLINOIS. 1914.

49. PROJECT: WOOD HOUSE, DECATUR, ILLINOIS. 1915.

50. PROJECT: AMERICAN SYSTEM READY-CUT HOUSES. 1913-15.

51, 52. PROJECT: AMERICAN SYSTEM READY-CUT HOUSES. 1913-15.

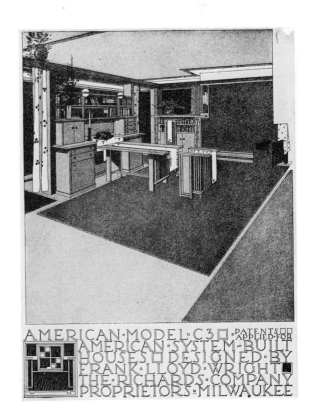

53. A. D. GERMAN WAREHOUSE, RICHLAND CENTER, WISCONSIN. 1915.

54. IMPERIAL HOTEL, TOKYO, JAPAN. 1915.

55. PROJECT: FRANK LLOYD WRIGHT HOUSE,
GOETHE STREET, CHICAGO, ILLINOIS. 1911.

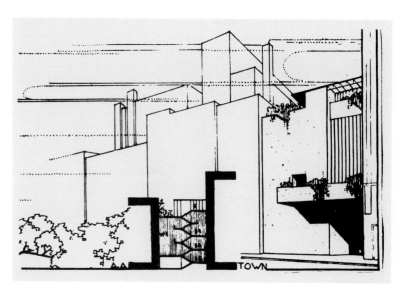

57. PROJECT: ZONED HOUSE, CITY VERSION. 1935.

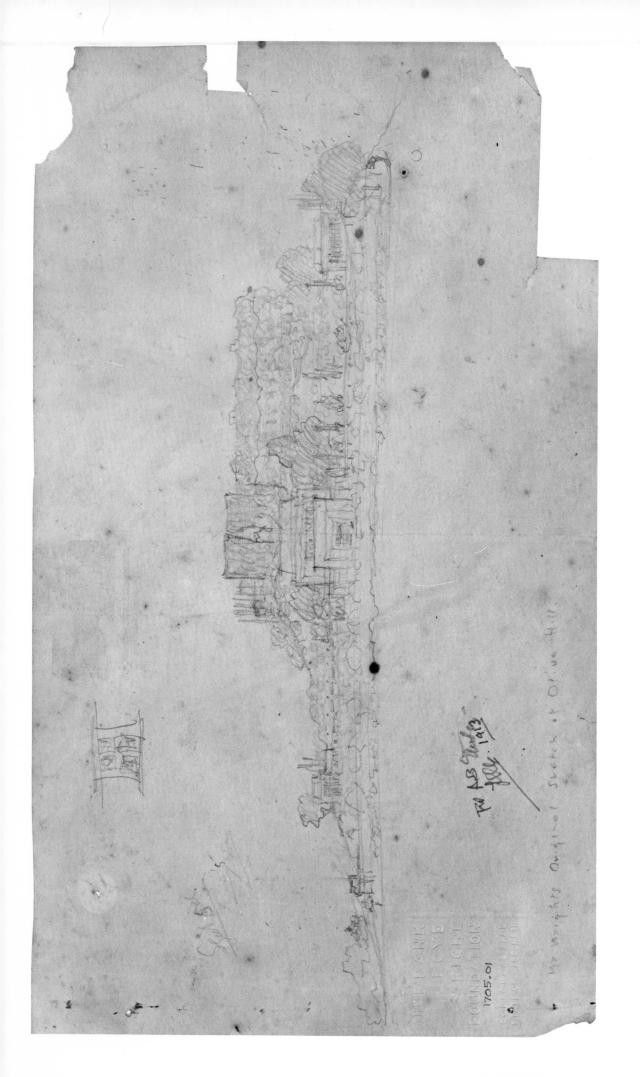

58. ALINE BARNSDALL "HOLLYHOCK HOUSE", OLIVE HILL, LOS ANGELES, CALIFORNIA. 1916-20.

59, 60. PROJECT: ALINE BARNSDALL THEATER, LOS ANGELES, CALIFORNIA. 1920.

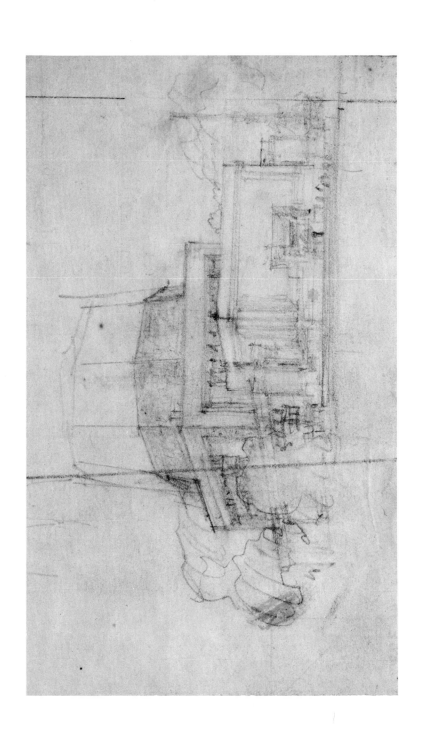

STUDY FOR BARNSDALL HOUSE 1913

61. ALINE BARNSDALL "HOLLYHOCK HOUSE", OLIVE HILL, LOS ANGELES, CALIFORNIA. 1916-20.

62. PROJECT: ALINE BARNSDALL THEATER, LOS ANGELES, CALIFORNIA. 1920.

(Club house)

63. ALINE BARNSDALL "HOLLYHOCK HOUSE", OLIVE HILL, LOS ANGELES, CALIFORNIA. 1916-20.

64. PROJECT: CEMENT BLOCK HOUSE, LOS ANGELES, CALIFORNIA. 1921.

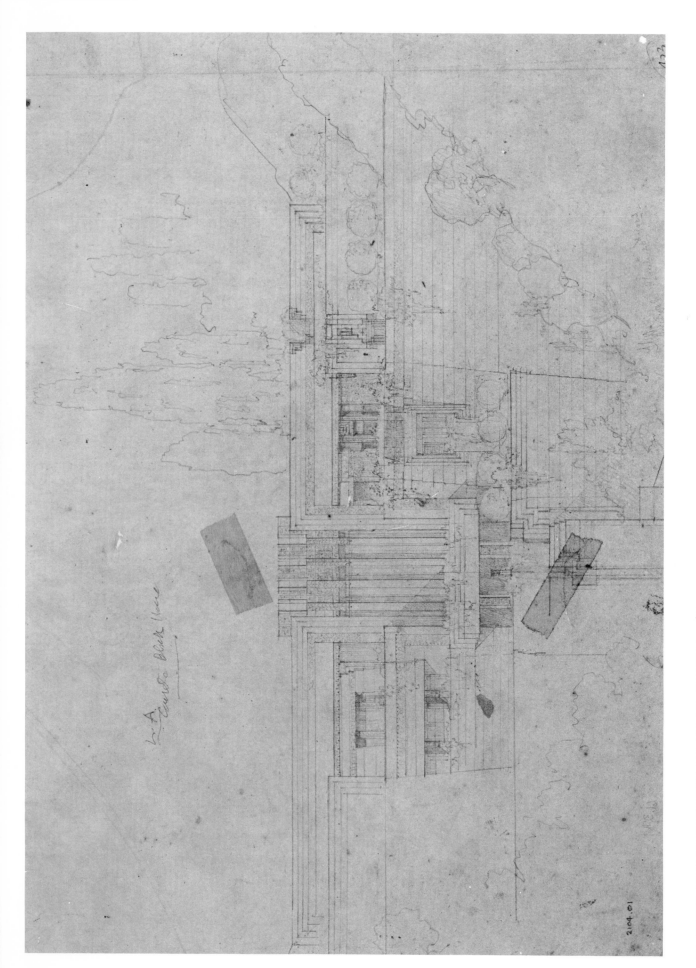

65. PROJECT: CONCRETE BLOCK HOUSE, LOS ANGELES, CALIFORNIA. 1923.

66. PROJECT: EDWARD H. DOHENY RANCH, SIERRA MADRE MOUNTAINS, CALIFORNIA. 1921.

67. PROJECT: EDWARD H. DOHENY RANCH, SIERRA MADRE MOUNTAINS, CALIFORNIA. 1921.

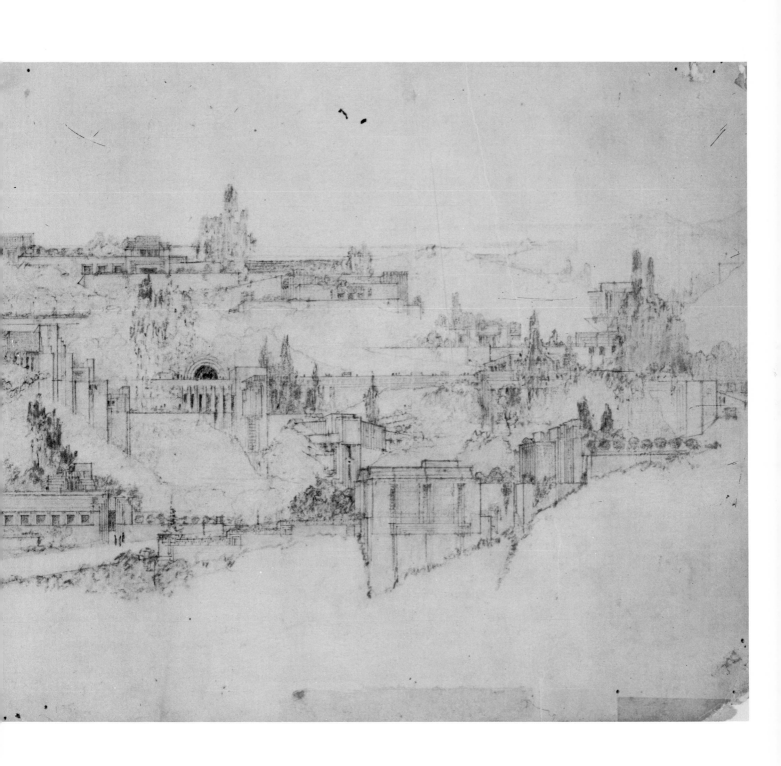

68. PROJECT: EDWARD H. DOHENY RANCH, SIERRA MADRE MOUNTAINS, CALIFORNIA. 1921.

69, 70. PROJECT: EDWARD H. DOHENY RANCH, SIERRA MADRE MOUNTAINS, CALIFORNIA. 1921.

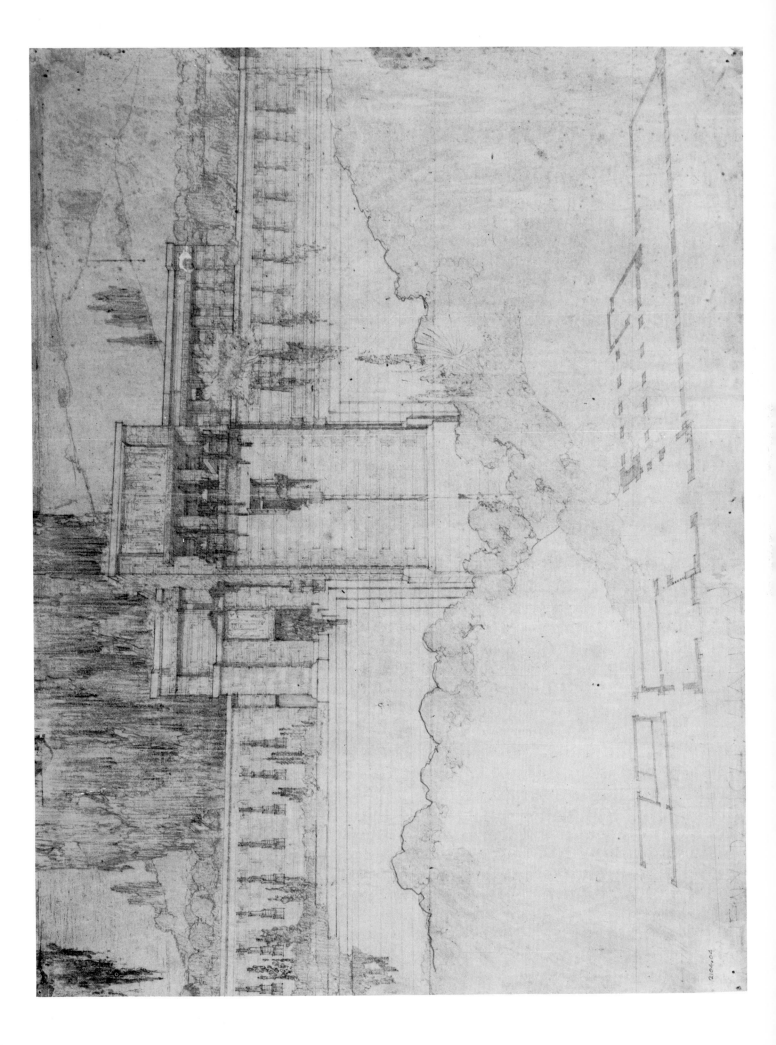

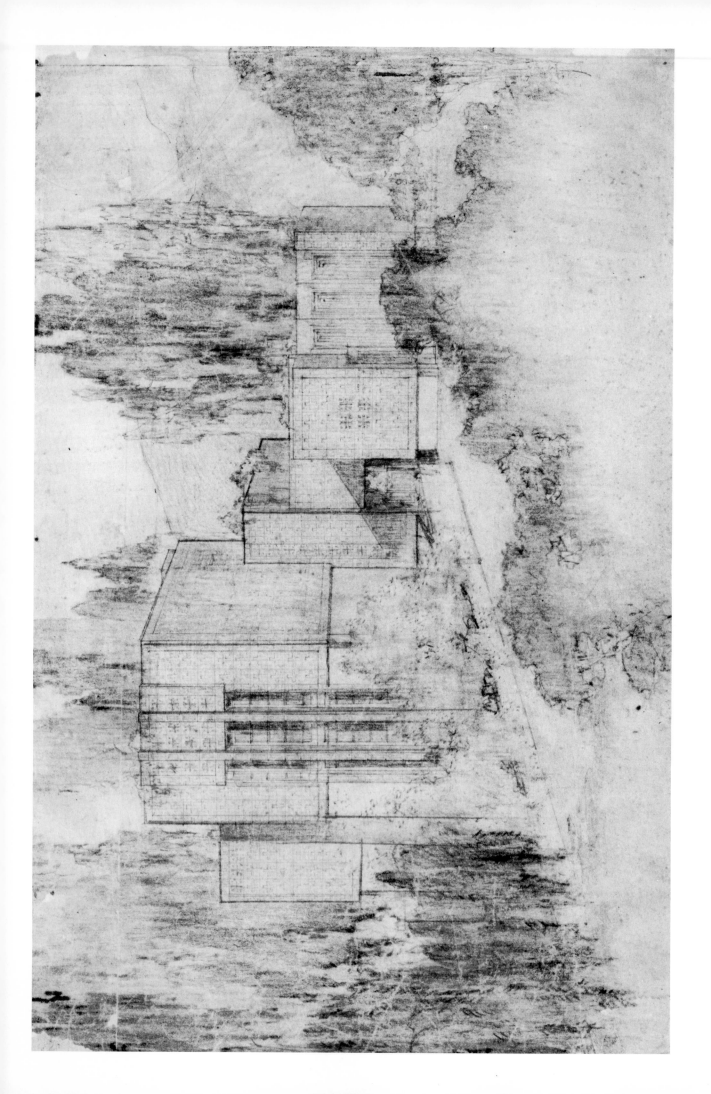

71, 72. MRS. GEORGE MADISON MILLARD HOUSE, PASADENA, CALIFORNIA. 1923.

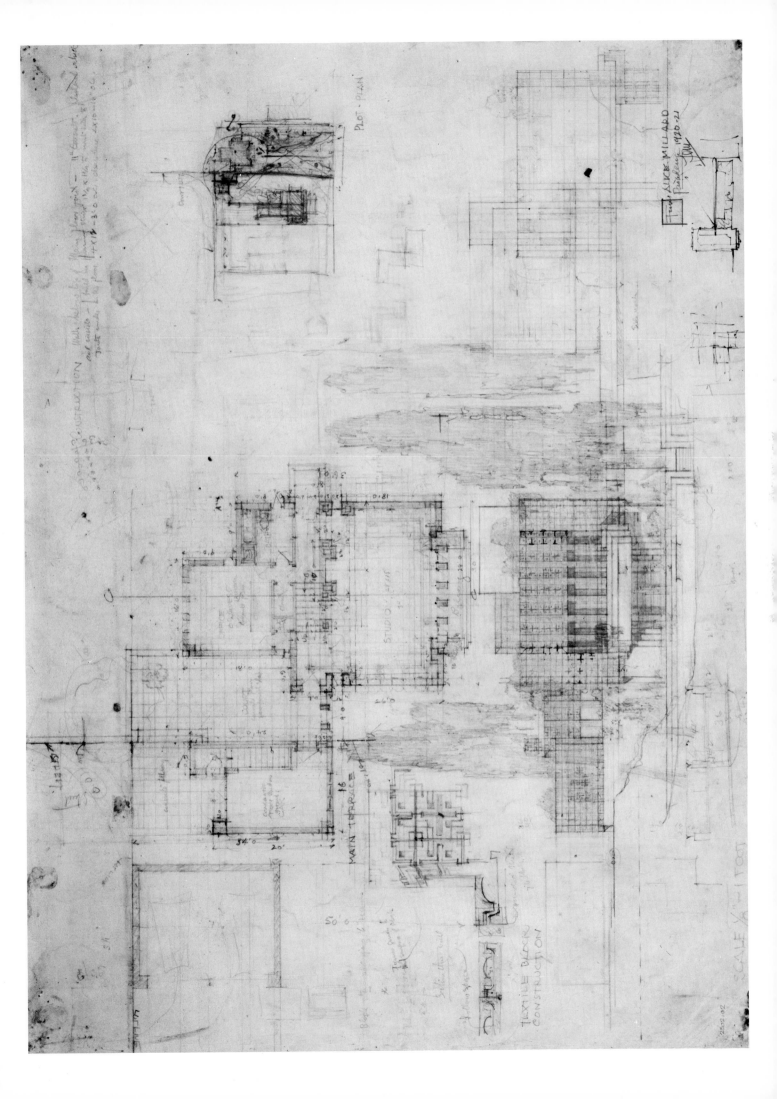

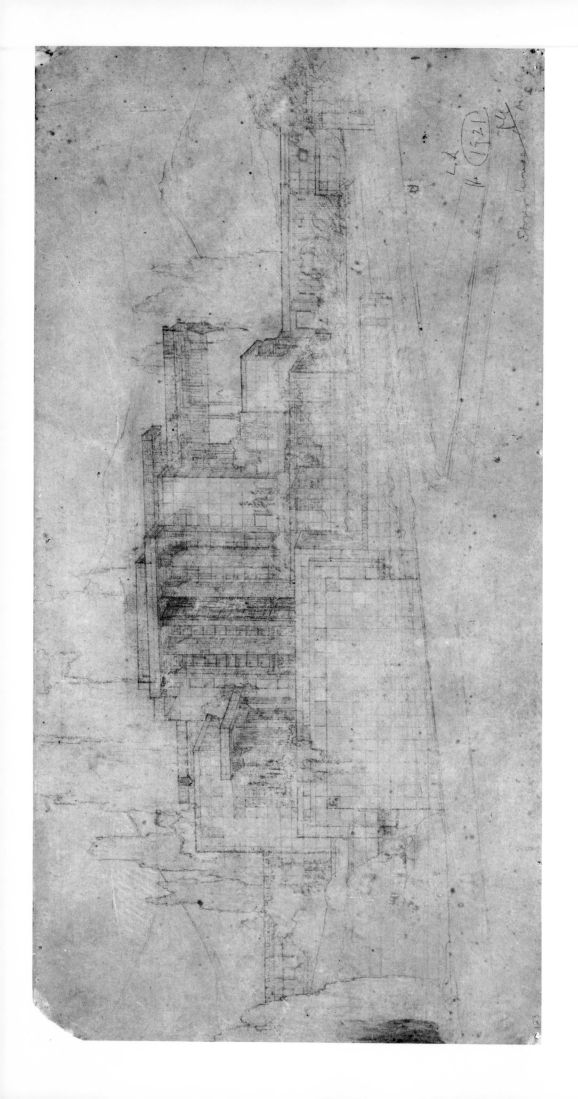

73. DR. JOHN STORER HOUSE, LOS ANGELES, CALIFORNIA. 1923.

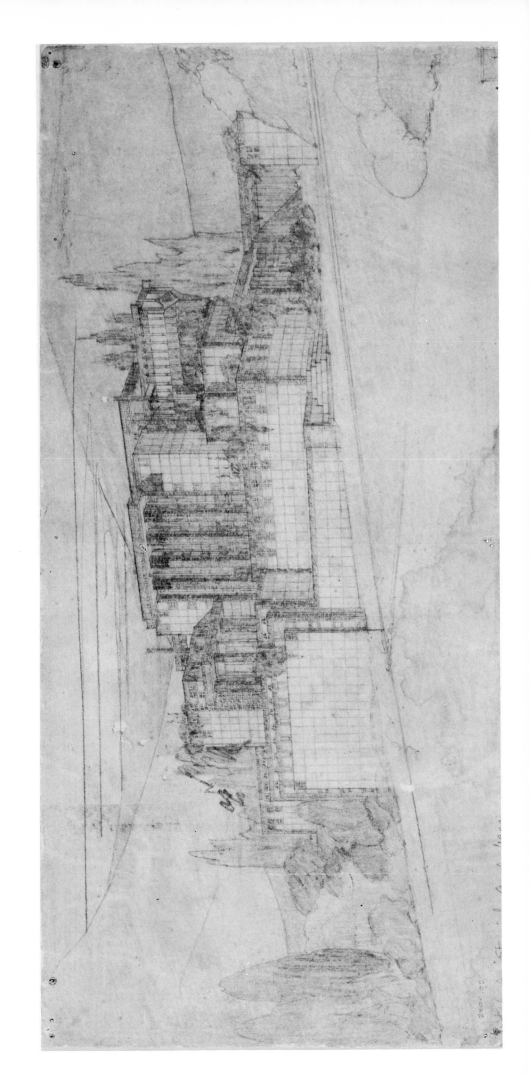

74. DR. JOHN STORER HOUSE, LOS ANGELES, CALIFORNIA. 1923.

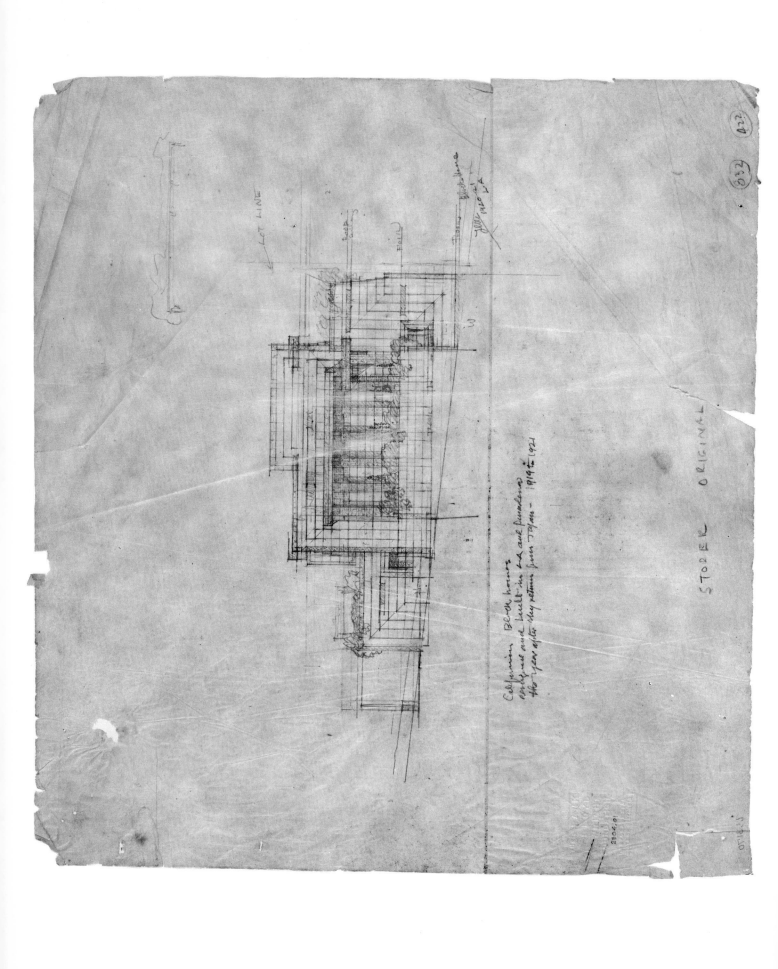

STODER ORIGINAL

California BLOCK houses
analysed and built in L.A. and founding
the year after they return from Japan — 1919 to 1921

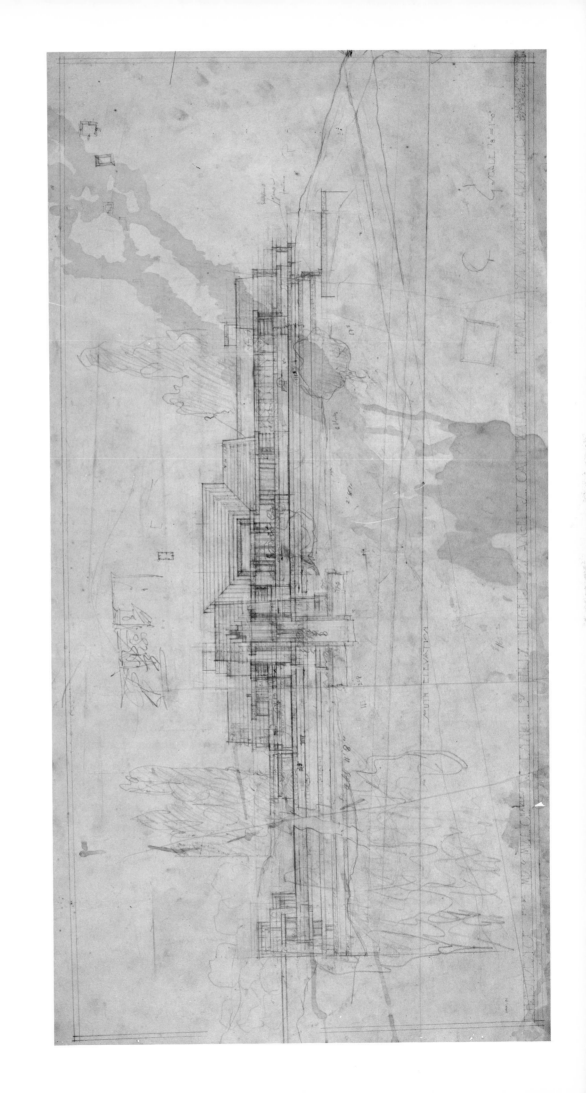

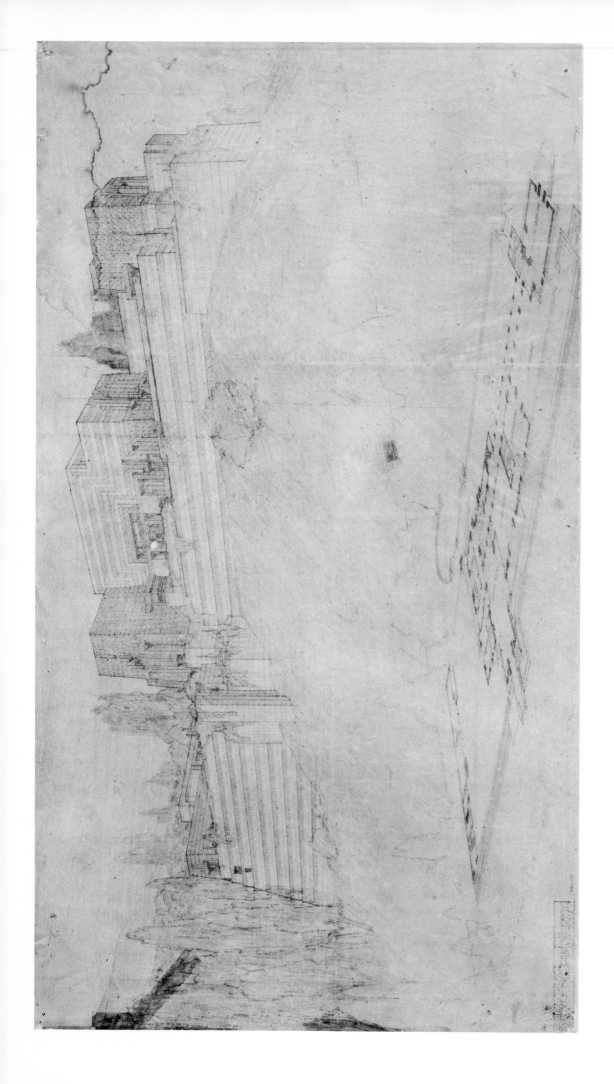

77. CHARLES ENNIS HOUSE, LOS ANGELES, CALIFORNIA. 1924.

78. CHARLES ENNIS HOUSE, LOS ANGELES, CALIFORNIA. 1924.

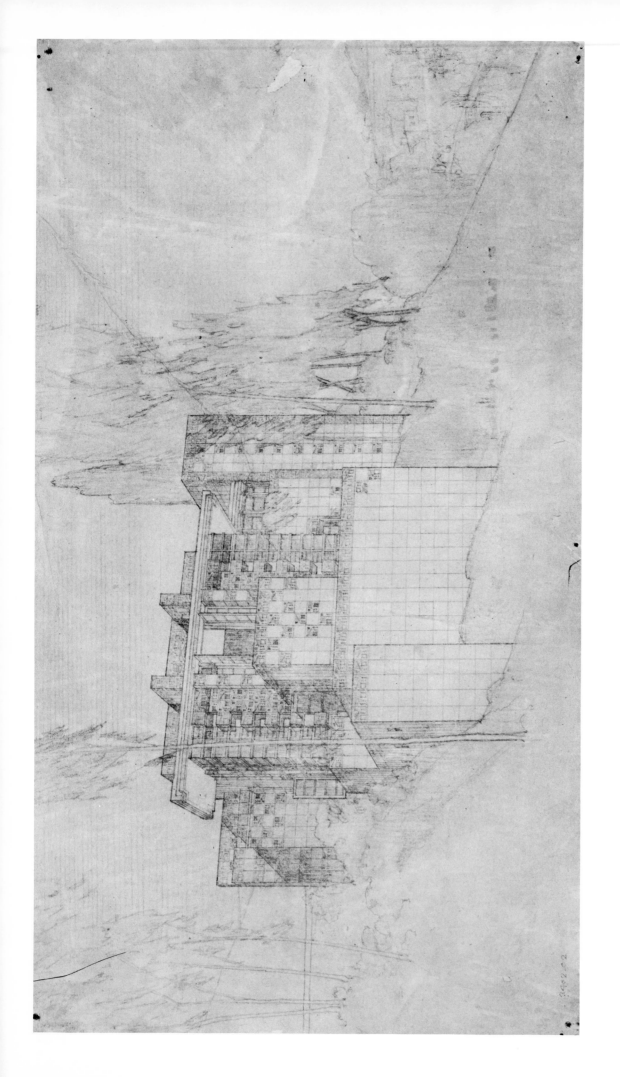

79. SAMUEL FREEMAN HOUSE, LOS ANGELES, CALIFORNIA. 1924.

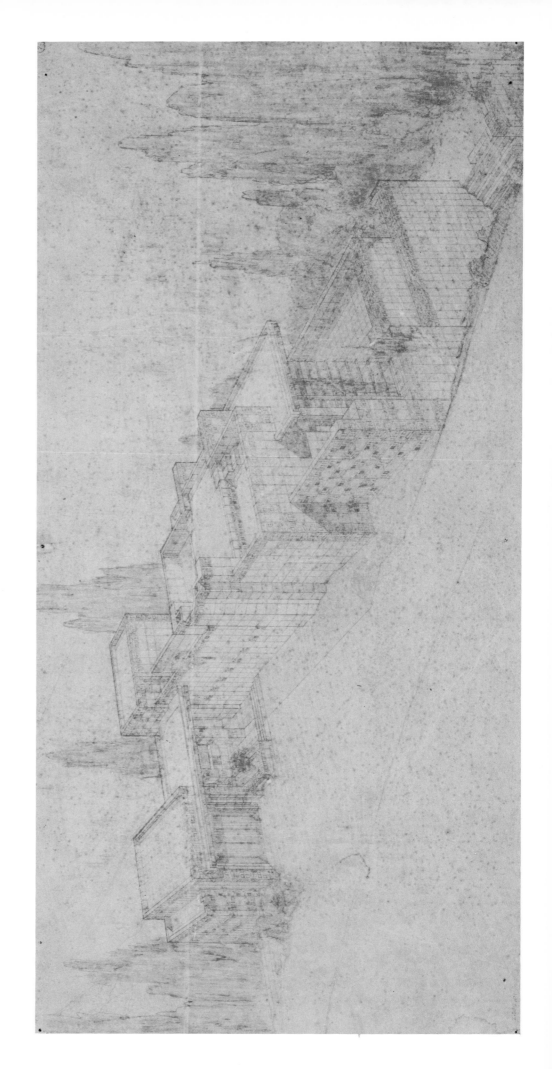

80. SAMUEL FREEMAN HOUSE, LOS ANGELES, CALIFORNIA. 1924.

81. PROJECT: DR. ALEXANDER CHANDLER SAN MARCOS-IN-THE-DESERT WINTER RESORT, CHANDLER, ARIZONA. 1927.

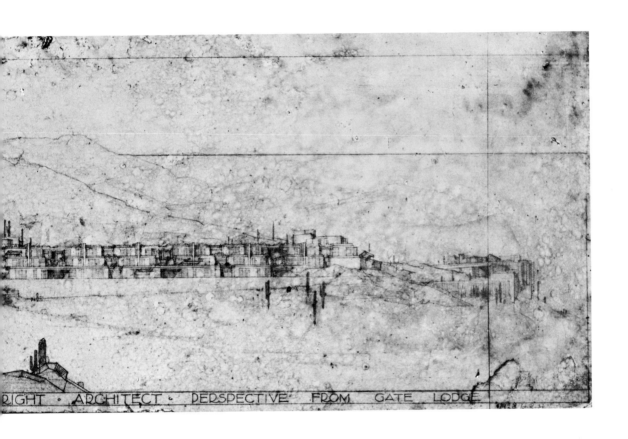

RIGHT · ARCHITECT · PERSPECTIVE · FROM · GATE LODGE

82. PROJECT: SAN MARCOS-IN-THE-DESERT WINTER RESORT, CHANDLER, ARIZONA. 1927.

83. PROJECT: SAN MARCOS-IN-THE-DESERT WINTER RESORT, CHANDLER, ARIZONA. 1927.

84. ALINE BARNSDALL KINDERGARTEN, "THE LITTLE DIPPER", OLIVE HILL, LOS ANGELES, CALIFORNIA. 1923.

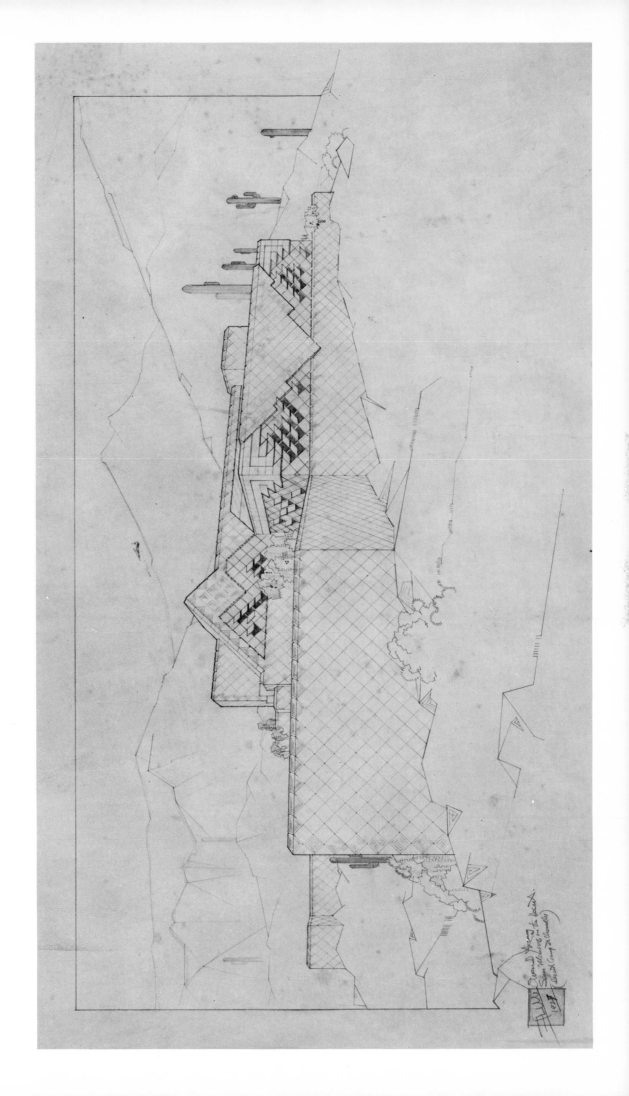

85. PROJECT: OWEN D. YOUNG HOUSE, SAN MARCOS-IN-THE-DESERT, ARIZONA. 1927.

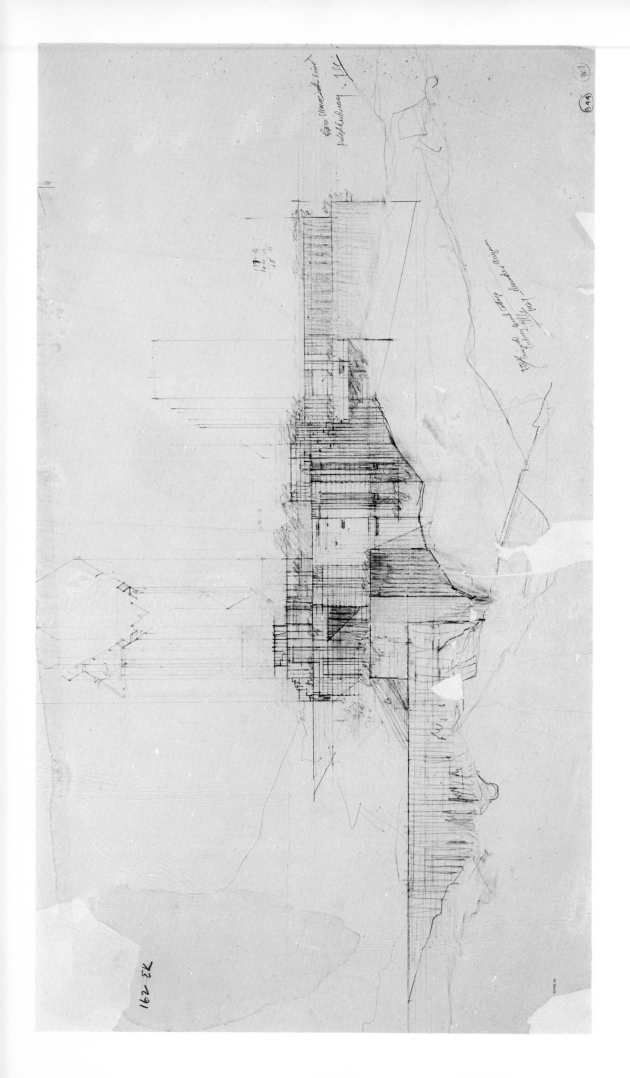

86. PROJECT: WELLINGTON AND RALPH CUDNEY HOUSE, SAN MARCOS-IN-THE-DESERT, ARIZONA. 1927.

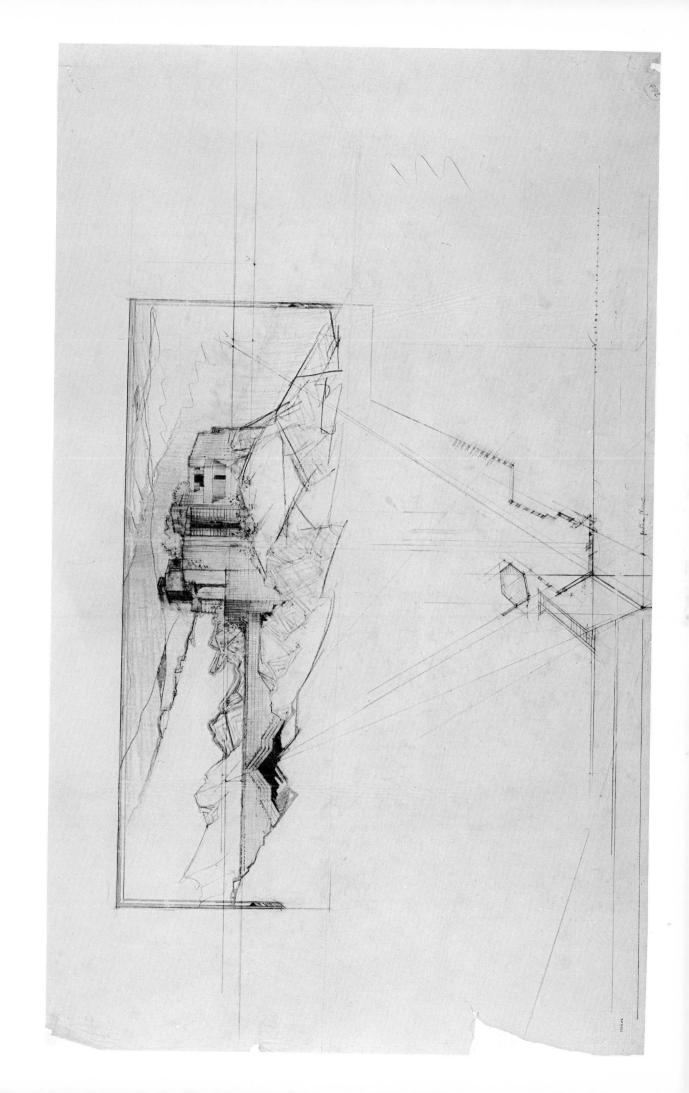

87. PROJECT: WELLINGTON AND RALPH CUDNEY HOUSE, SAN MARCOS-IN-THE-DESERT, ARIZONA. 1927.

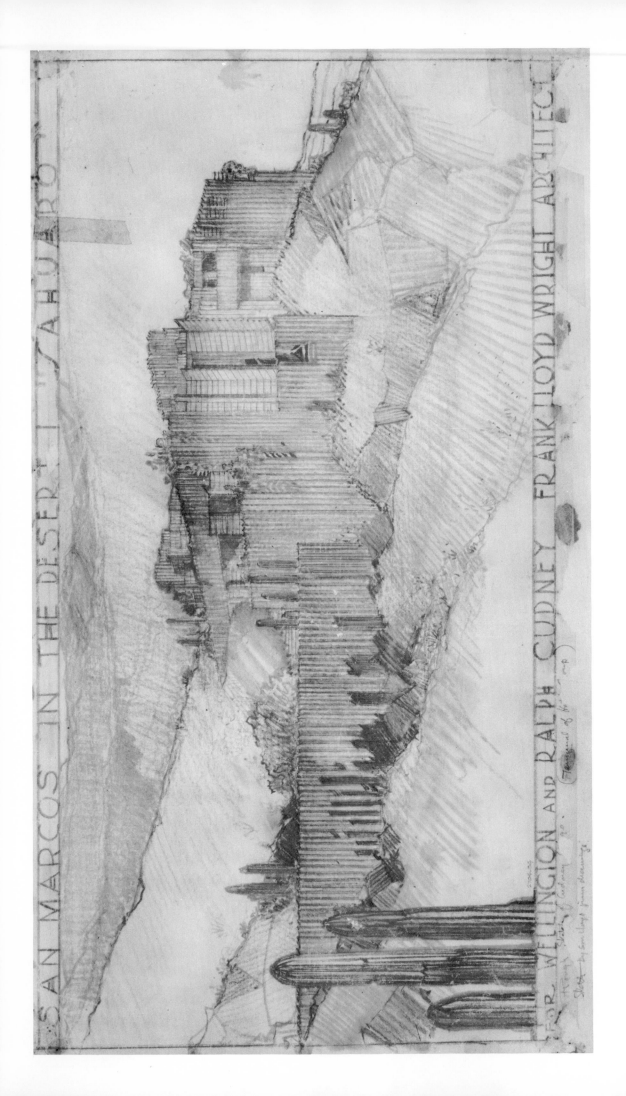

88. PROJECT: WELLINGTON AND RALPH CUDNEY HOUSE, SAN MARCOS-IN-THE-DESERT, ARIZONA. 1927.

89. PROJECT: WELLINGTON AND RALPH CUDNEY HOUSE, SAN MARCOS-IN-THE-DESERT, ARIZONA. 1927.

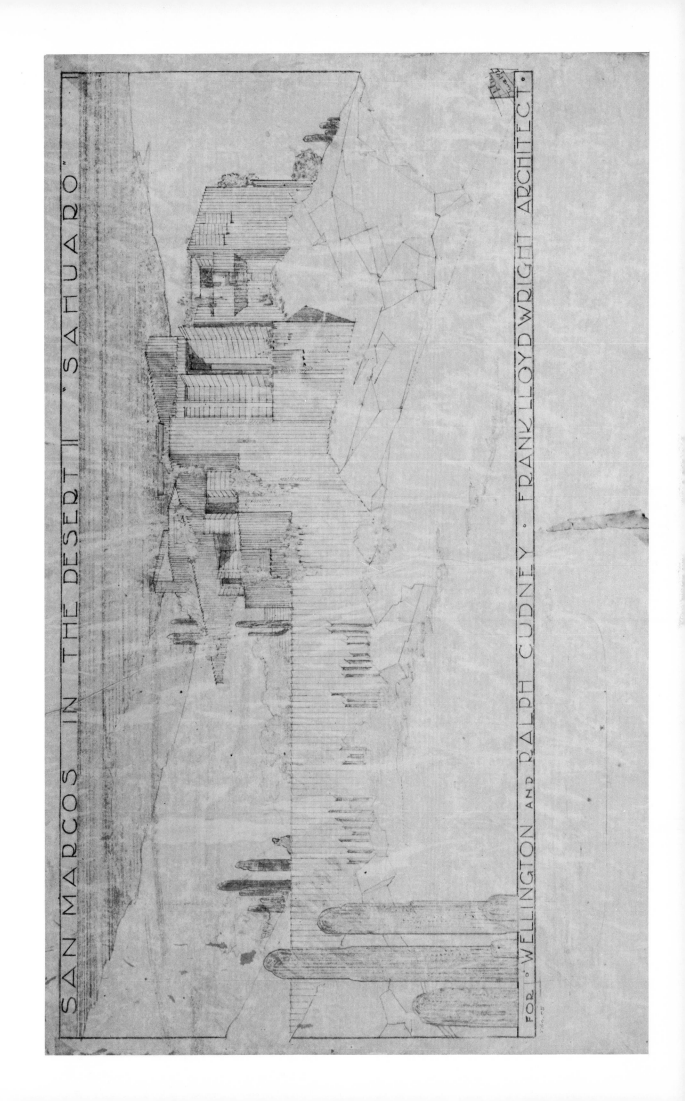

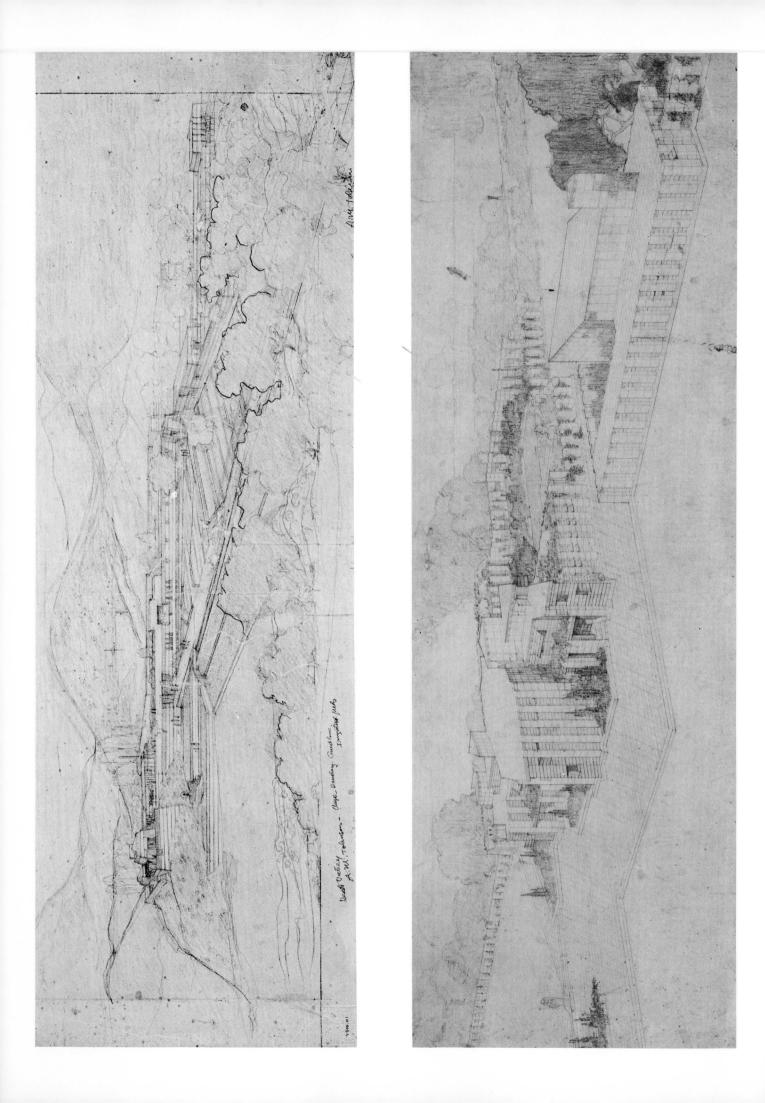

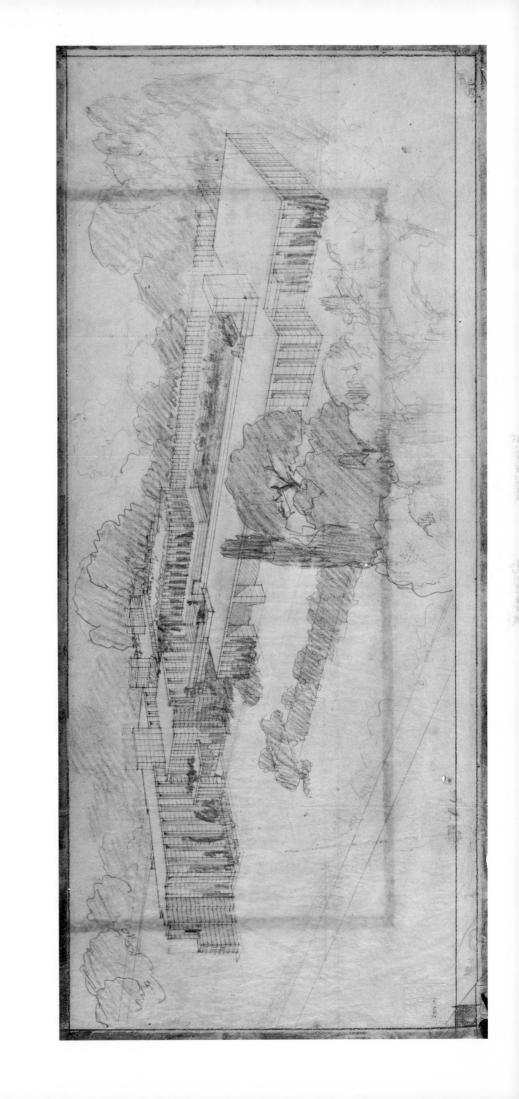

90. PROJECT: A. M. JOHNSON DESERT COMPOUND AND SHRINE, DEATH VALLEY, CALIFORNIA. 1922.

91. PROJECT: RICHARD LLOYD JONES HOUSE, "WESTHOPE", TULSA, OKLAHOMA. 1929.

92. RICHARD LLOYD JONES HOUSE, "WESTHOPE", TULSA, OKLAHOMA. 1929.

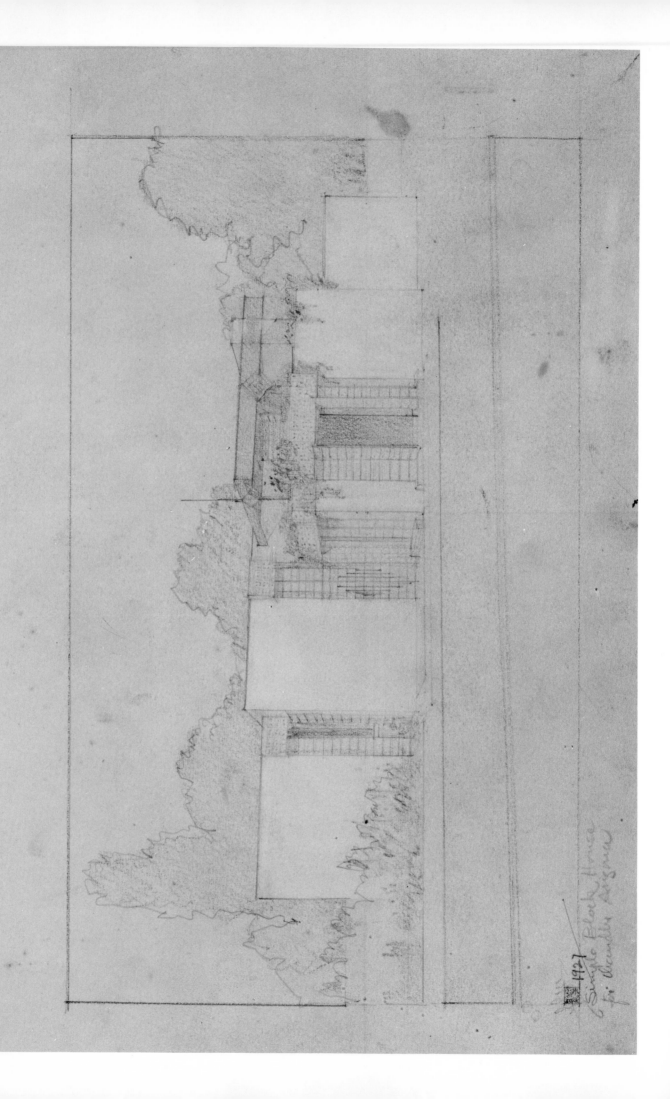

Single Plank House
for Arcadia Arizona

93. PROJECT: SINGLE BLOCK HOUSE, CHANDLER, ARIZONA. 1927.

94. PROJECT: ROSENWALD FOUNDATION SCHOOL FOR NEGRO CHILDREN. 1929.

95. PROJECT: OAK PARK PLAYGROUND ASSOCIATION PLAY HOUSES (NO. 4), OAK PARK, ILLINOIS. 1926.

96. PROJECT: DR. ALEXANDER CHANDLER SAN MARCOS WATER GARDENS TOURIST CAMP, CHANDLER, ARIZONA. 1927-8.

97. PROJECT: FLOATING CABIN, TAHOE SUMMER COLONY, LAKE TAHOE, CALIFORNIA. 1922.

98. PROJECT: FLOATING CABIN, TAHOE SUMMER COLONY, LAKE TAHOE, CALIFORNIA. 1922.

99. PROJECT: CABIN, TAHOE SUMMER COLONY, LAKE TAHOE, CALIFORNIA. 1922.

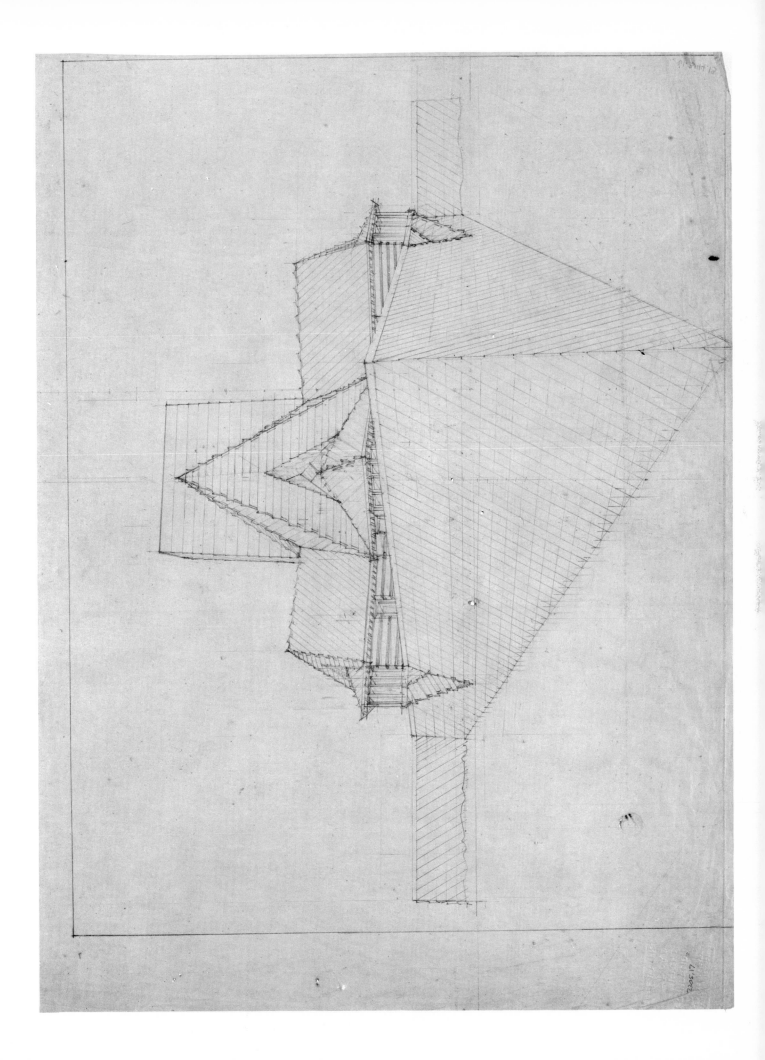

100. PROJECT: CABIN, TAHOE SUMMER COLONY, LAKE TAHOE, CALIFORNIA. 1923.

101. PROJECT: HUNTING LODGE, TAHOE SUMMER COLONY, LAKE TAHOE, CALIFORNIA. 1923.

E CABIN

102. PROJECT: CABIN, TAHOE SUMMER COLONY, LAKE TAHOE, CALIFORNIA. 1922.

103. PROJECT: E. A. SMITH HOUSE, PIEDMONT PINES, CALIFORNIA. 1938.

HOUSE FOR MR. AND MRS. E. A. SMITH PIEDMONT PINES
FRANK LLOYD WRIGHT ARCHITECT

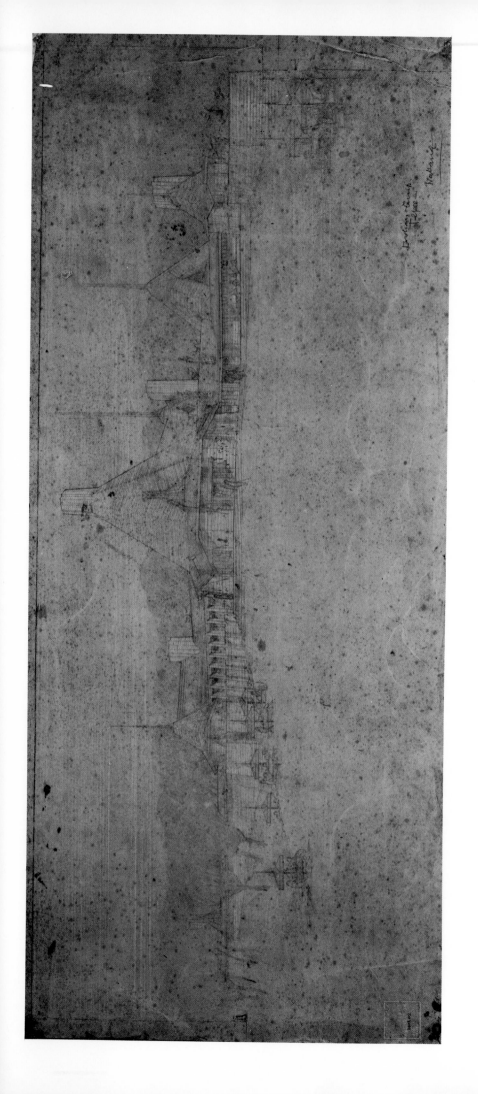

104. PROJECT: NAKOMA COUNTRY CLUB AND WINNEBAGO CAMPING GROUND INDIAN MEMORIAL, MADISON, WISCONSIN. 1924.

105. PROJECT: MRS. SAMUEL WILLIAM GLADNEY HOUSE, FORT WORTH, TEXAS. 1925.

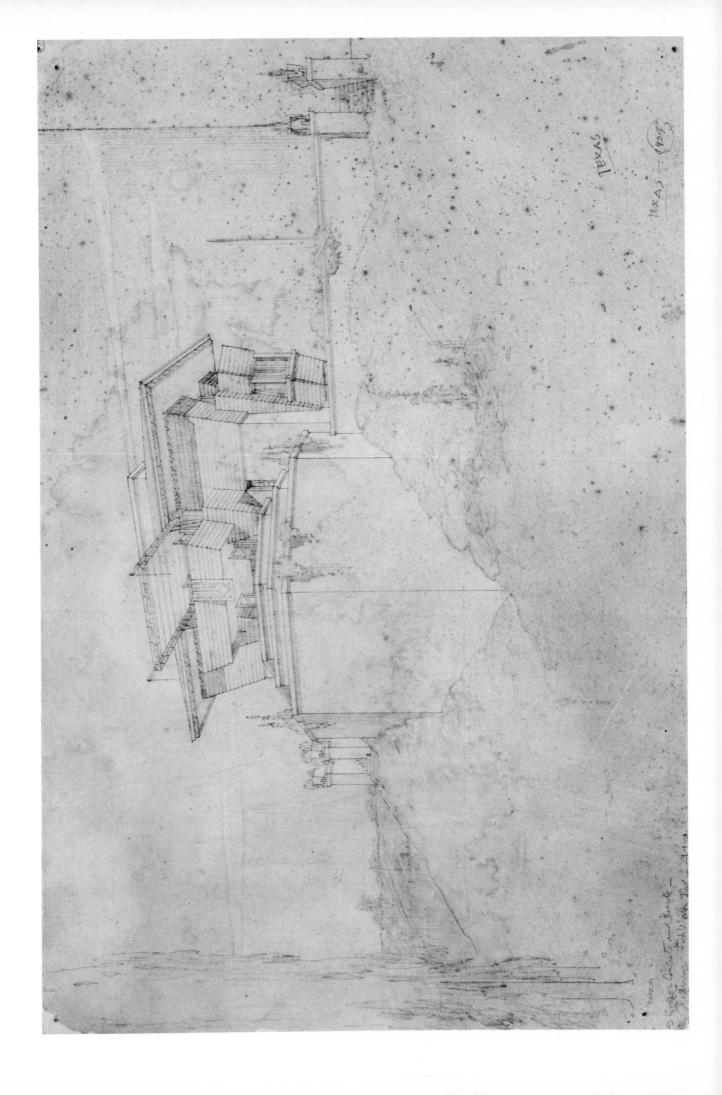

TEXAS

TEXAS — 1925

2505.23

Small Scale Study
(Birds eye.)

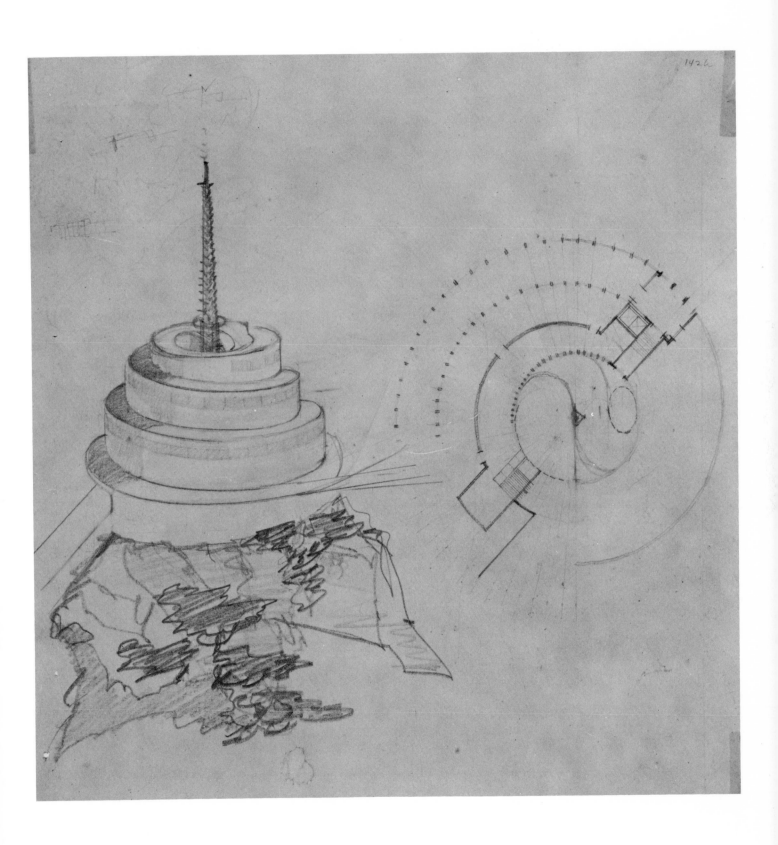

106, 107. PROJECT: GORDON STRONG AUTOMOBILE OBJECTIVE AND PLANETARIUM, SUGAR LOAF MOUNTAIN, MARYLAND. 1925.

108, 109. PROJECT: GORDON STRONG AUTOMOBILE OBJECTIVE AND PLANETARIUM, SUGAR LOAF MOUNTAIN, MARYLAND. 1925.

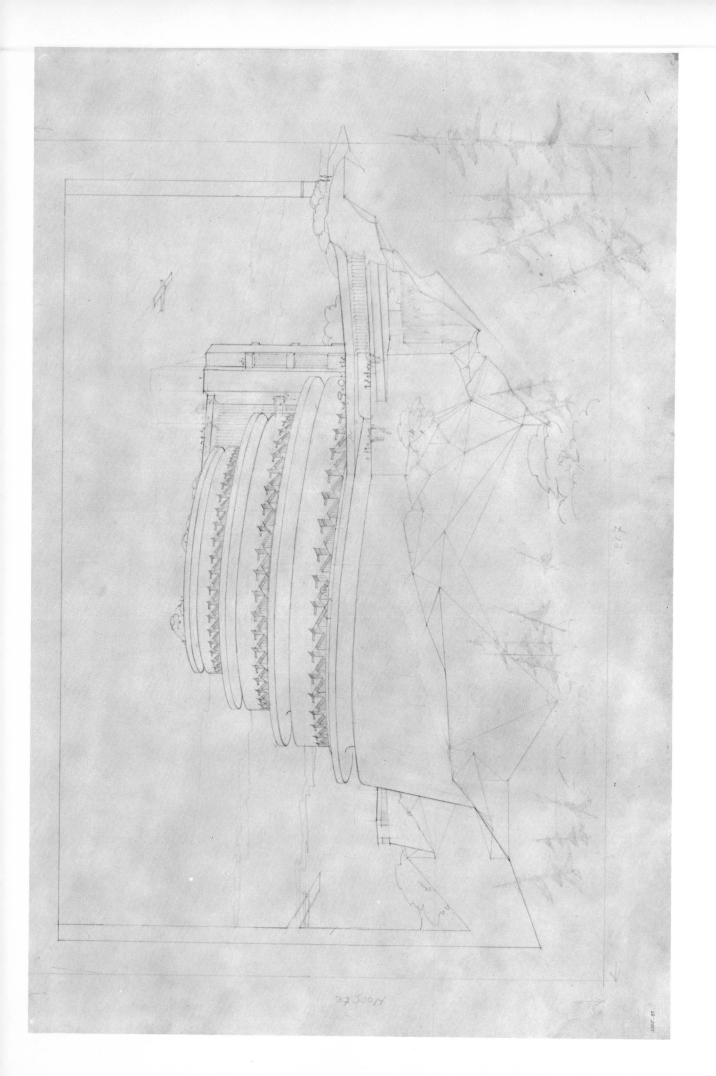

110, 111. PROJECT: GORDON STRONG AUTOMOBILE OBJECTIVE AND PLANETARIUM, SUGAR LOAF MOUNTAIN, MARYLAND. 1925.

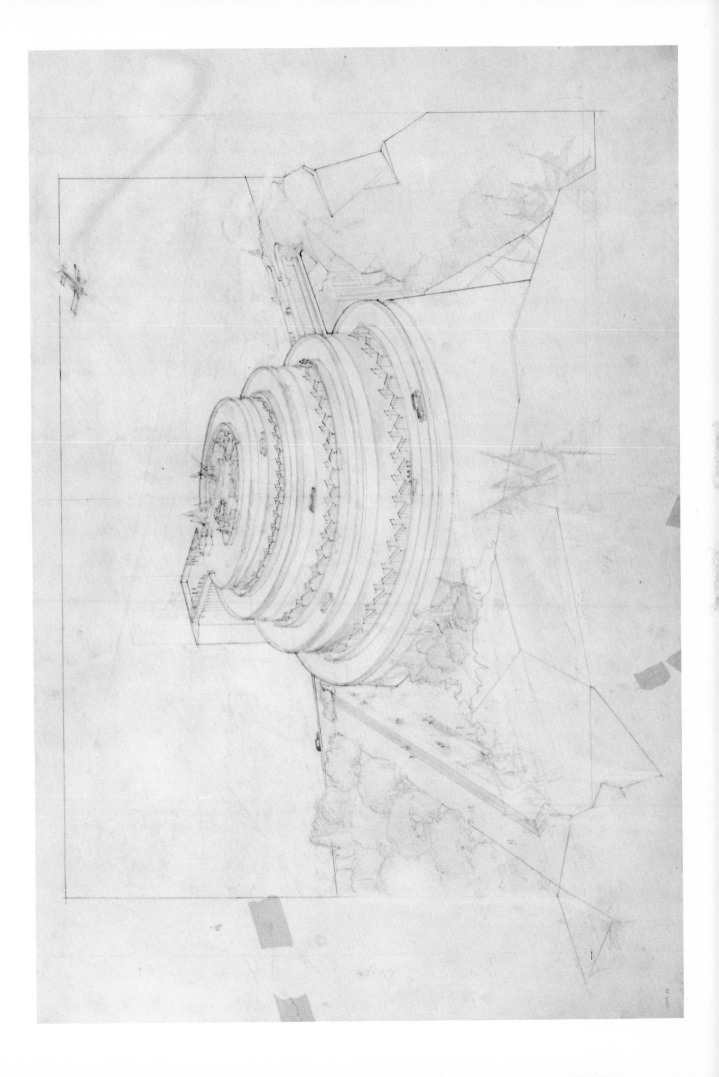

112, 113. PROJECT: GORDON STRONG AUTOMOBILE OBJECTIVE AND PLANETARIUM, SUGAR LOAF MOUNTAIN, MARYLAND. 1925.

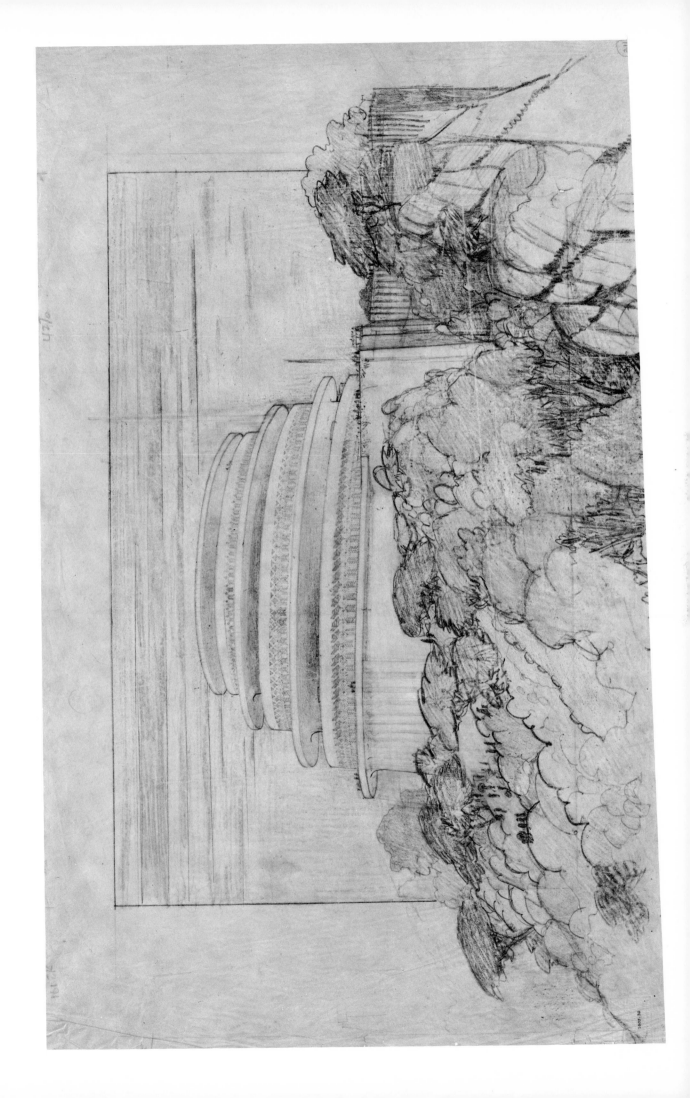

114. PROJECT: STEEL CATHEDRAL INCLUDING MINOR CATHEDRALS

FOR A MILLION PEOPLE, NEW YORK CITY, N. Y. 1926.

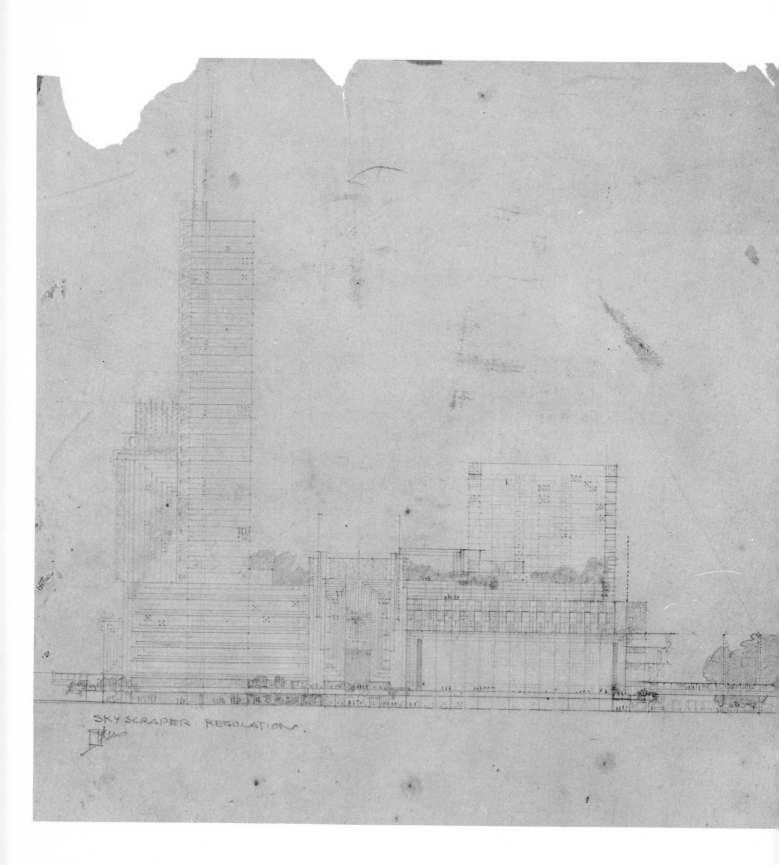

SKYSCRAPER REGULATION.

115. PROJECT: SKYSCRAPER REGULATIONS, CHICAGO, ILLINOIS. 1926.

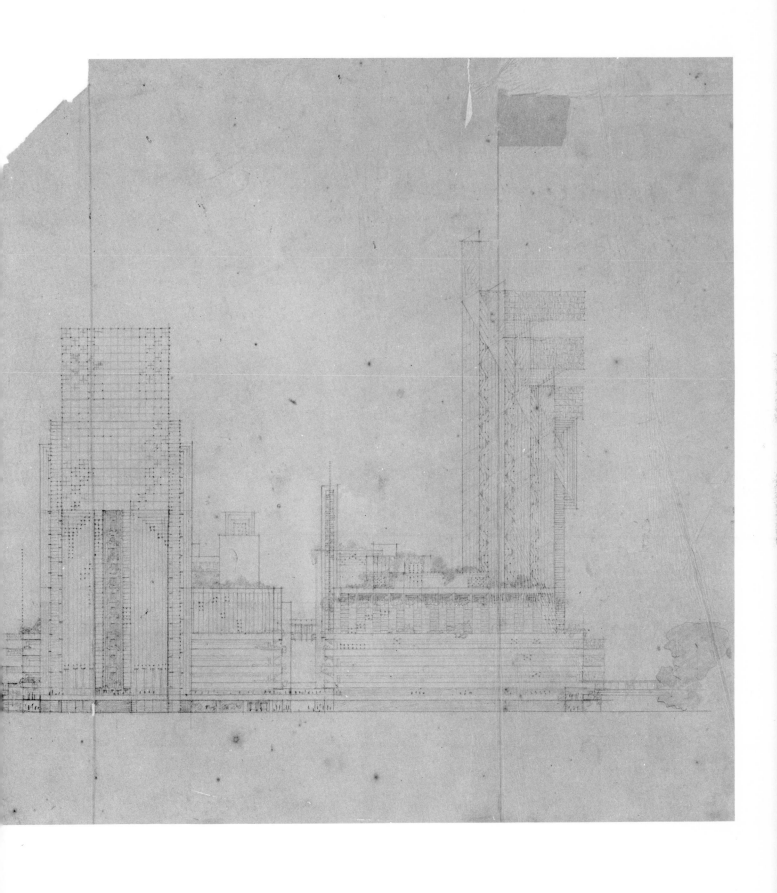

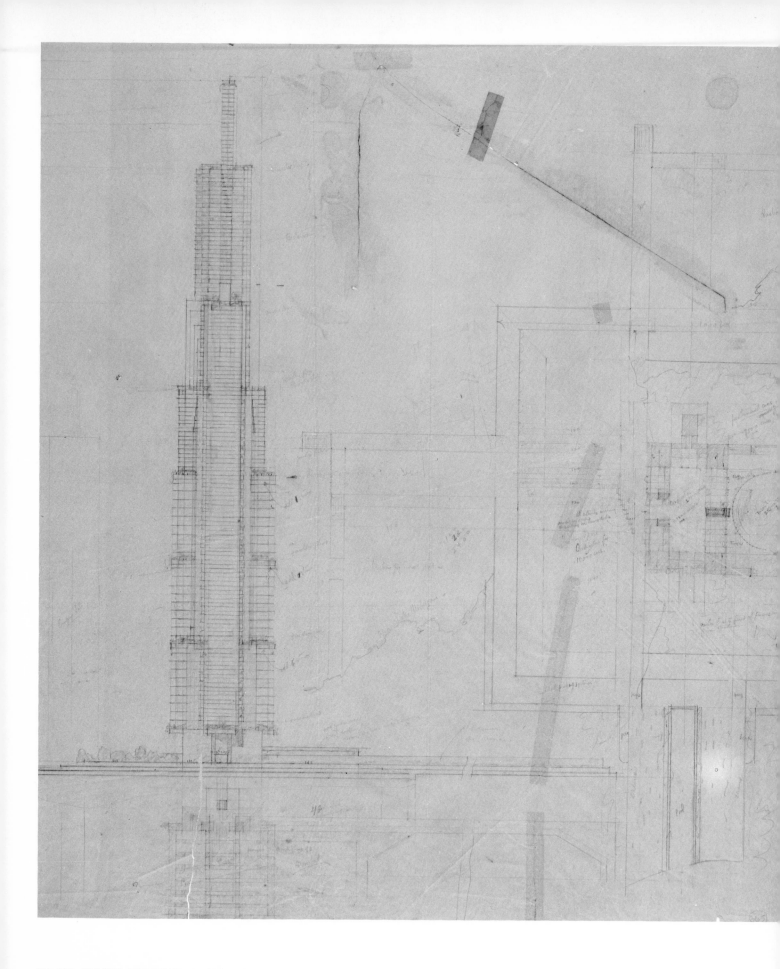

116, 117. PROJECT: SKYSCRAPER, CHICAGO, ILLINOIS. 1931.

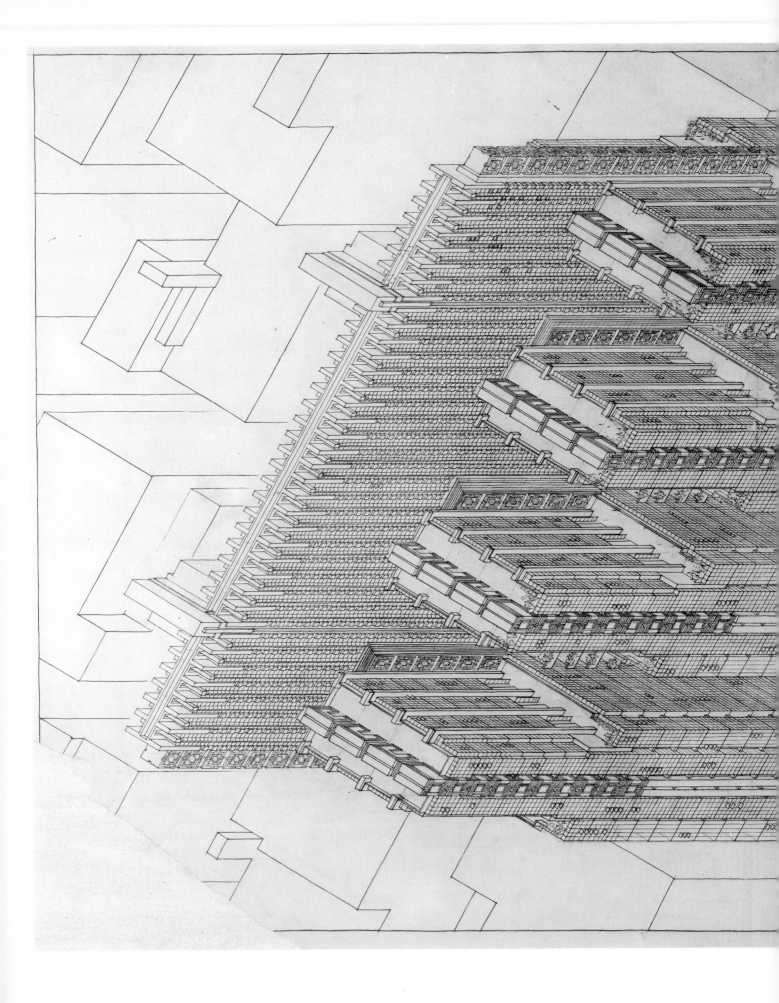

118. PROJECT: NATIONAL LIFE INSURANCE COMPANY SKYSCRAPER, CHICAGO, ILLINOIS. 1924.

119. PROJECT: NATIONAL LIFE INSURANCE COMPANY SKYSCRAPER, CHICAGO, ILLINOIS. 1924.

FIRST GROVP

IN THE BOUWERIE. NEW YORK CITY FRANK LLOYD WRIGHT. ARCHITECT

120. PROJECT: ST. MARK'S APARTMENT TOWER, ST. MARK'S-IN-THE-BOUWERIE, NEW YORK CITY, N. Y. 1929.

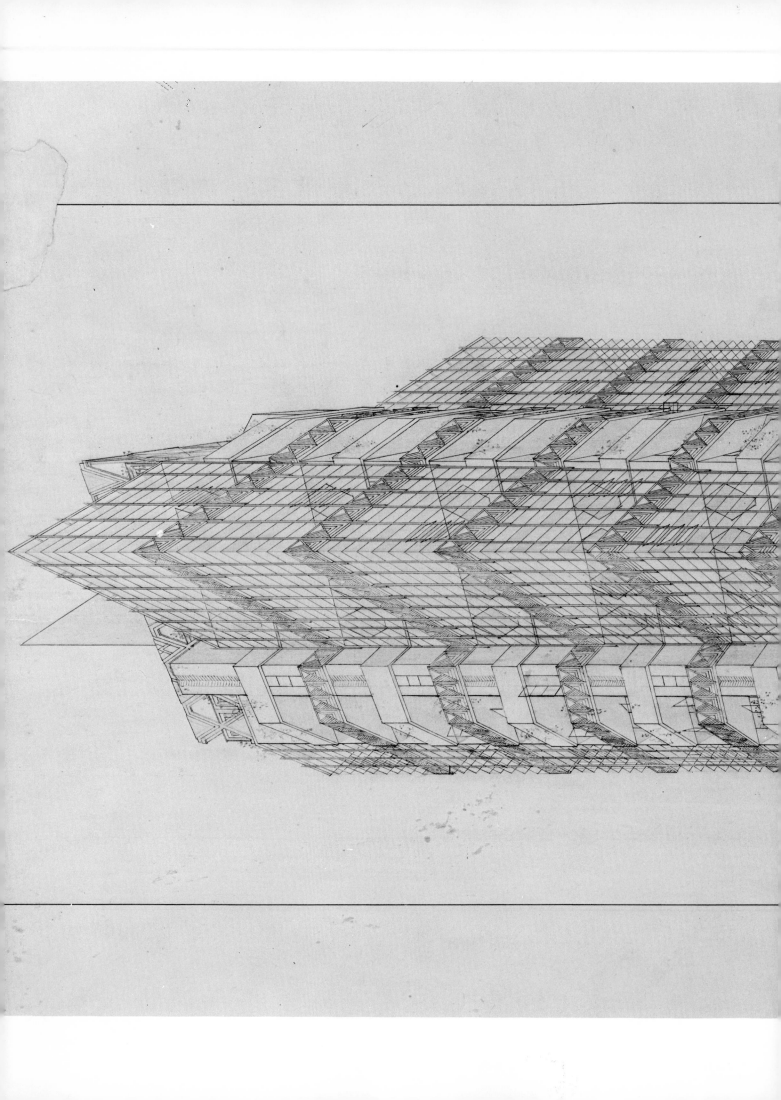

121. PROJECT: ST. MARK'S APARTMENT TOWER, ST. MARK'S-IN-THE-BOUWERIE, NEW YORK CITY, N. Y. 1929.

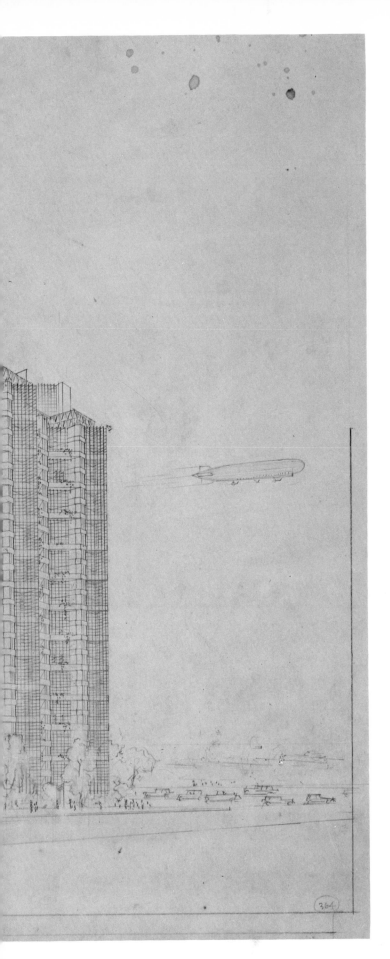

122. PROJECT: GROUPED APARTMENT TOWERS, CHICAGO, ILLINOIS. 1930.

123. PROJECT: ST. MARK'S APARTMENT TOWER, ST. MARK'S-IN-THE-BOUWERIE, NEW YORK CITY, N. Y. 1929.

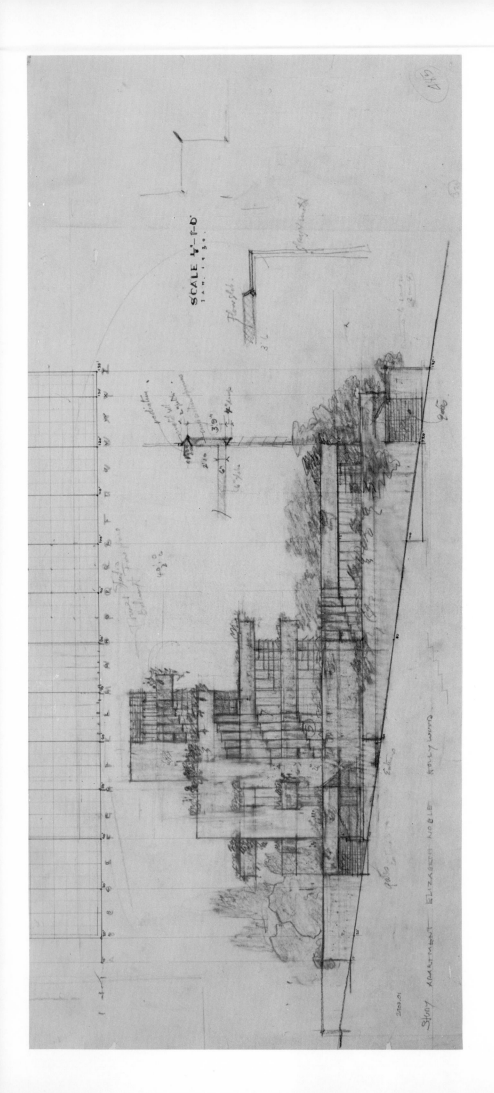

124. PROJECT: ELIZABETH NOBLE APARTMENT HOUSE, LOS ANGELES, CALIFORNIA. 1929.

125. PROJECT: ELIZABETH NOBLE APARTMENT HOUSE, LOS ANGELES, CALIFORNIA. 1929.

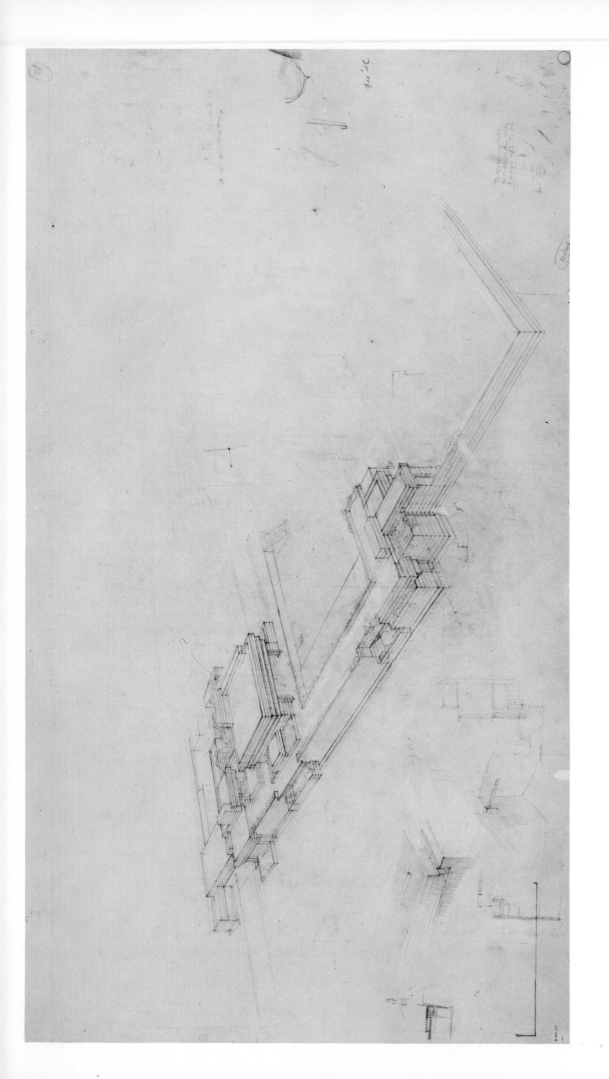

126. PROJECT: "HOUSE ON THE MESA", DENVER, COLORADO. 1931.

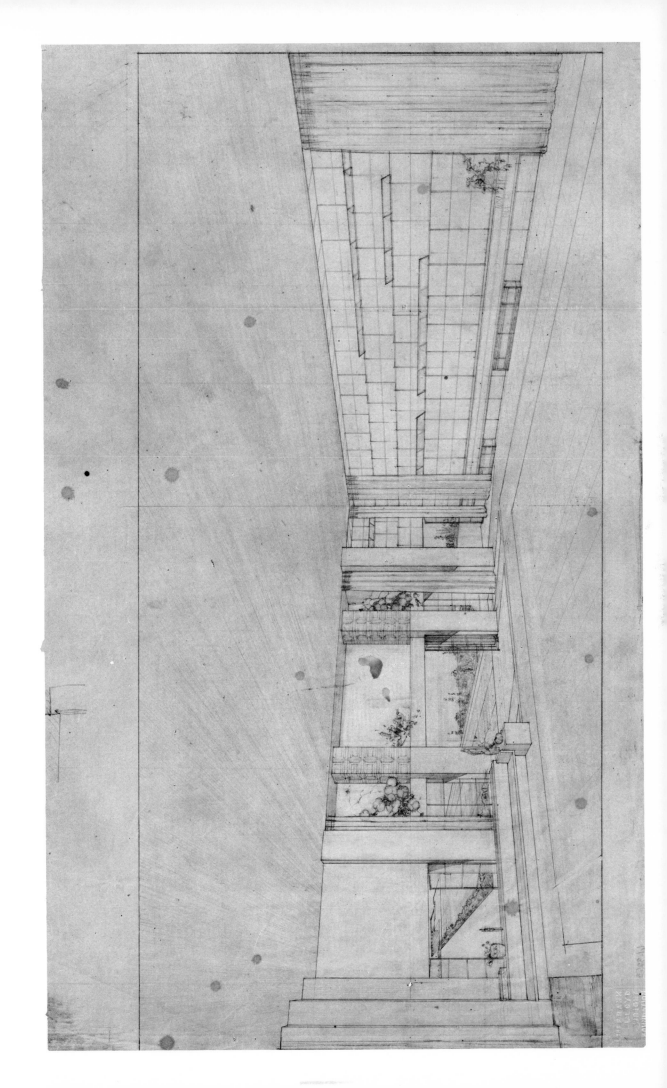

127. PROJECT: "HOUSE ON THE MESA", DENVER, COLORADO. 1931.

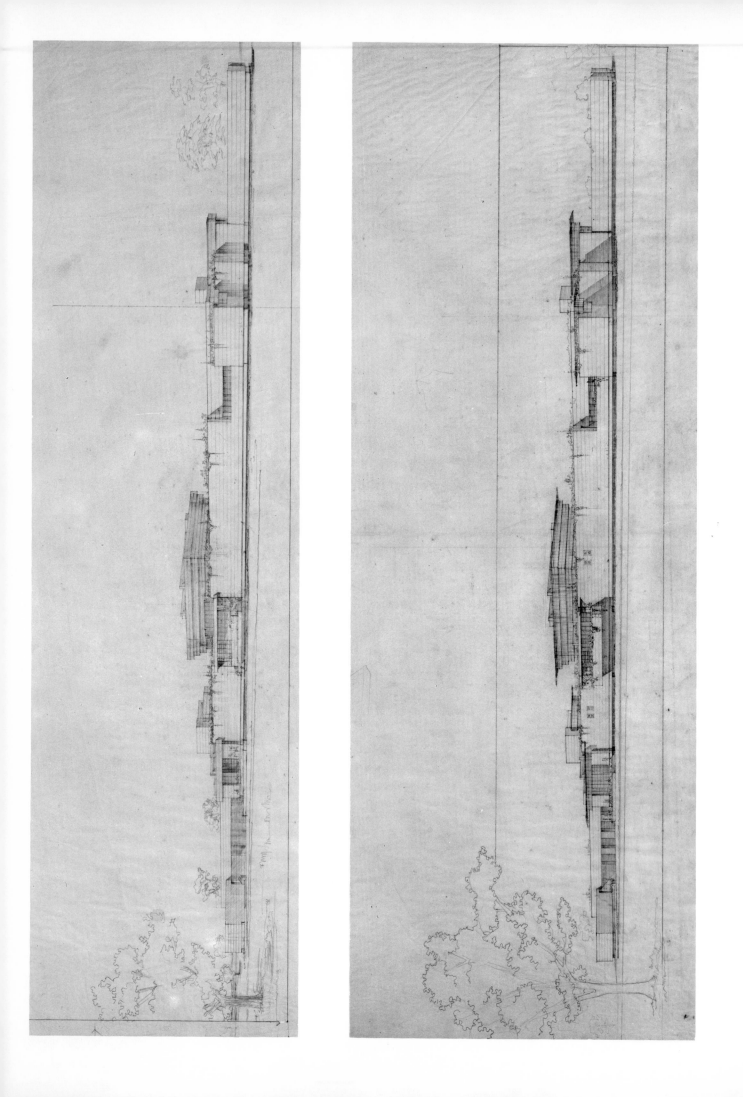

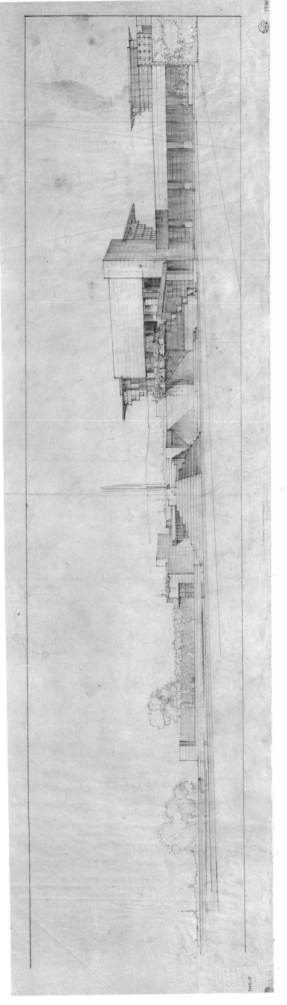

128, 129, 130, 131. PROJECT: "HOUSE ON THE MESA", DENVER, COLORADO. 1931.

132. PROJECT: DEAN MALCOLM M. WILLEY HOUSE, MINNEAPOLIS, MINNESOTA. 1934.

133. HILLSIDE BUILDINGS, TALIESIN FELLOWSHIP, SPRING GREEN, WISCONSIN. 1933.

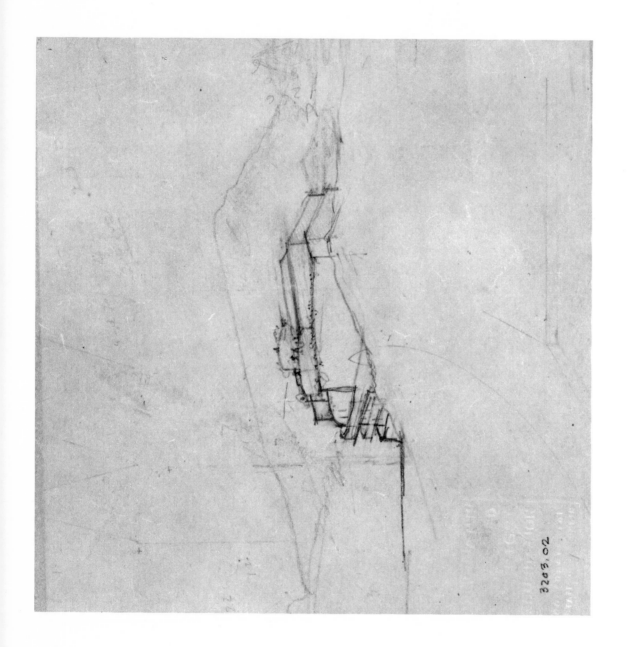

134, 135, 136. PROJECT: NEW THEATRE. 1932.

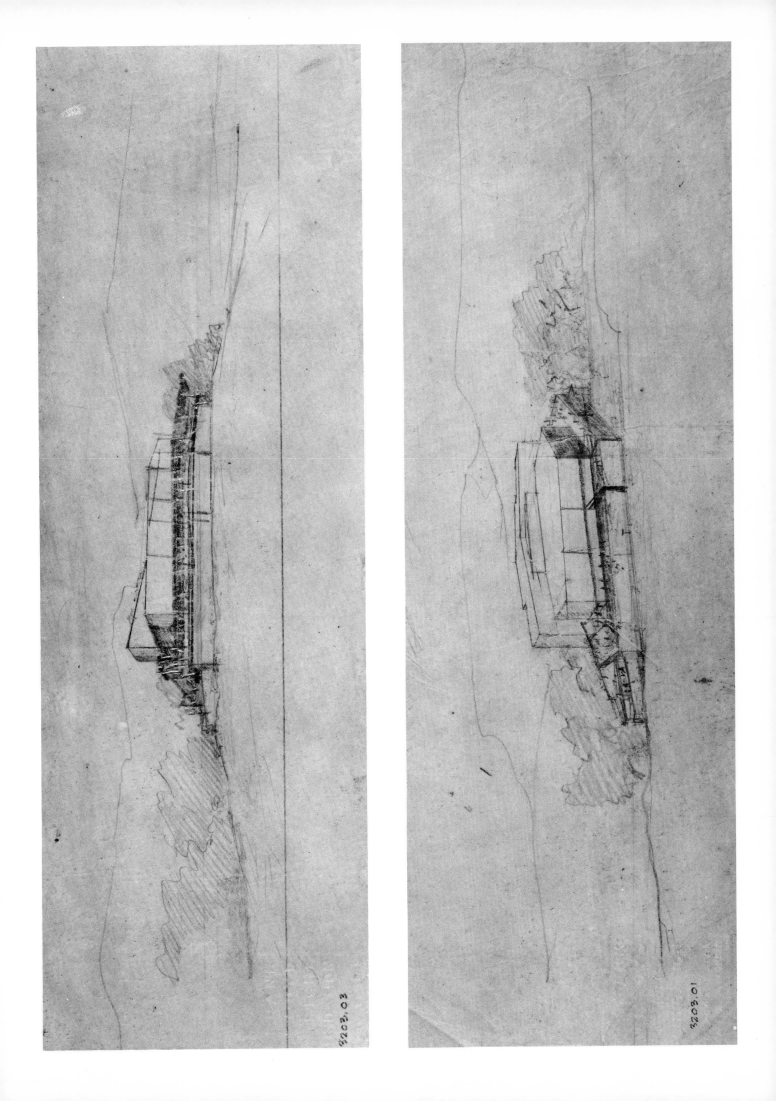

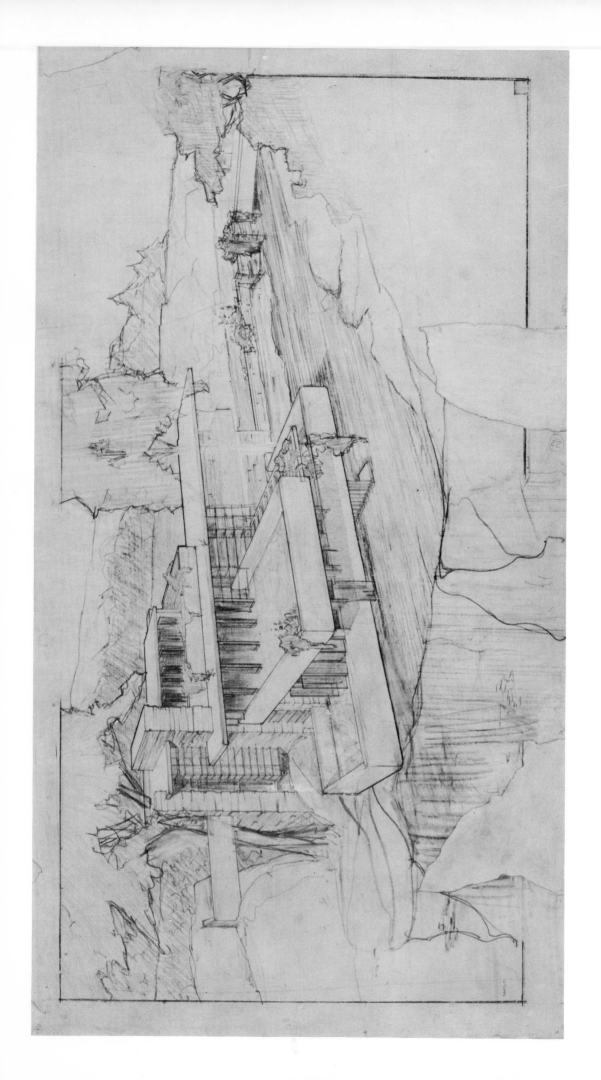

137. EDGAR J. KAUFMANN HOUSE "FALLINGWATER", BEAR RUN, PENNSYLVANIA. 1936.

138. EDGAR J. KAUFMANN HOUSE "FALLINGWATER", BEAR RUN, PENNSYLVANIA. 1936.

139. EDGAR J. KAUFMANN HOUSE "FALLINGWATER", BEAR RUN, PENNSYLVANIA. 1936.

140. EDGAR J. KAUFMANN HOUSE "FALLINGWATER", BEAR RUN, PENNSYLVANIA. 1936.

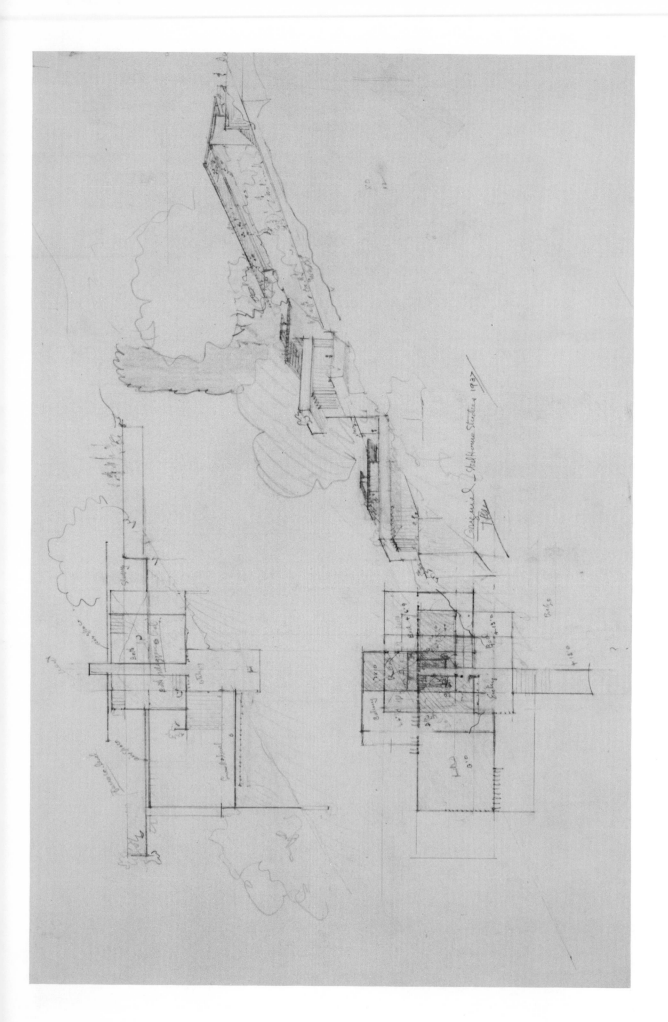

141, 142. PROJECT: "ALL STEEL" HOUSES DEVELOPMENT, LOS ANGELES, CALIFORNIA. 1937.

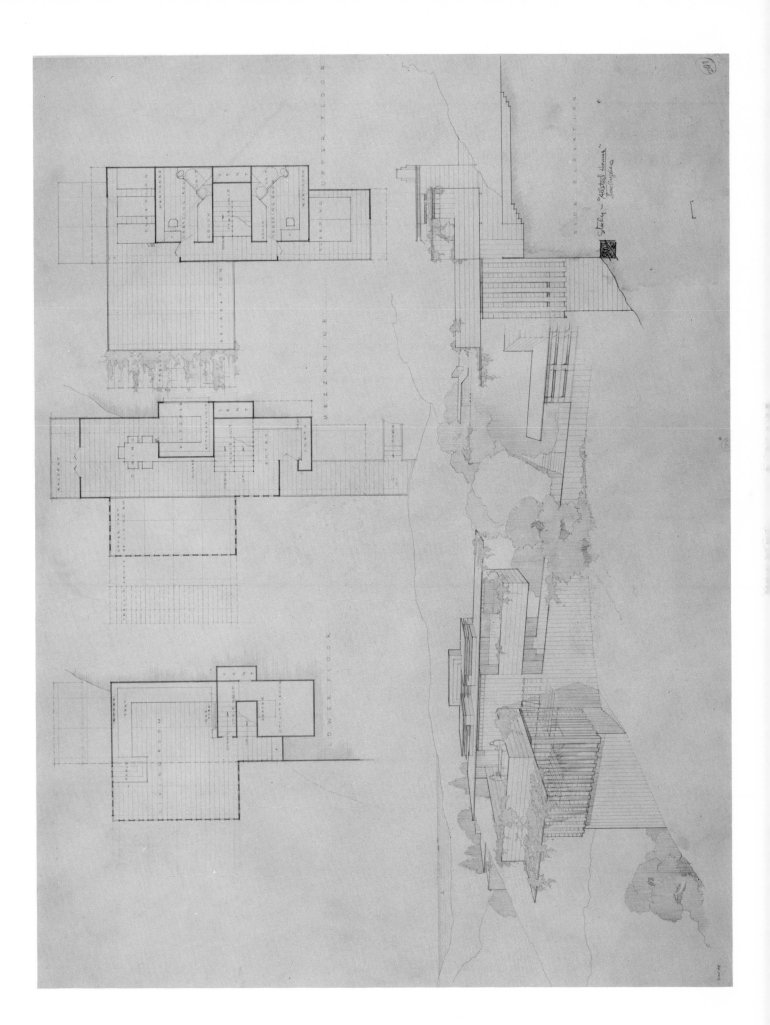

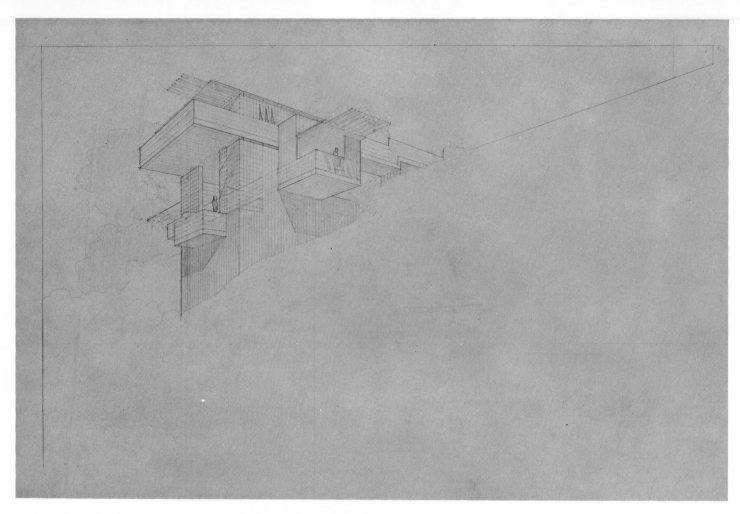

143, 144. PROJECT: "ALL STEEL" HOUSES DEVELOPMENT, LOS ANGELES, CALIFORNIA. 1937.

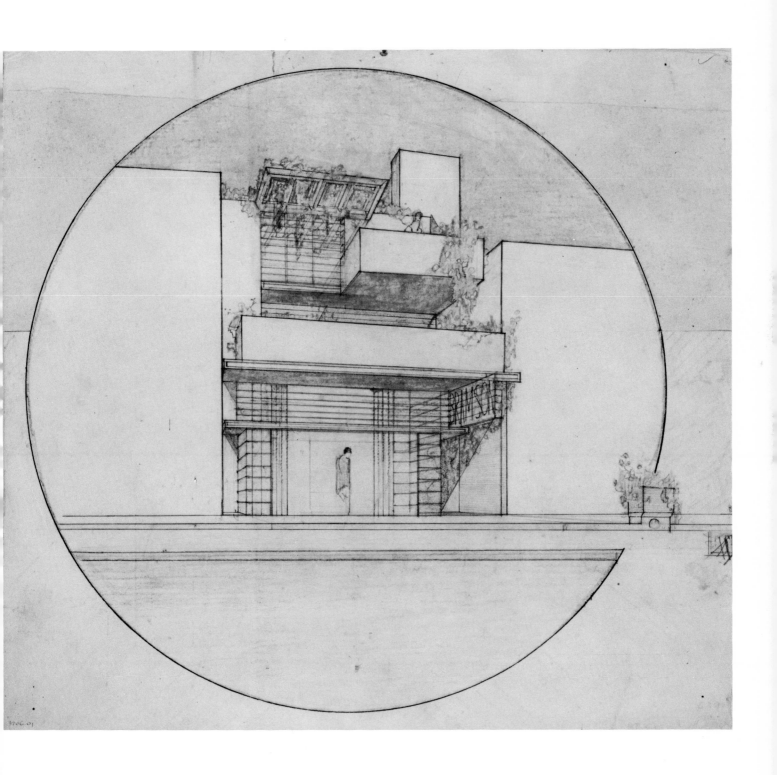

145. PROJECT: LEO BRAMSON DRESS SHOP, OAK PARK, ILLINOIS. 1937.

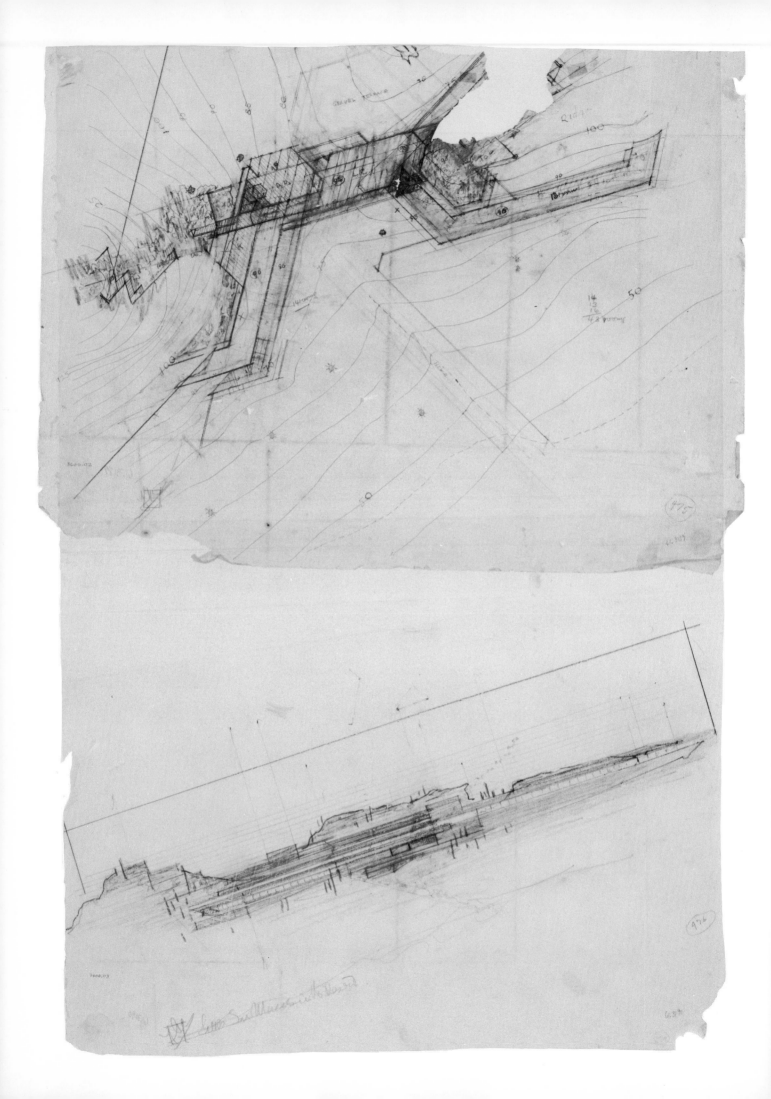

146, 147. PROJECT: LITTLE SAN MARCOS, CHANDLER, ARIZONA. 1936.

148. PROJECT: LITTLE SAN MARCOS, CHANDLER, ARIZONA. 1936.

149. "TALIESIN WEST", FRANK LLOYD WRIGHT WINTER RESIDENCE AND STUDIO, PARADISE VALLEY, ARIZONA. 1938.

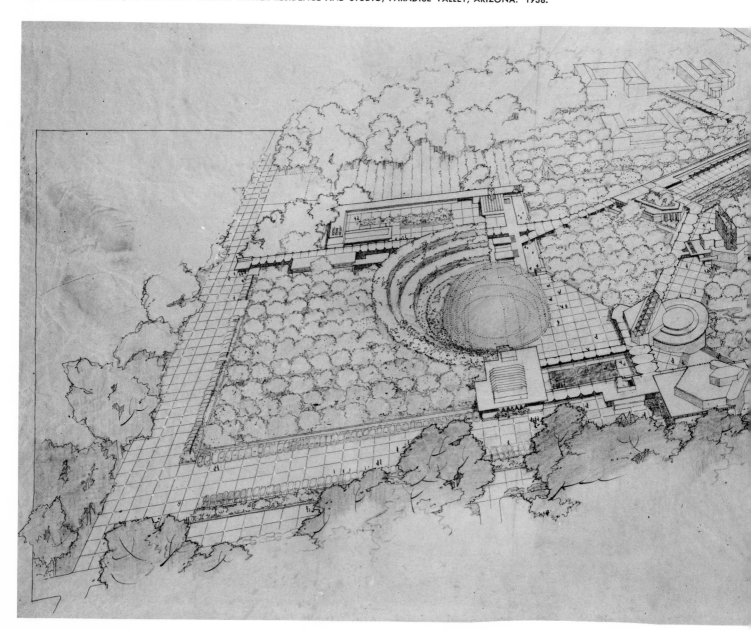

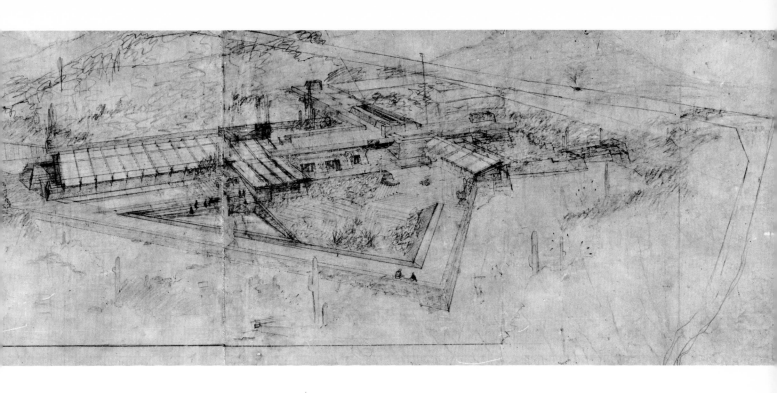

150. FLORIDA SOUTHERN COLLEGE, LAKELAND, FLORIDA. 1938.

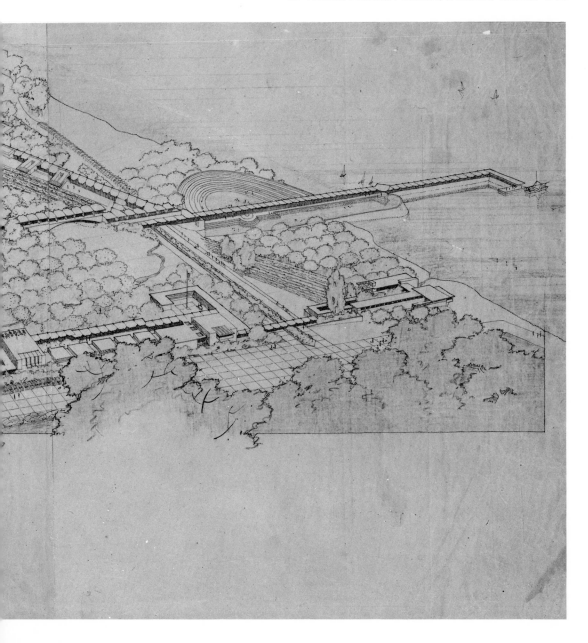

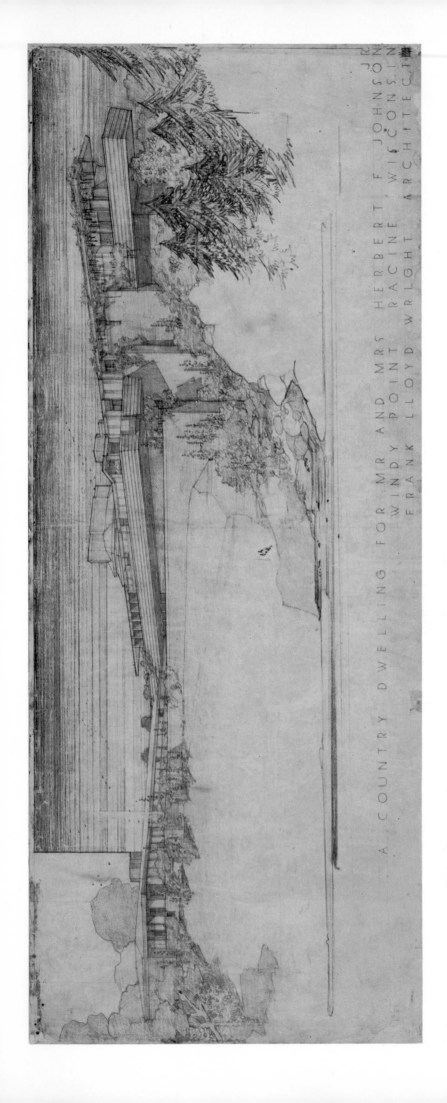

A COUNTRY DWELLING FOR MR AND MRS HERBERT F JOHNSON JR
WINDY POINT RACINE WISCONSIN
FRANK LLOYD WRIGHT ARCHITECT

151, 152. HERBERT F. JOHNSON, JR. HOUSE, "WINGSPREAD", WINDY POINT, WISCONSIN. 1937.

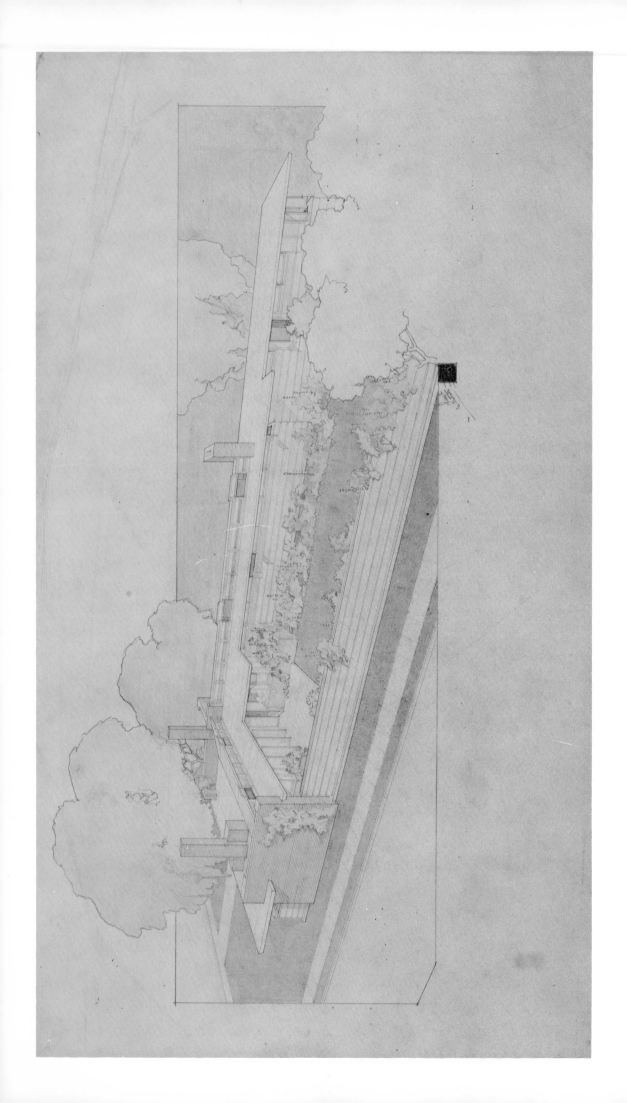

153. PROJECT: ROBERT D. LUSK HOUSE, HURON, S. DAKOTA. 1936.

154, 155. HERBERT JACOBS HOUSE, MADISON, WISCONSIN. 1937.

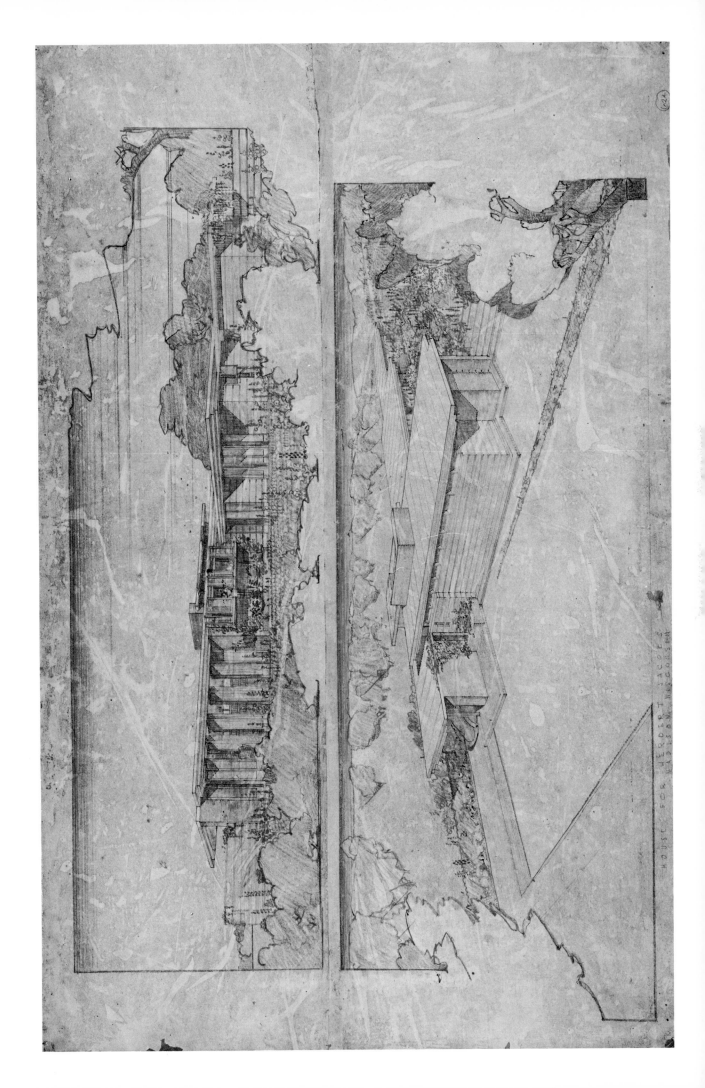

156.   PAUL R. HANNA HOUSE, PALO ALTO, CALIFORNIA. 1937.

157.   PAUL R. HANNA HOUSE, PALO ALTO, CALIFORNIA. 1937.

158.   CARL WALL HOUSE, PLYMOUTH, MICHIGAN. 1939.

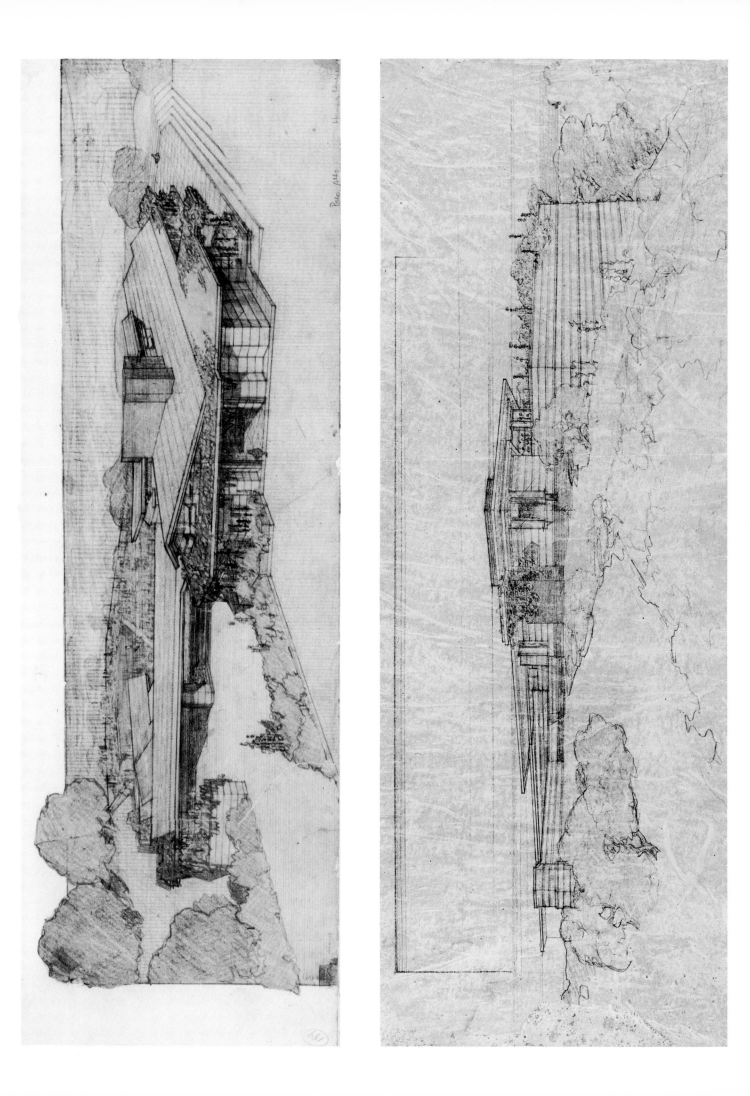

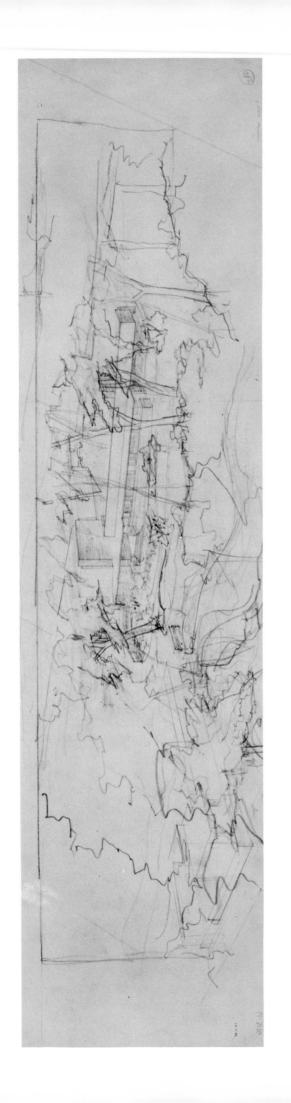

159. EDGAR J. KAUFMANN GUEST HOUSE, BEAR RUN, PENNSYLVANIA. 1939.

160. PROJECT: "HOUSE FOR A FAMILY OF $5,000-$6,000 INCOME", FOR *LIFE* MAGAZINE. 1938.

161. BERNARD SCHWARTZ HOUSE, STILL BEND, WISCONSIN. 1939.

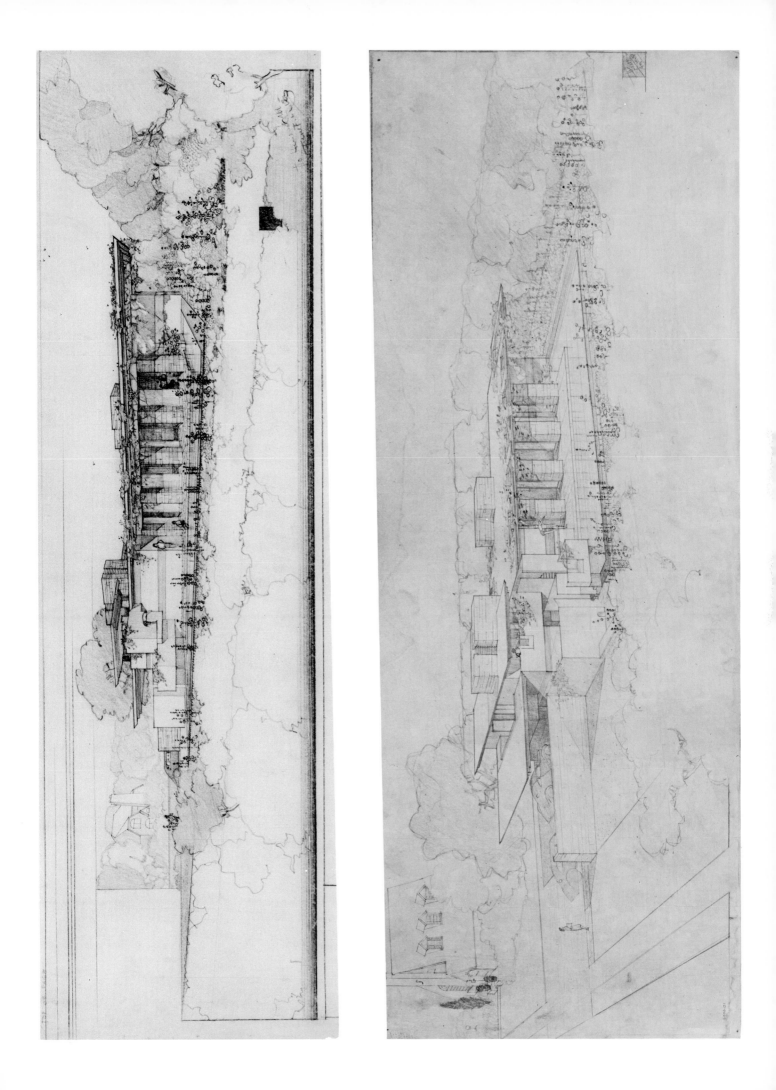

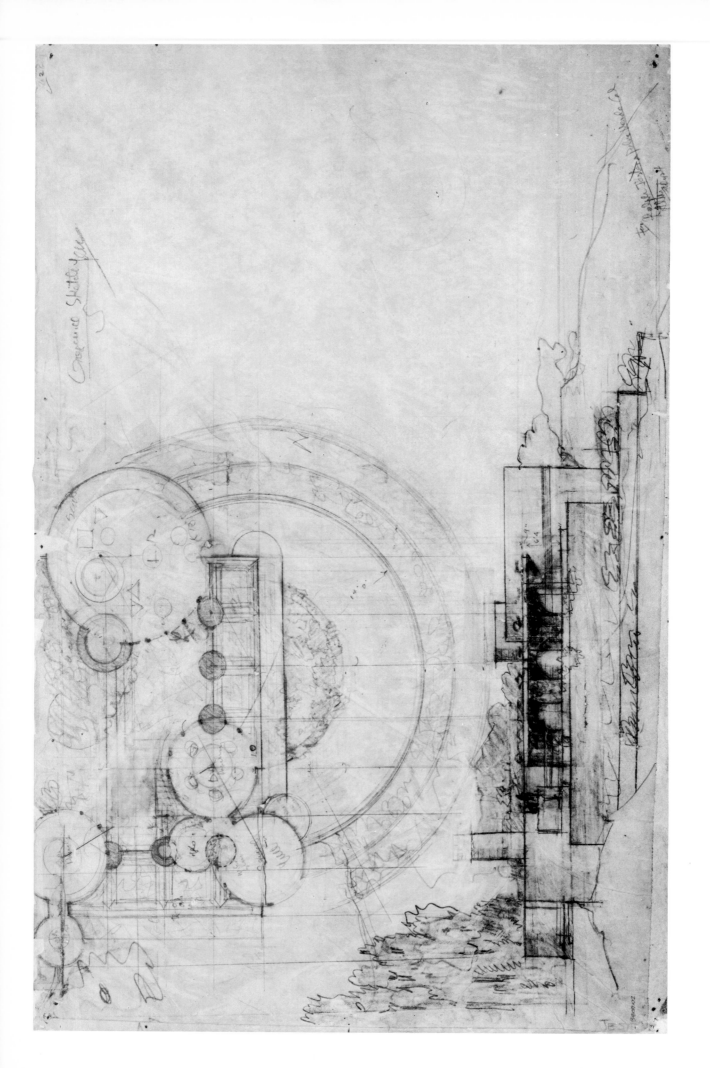

162. PROJECT: RALPH JESTER HOUSE, PALOS VERDES, CALIFORNIA. 1938.

163. PROJECT: RALPH JESTER HOUSE, PALOS VERDES, CALIFORNIA. 1938.

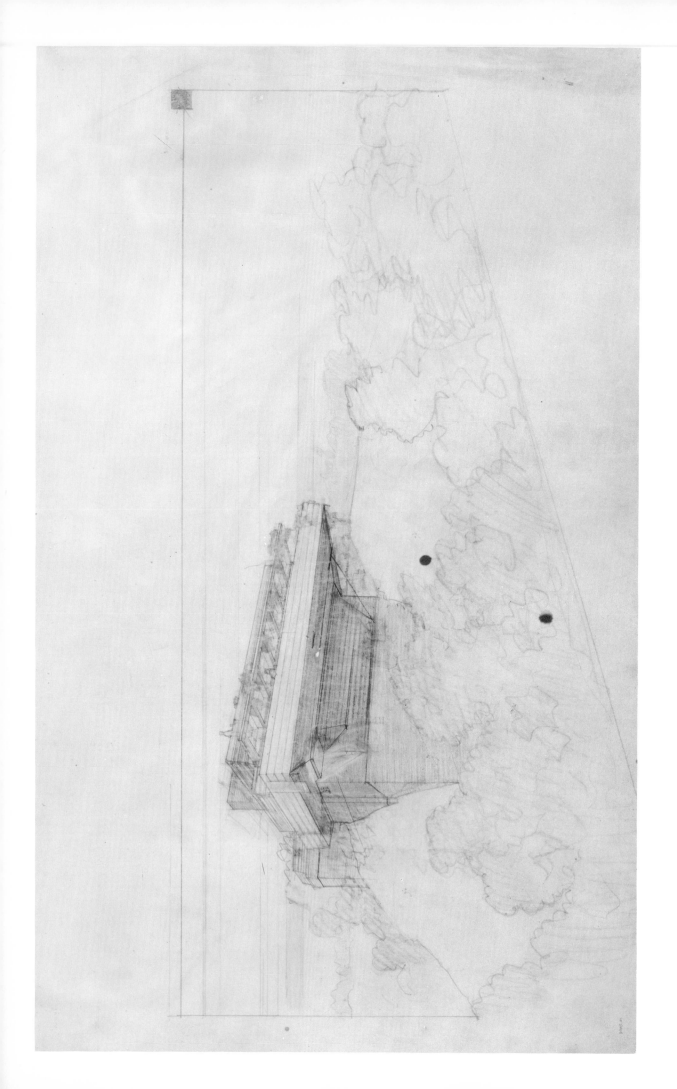

164. GEORGE D. STURGES HOUSE, BRENTWOOD HEIGHTS, CALIFORNIA. 1939.

165. GEORGE D. STURGES HOUSE, BRENTWOOD HEIGHTS, CALIFORNIA. 1939.

HOUSE FOR MR. AND MRS. GEORGE D. STURGES
LOS ANGELES · CALIFORNIA
FRANK LLOYD WRIGHT

166. ROSE PAUSON HOUSE, PHOENIX, ARIZONA. 1940.

167. ROSE PAUSON HOUSE, PHOENIX, ARIZONA. 1940.

168. LLOYD LEWIS HOUSE, LIBERTYVILLE, ILLINOIS. 1940.

169. JOHN C. PEW HOUSE, SHOREWOOD HILLS, MADISON, WISCONSIN. 1940.

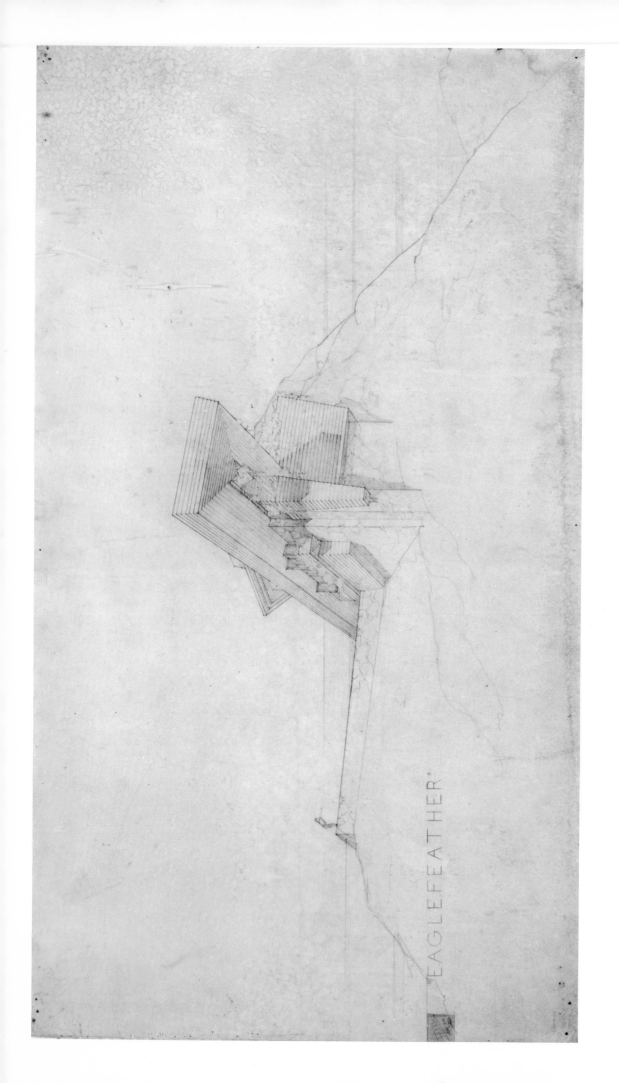

"EAGLEFEATHER"

170. PROJECT: ARCH OBOLER HOUSE, "EAGLE FEATHER", CALIFORNIA. 1940.

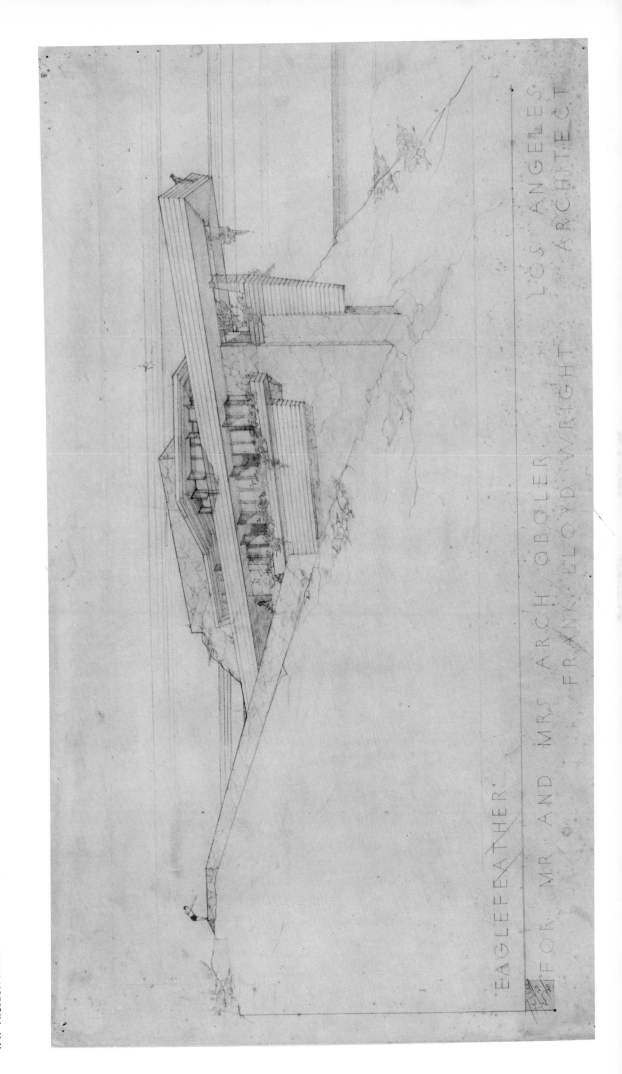

171. PROJECT: ARCH OBOLER HOUSE, "EAGLE FEATHER", CALIFORNIA. 1940.

172. S. C. JOHNSON & SON, INC. ADMINISTRATION BUILDING, RACINE, WISCONSIN. 1936-39.

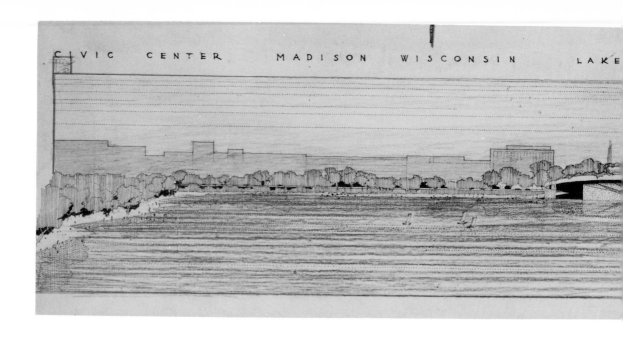

CIVIC CENTER MADISON WISCONSIN LAKE

173, 174. PROJECT: MADISON CIVIC CENTER, LAKE MONONA, MADISON, WISCONSIN. 1938.

EXTENSION AND TERMINAL OF MONONA AVENUE

SEVEN ACRES OF MADE OVER EXISTING RAILROAD TRACKS FOR PARKING.
LAKE WATER THROWN UP INTO MONUMENTAL FOUNTAINS.
CIVIC AUDITORIUM SEATING 10,000, FRONTING OLIN TERRACE.
COUNTY JAIL AND OFFICES, CITY HALL, UNION RAILROAD DEPOT.

MONONA AVE.

COST $17,500,000, RAISE

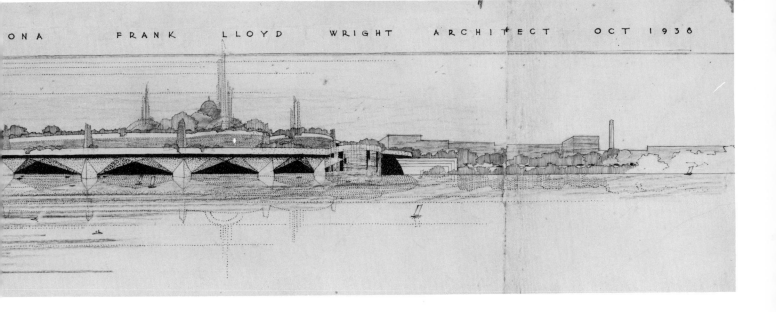

ONA   FRANK   LLOYD   WRIGHT   ARCHITECT   OCT 1938

WILSON ST.   CARROLL

"THE CITY GOES TO THE LAKE"   SEVEN MONTHS WATERDOMES, FIVE MONTHS EVERGREENS. INSTEAD

(SEE KAUFMANN A LA PITTSBURG)

CONNECTICUT AVENUE EL

FLORIDA AVENUE ELE

175, 176. PROJECT: CRYSTAL HEIGHTS HOTEL TOWERS, WASHINGTON, D. C. 1940.

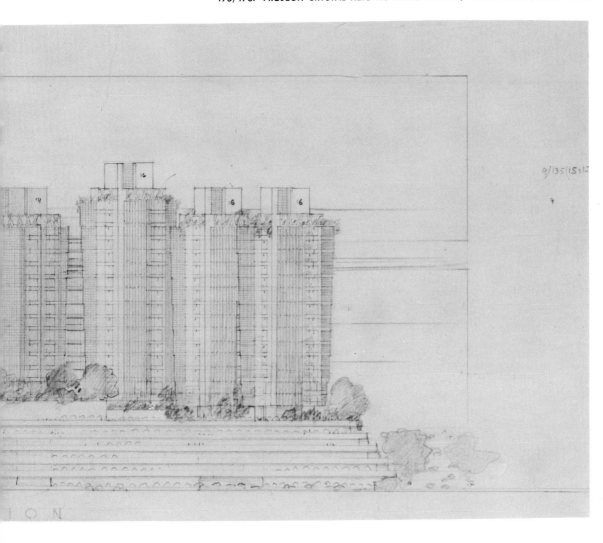

177. PROJECT: CRYSTAL HEIGHTS HOTEL TOWERS, WASHINGTON, D. C. 1940.

178. PROJECT: CRYSTAL HEIGHTS HOTEL TOWERS, WASHINGTON, D. C. 1940.

CRYSTAL HEIGHTS WASH

TON D.C.   FRANK LLOYD WRIGHT   ARCHITECT

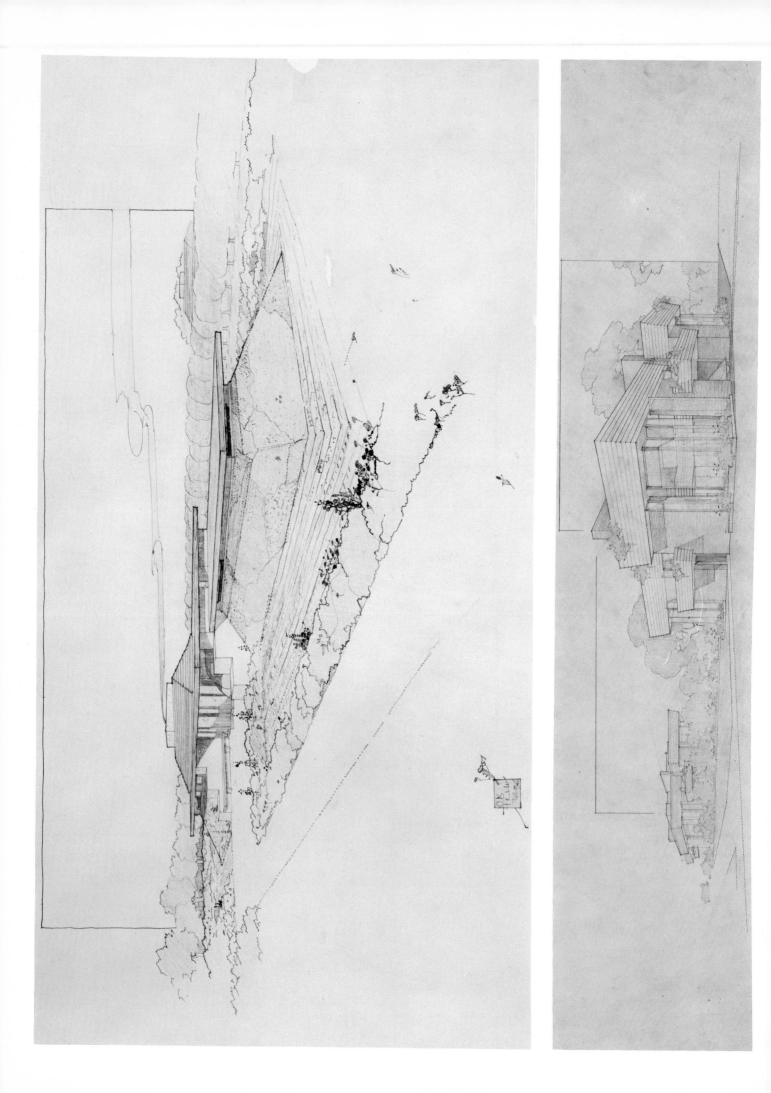

179. PROJECT: COOPERATIVE HOMESTEADS. 1942.

180. QUADRUPLE HOUSE, "SUNTOP HOMES", ARDMORE, PENNSYLVANIA. 1939.

181. QUADRUPLE HOUSE, "SUNTOP HOMES", ARDMORE, PENNSYLVANIA. 1939.

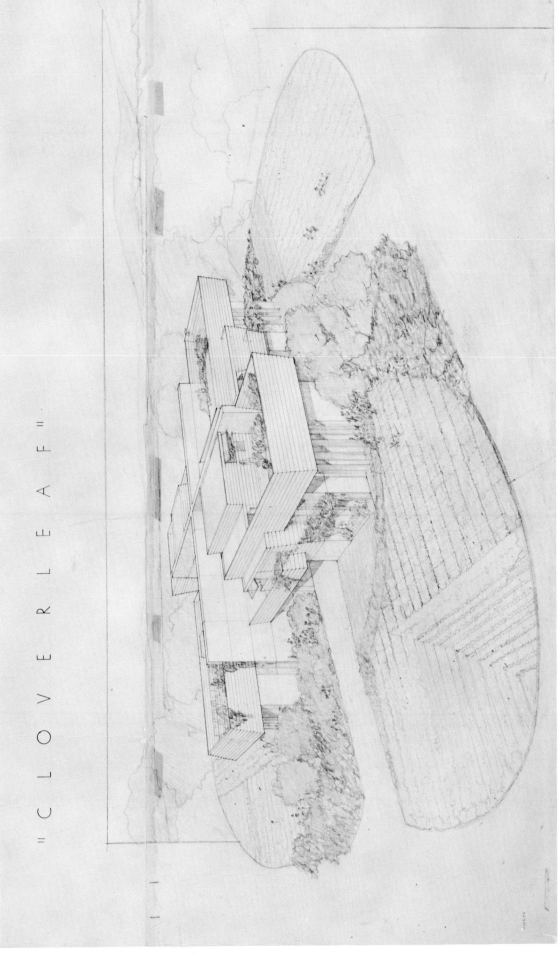

"CLOVERLEAF"

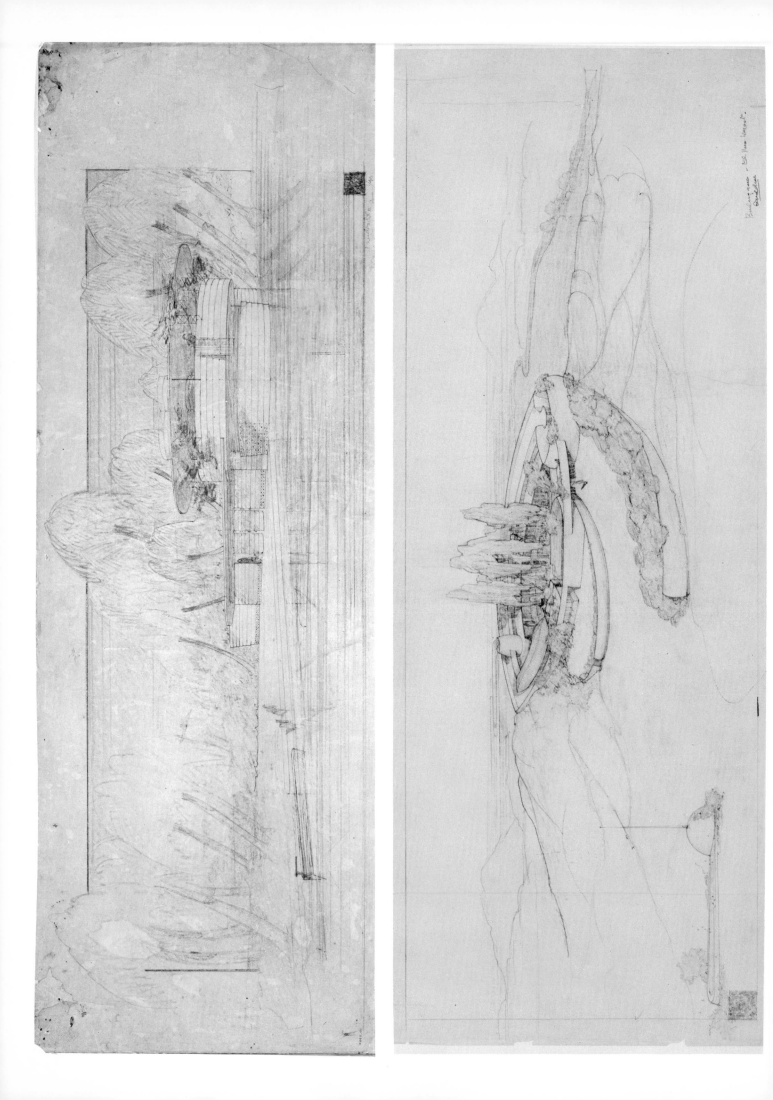

182. PROJECT: LUDD M. SPIVEY HOUSE, FT. LAUDERDALE, FLORIDA. 1939.

183. PROJECT: LLOYD BURLINGHAM HOUSE, EL PASO, TEXAS. 1941.

184. PROJECT: V. C. MORRIS HOUSE, SAN FRANCISCO, CALIFORNIA. 1946.

SEACLIFF

HOUSE FOR MR. & MRS. V. C. MORRIS
SAN FRANCISCO, CALIFORNIA

FRANK LLOYD WRIGHT ARCHITECT

HOUSE FOR MR AND MRS V.C. MORRIS · SAN FRANCISCO, CAL. · FRANK LLOYD WRIGHT · ARCHITECT

185. PROJECT: V. C. MORRIS HOUSE, SAN FRANCISCO, CALIFORNIA. 1946.

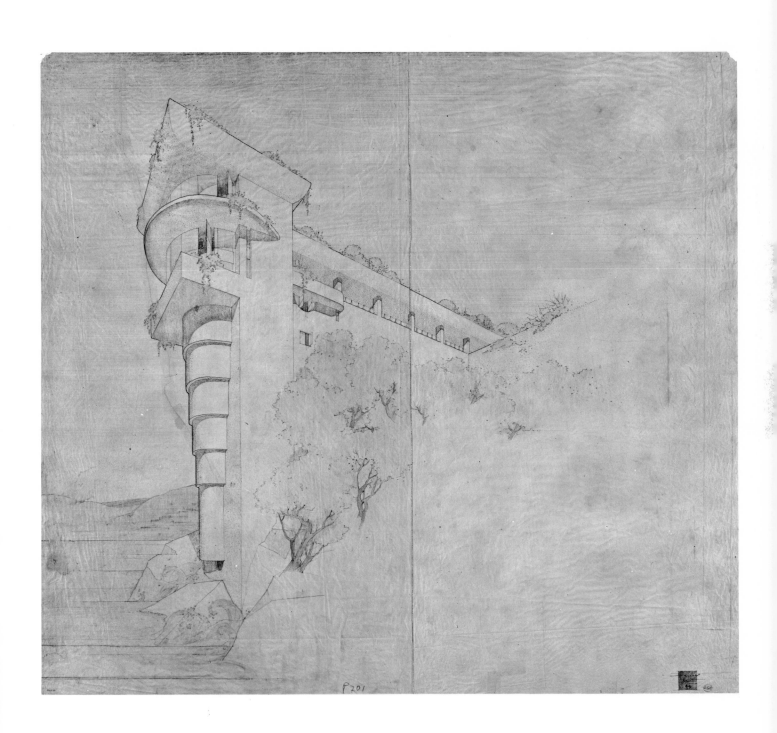

P 201

186. PROJECT: V. C. MORRIS HOUSE, SAN FRANCISCO, CALIFORNIA. 1943.

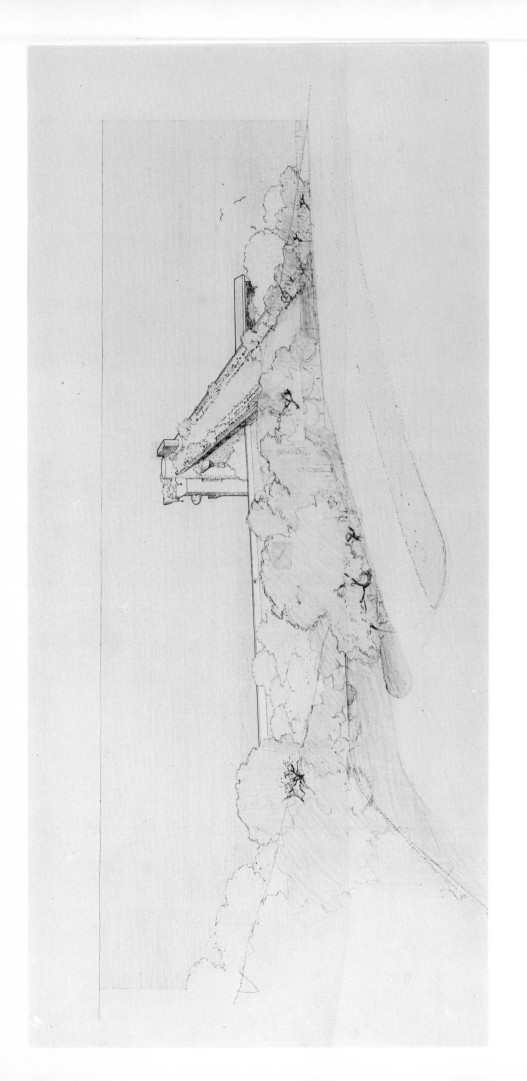

187. PROJECT: V. C. MORRIS HOUSE, SAN FRANCISCO, CALIFORNIA. 1946.

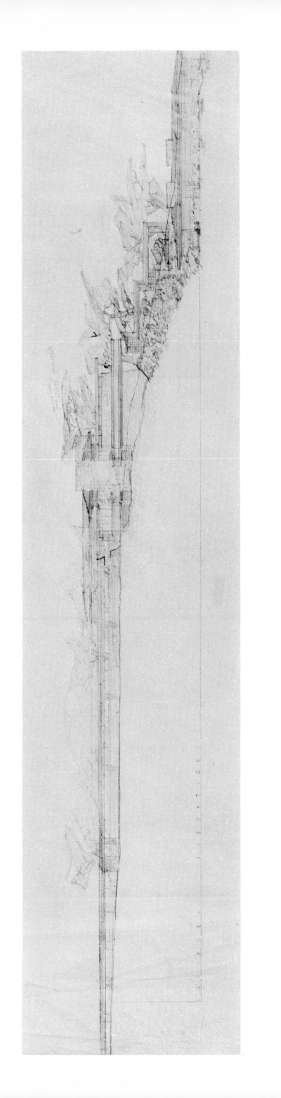

188, 189. PROJECT: JOHN NESBITT HOUSE, CARMEL BAY, CALIFORNIA. 1940.

190, 191. SOLOMON R. GUGGENHEIM MUSEUM, NEW YORK CITY, N. Y. 1943.

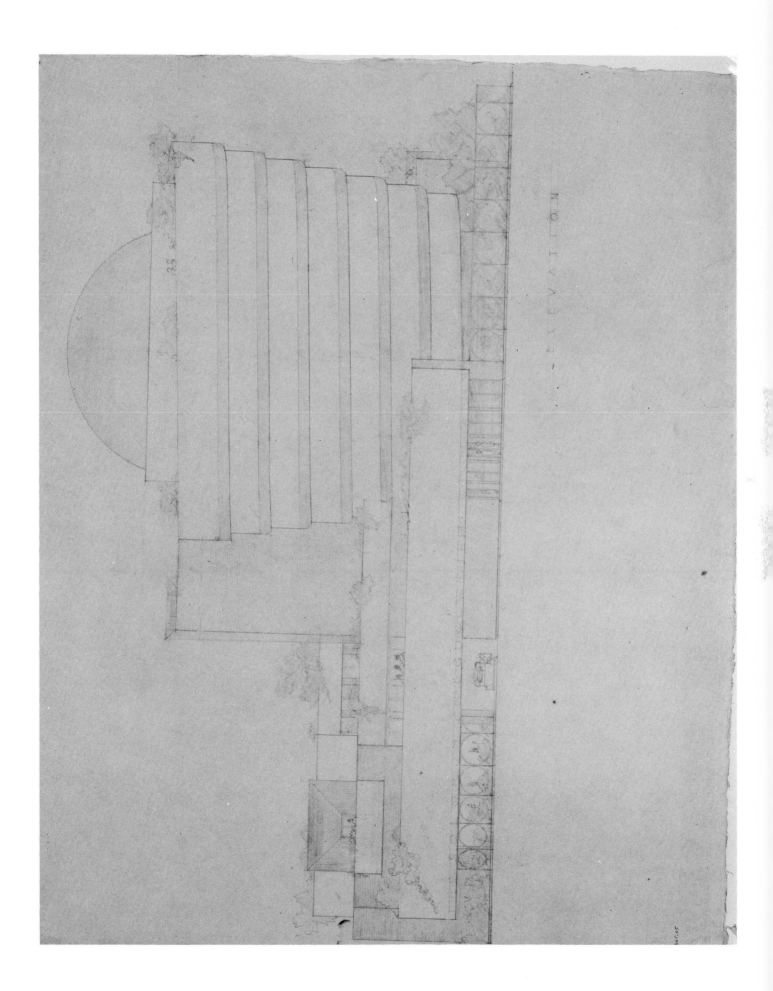

ELEVATION

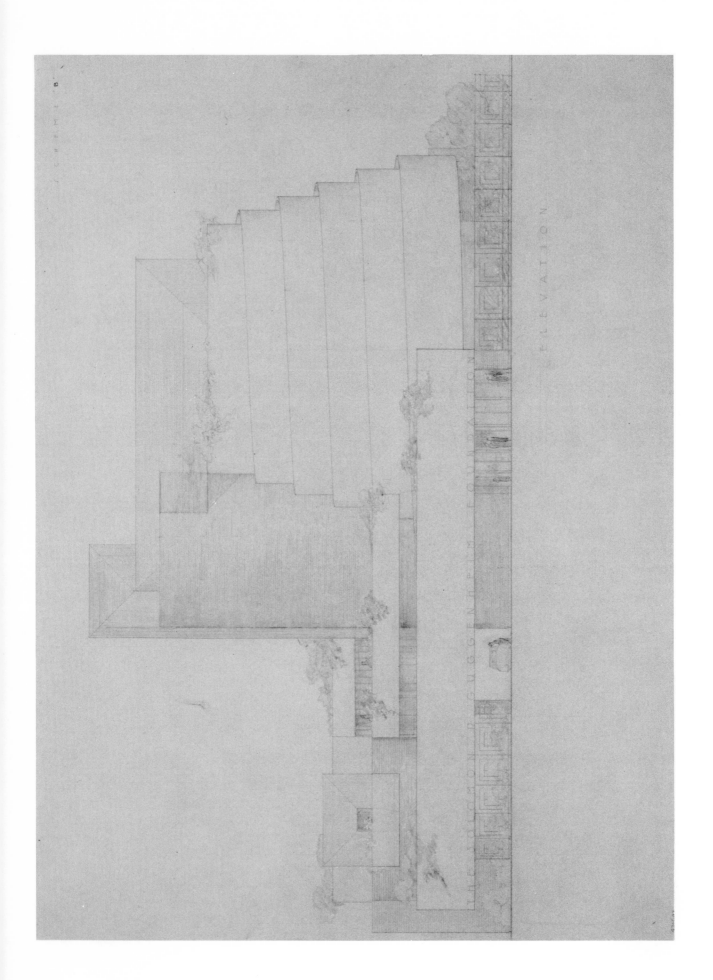

192, 193. SOLOMON R. GUGGENHEIM MUSEUM, NEW YORK CITY, N. Y. 1943.

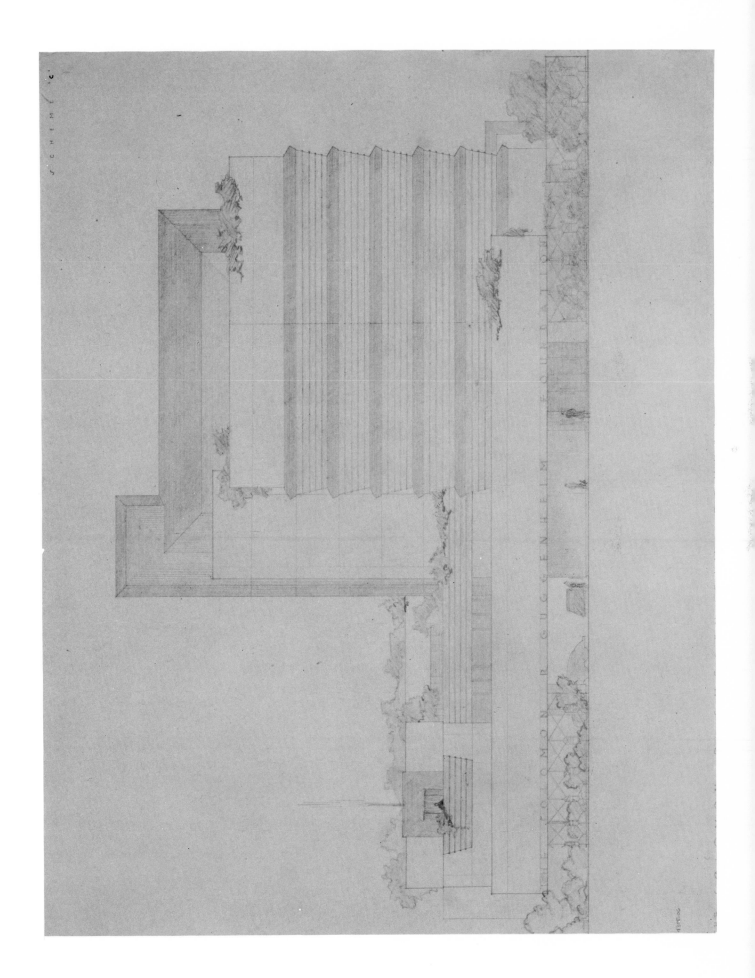

SCHEME C

THE SOLOMON R. GUGGENHEIM FOUNDATION

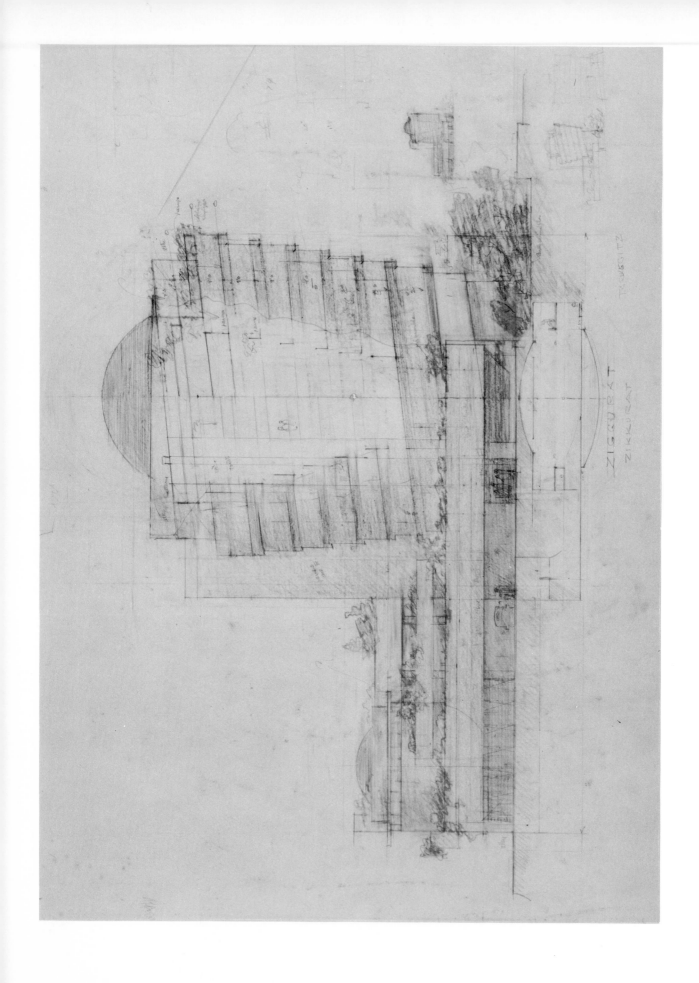

194. SOLOMON R. GUGGENHEIM MUSEUM, NEW YORK CITY, N. Y. 1943.

195, 196. SOLOMON R. GUGGENHEIM MUSEUM, NEW YORK CITY, N. Y. 1948.

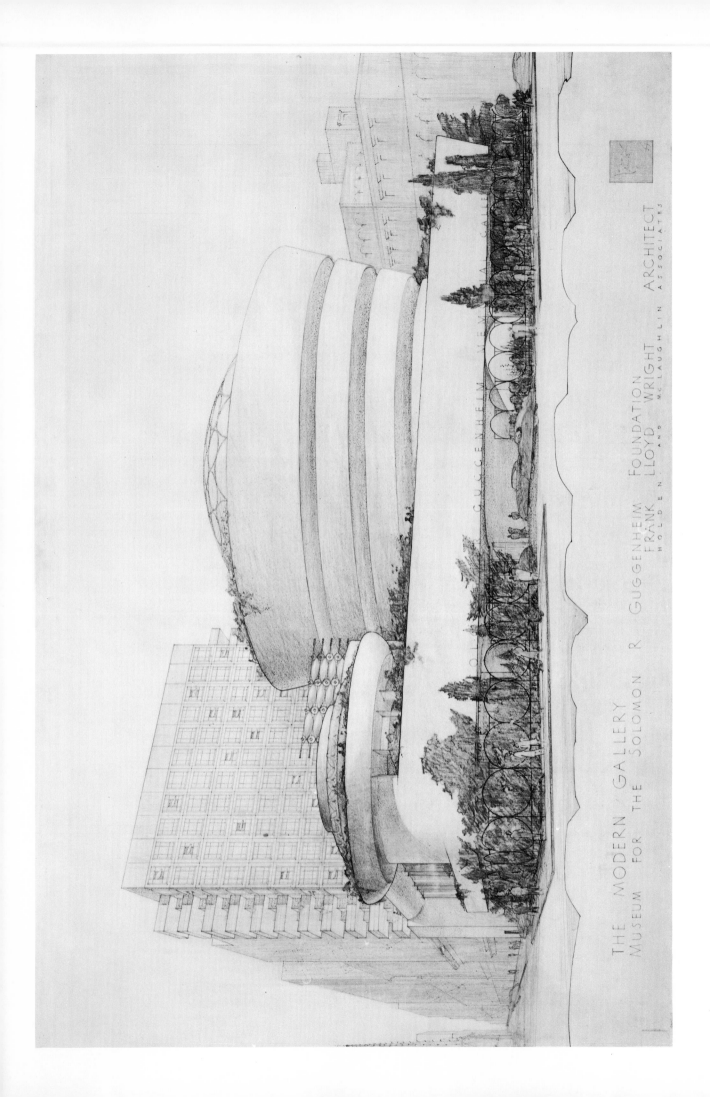

THE MODERN GALLERY
MUSEUM FOR THE SOLOMON R GUGGENHEIM FOUNDATION
FRANK LLOYD WRIGHT ARCHITECT
HOLDEN AND McLAUGHLIN ASSOCIATES

197. SOLOMON R. GUGGENHEIM MUSEUM, NEW YORK CITY, N. Y. 1949.

198. SOLOMON R. GUGGENHEIM MUSEUM, NEW YORK CITY, N. Y. 1957.

THE SOLOMON R. GUGGENHEIM MUSEUM

THE SOLOMON R. GUGGENHEIM MUSEUM

FRANK LLOYD WRIGHT ARCHITECT

TOP RAMP
THE
WATERCOLOR
SOCIETY

NOTE:
PICTURES-
4' × 6'
4' × 10'
3 × 7
3 × 5

199, 200. SOLOMON R. GUGGENHEIM MUSEUM, NEW YORK CITY, N.Y. 1956.

AVERAGE SCULPTURE & PAINTING

NOTE:
CANVASES —
7' X 9'
5' X 6'
4'6" X 4'6"
4' X 4'

MIDDLE OF THE ROAD

NOTE:
CANVASES:
10½ x 12'
5' x 5'
5' x 4'
4' x 4'

201, 202. SOLOMON R. GUGGENHEIM MUSEUM, NEW YORK CITY, N. Y. 1956.

THE MASTERPIECE

NOTE:
CANVASES—
9' x 8'
9' x 9'

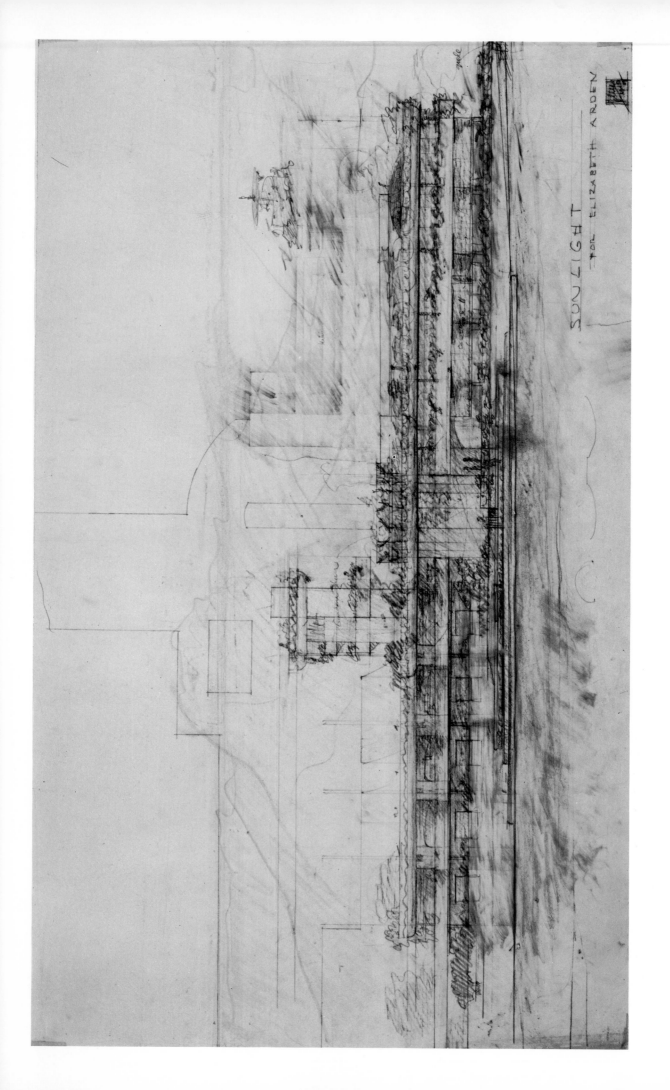

203. PROJECT: ELIZABETH ARDEN RESORT HOTEL, "SUNLIGHT", PHOENIX, ARIZONA. 1945.

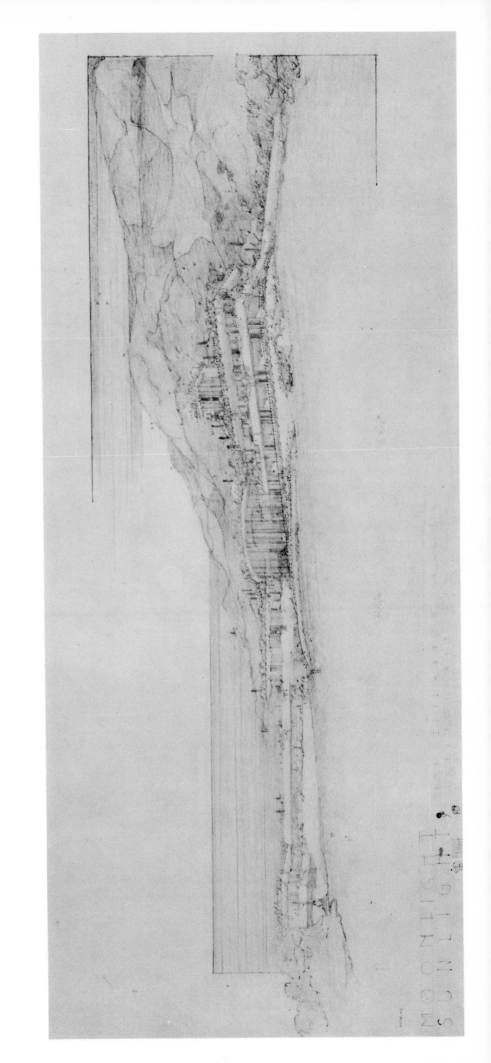

204. PROJECT: ELIZABETH ARDEN RESORT HOTEL, "SUNLIGHT", PHOENIX, ARIZONA. 1945.

205. PROJECT: CALICO MILLS OFFICE BUILDING, AHMEDABAD, INDIA. 1946.

206. PROJECT: CALICO MILLS OFFICE BUILDING, AHMEDABAD, INDIA. 1946.

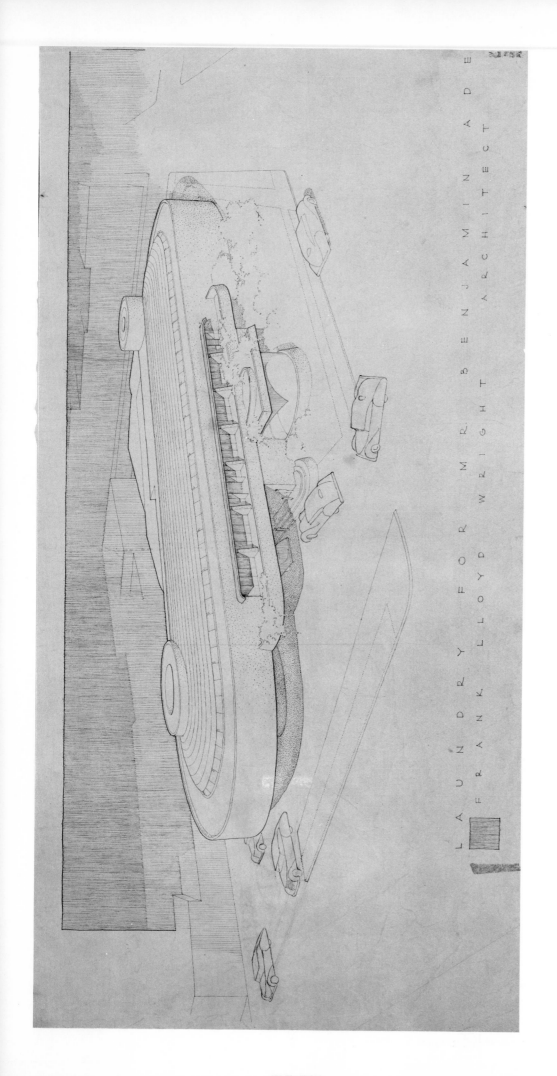

LAUNDRY FOR MR. BENJAMIN A DE
FRANK LLOYD WRIGHT ARCHITECT

207. PROJECT: BENJAMIN ADELMAN LAUNDRY, MILWAUKEE, WISCONSIN. 1946.

208. E. L. MARTING HOUSE, AKRON, OHIO. 1947.

209. ROBERT LLEWELLYN WRIGHT HOUSE, BETHESDA, MARYLAND. 1953.

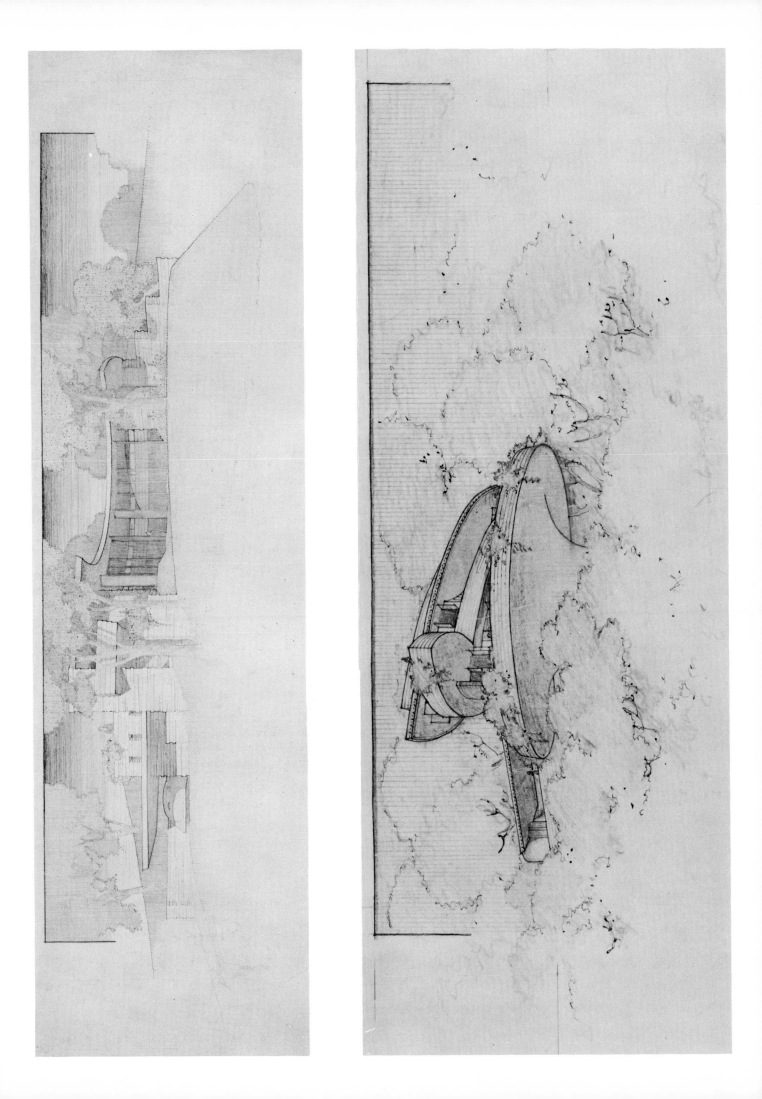

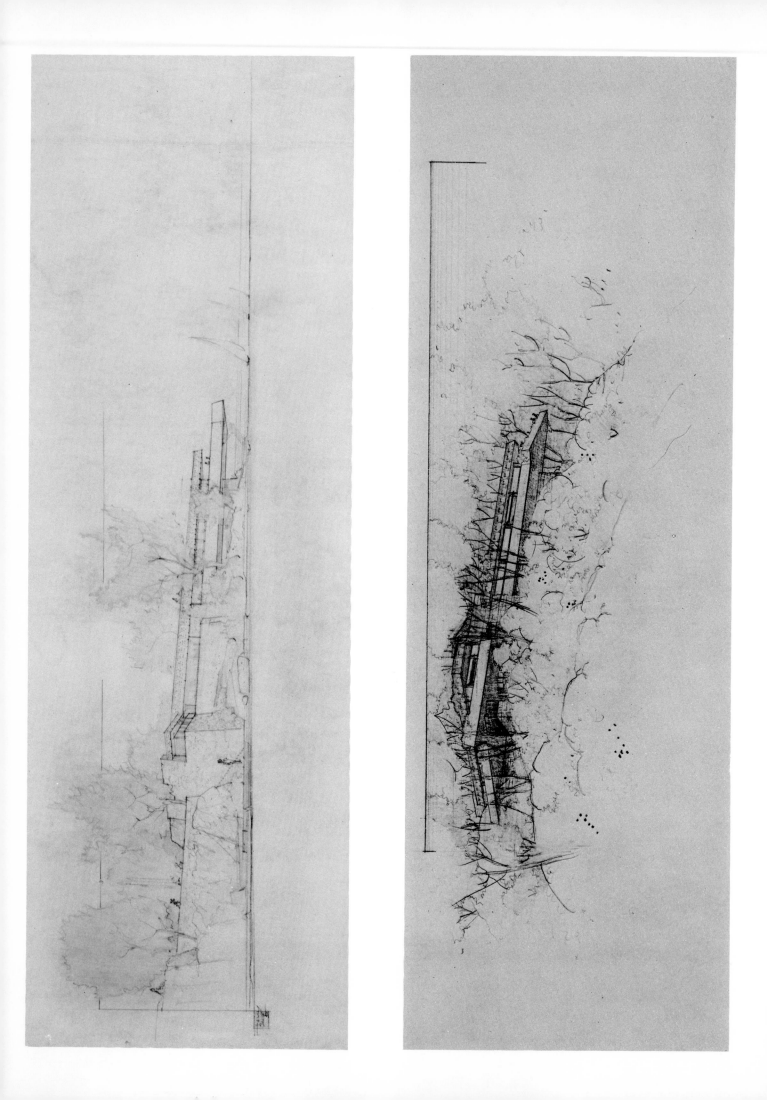

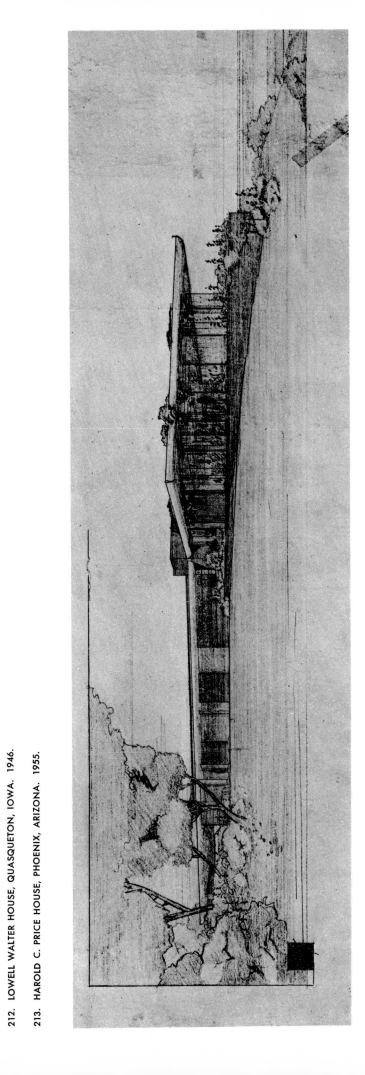

210. PROJECT: A. K. CHAHROUDI HOUSE, PETRA ISLAND, LAKE MAHOPAC, NEW YORK. 1950.

211. PROJECT: JOSEPH H. BREWER HOUSE. 1953.

212. LOWELL WALTER HOUSE, QUASQUETON, IOWA. 1946.

213. HAROLD C. PRICE HOUSE, PHOENIX, ARIZONA. 1955.

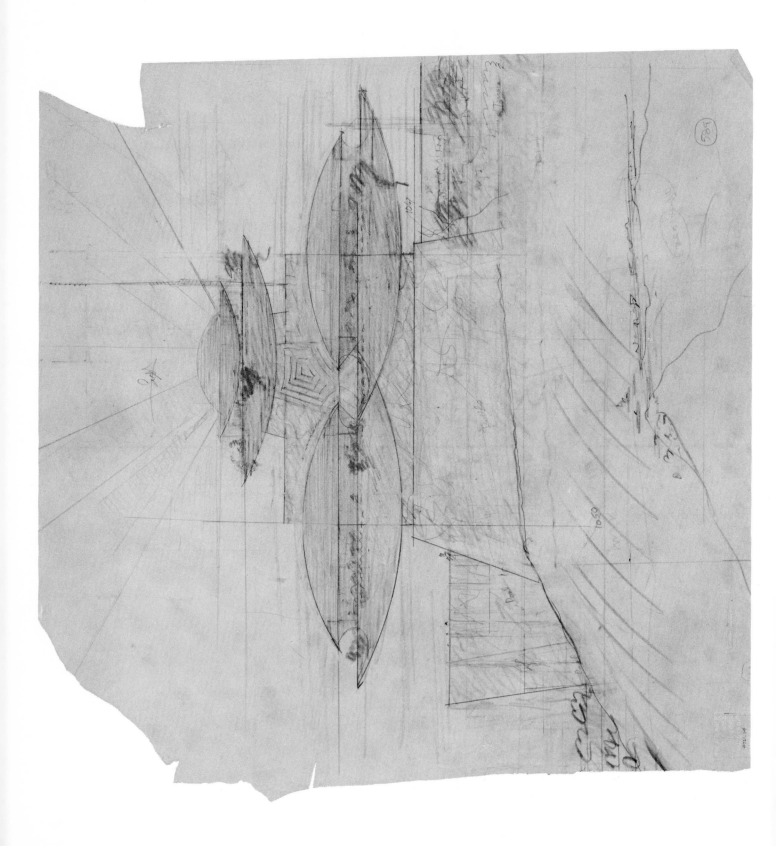

214, 215. PROJECT: HUNTINGTON HARTFORD PLAY RESORT, HOLLYWOOD HILLS, CALIFORNIA. 1947.

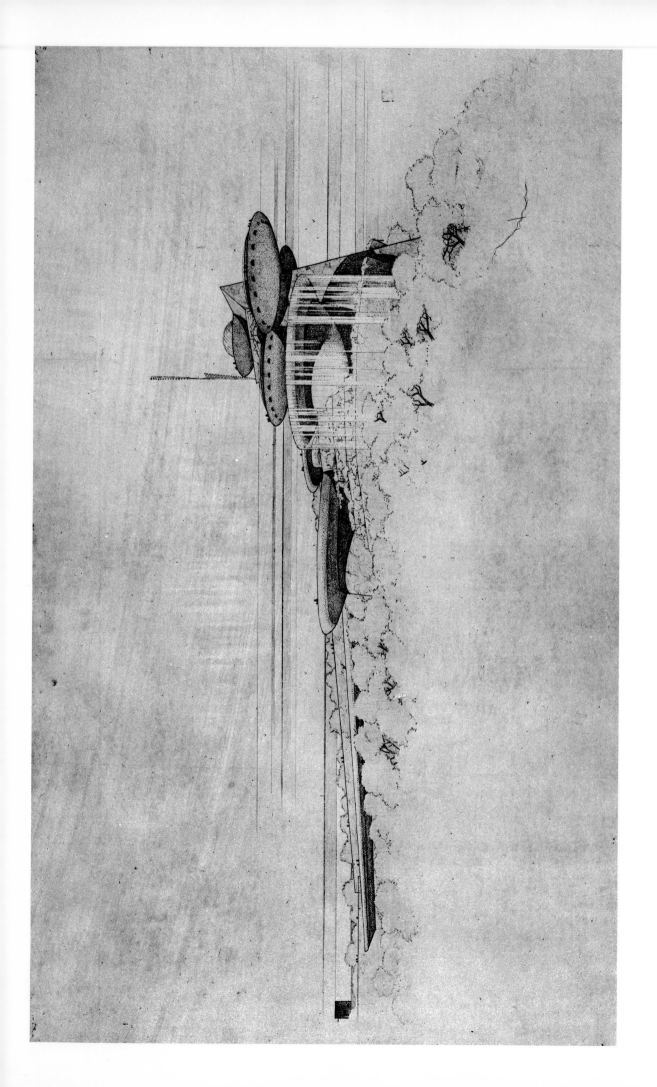

216. PROJECT: HUNTINGTON HARTFORD PLAY RESORT, HOLLYWOOD HILLS, CALIFORNIA. 1947.

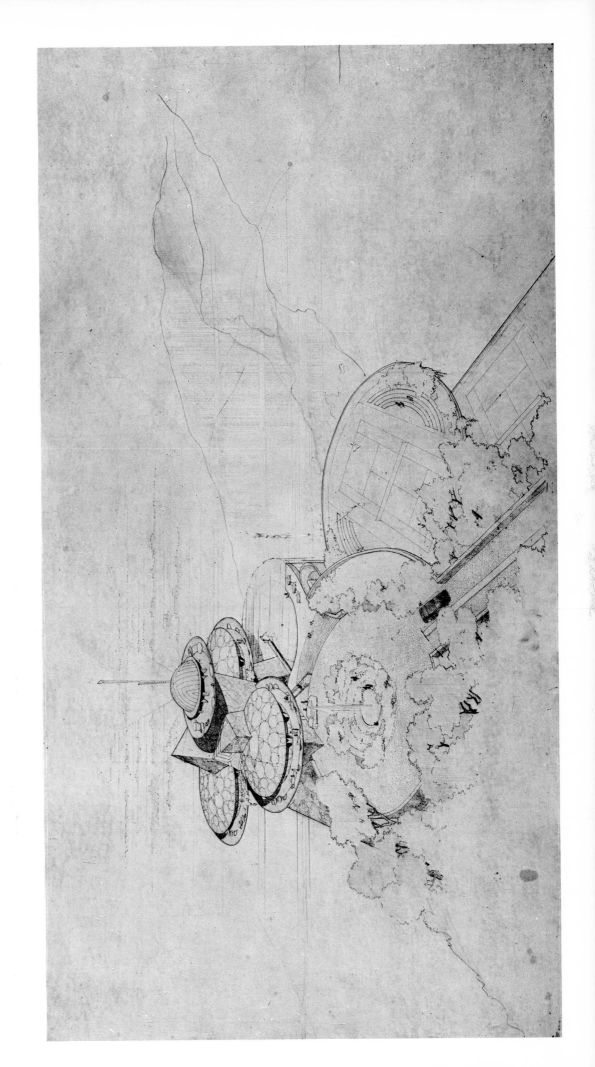

217. PROJECT: HUNTINGTON HARTFORD PLAY RESORT, HOLLYWOOD HILLS, CALIFORNIA. 1947.

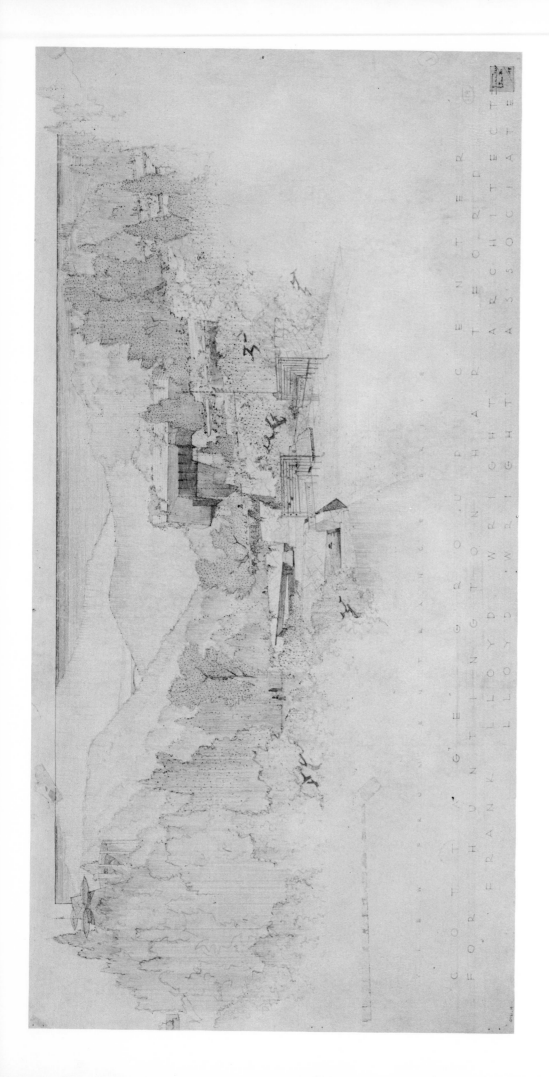

218. PROJECT: COTTAGE GROUP CENTER, HUNTINGTON HARTFORD PLAY RESORT, HOLLYWOOD HILLS, CALIFORNIA. 1947.

219. PROJECT: COTTAGE GROUP CENTER, HUNTINGTON HARTFORD PLAY RESORT, HOLLYWOOD HILLS, CALIFORNIA. 1947.

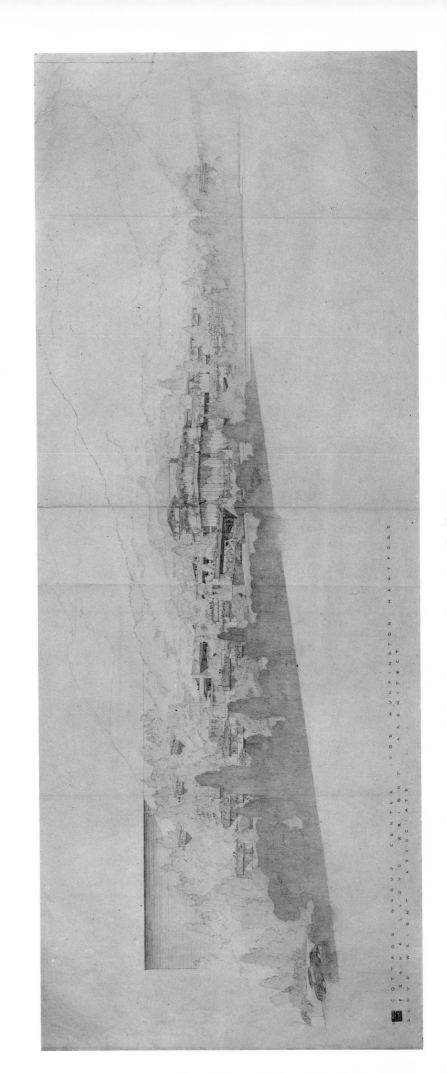

COTTAGE GROUP CENTER FOR HUNTINGTON HARTFORD
FRANK LLOYD WRIGHT ARCHITECT
LLOYD WRIGHT ASSOCIATE

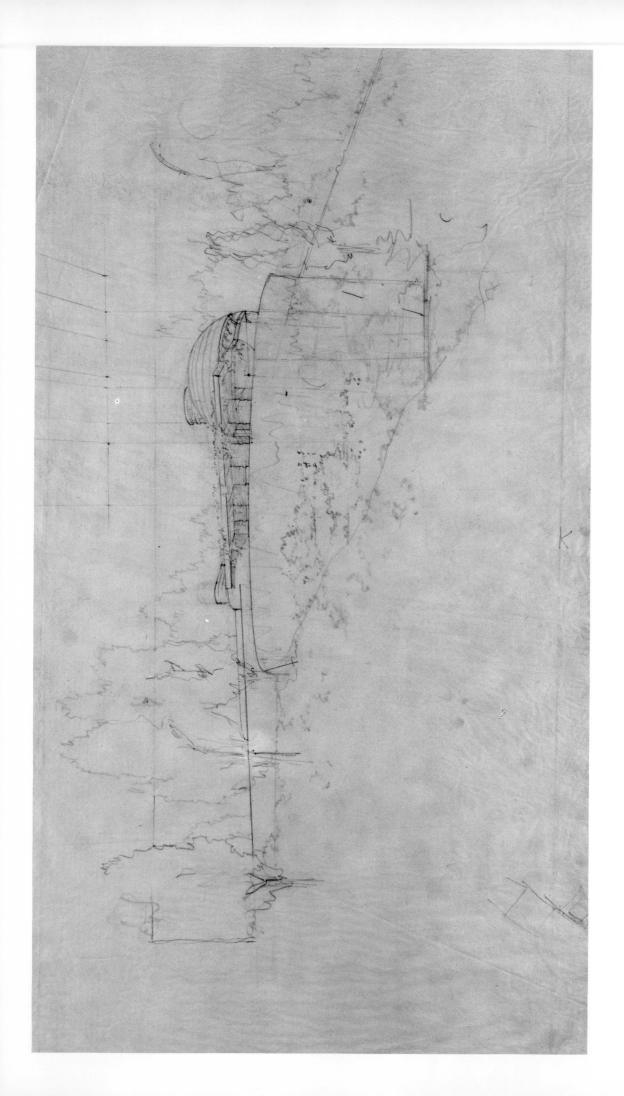

220. PROJECT: HUNTINGTON HARTFORD HOUSE, HOLLYWOOD HILLS, CALIFORNIA. 1947.

221. PROJECT: ARNOLD FRIEDMAN HOUSE, PECOS, NEW MEXICO. 1945.

THE FIR-TREE FOR ARNOLD FRIEDMAN, PECOS, NEW MEXICO

222, 223. PROJECT: WARREN TREMAINE OBSERVATORY, METEOR CRATER, METEOR, ARIZONA. 1948.

224. PROJECT: NICHOLAS P. DAPHNE FUNERAL CHAPELS, SAN FRANCISCO, CALIFORNIA. 1948.

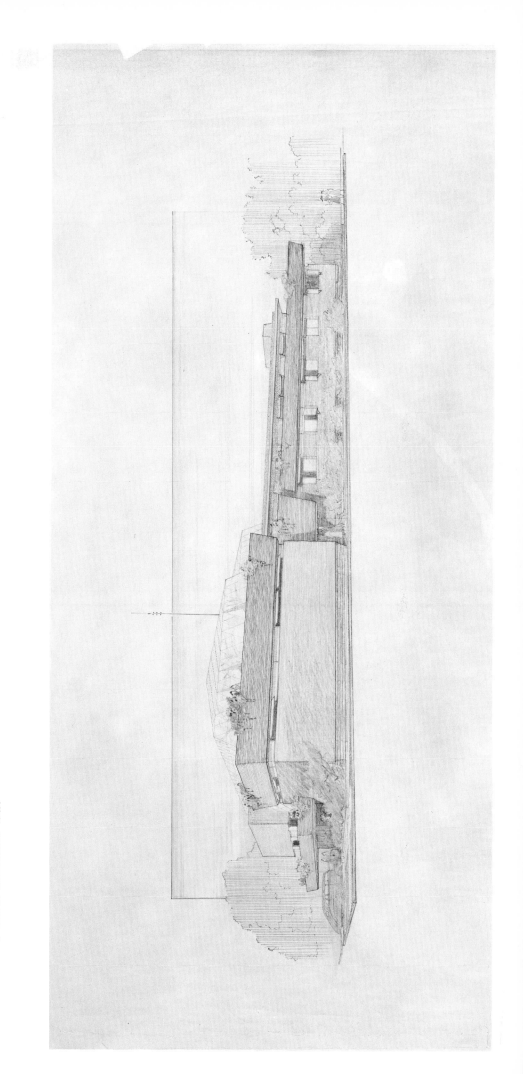

225. PROJECT: Y.W.C.A., RACINE, WISCONSIN. 1949.

226. PROJECT: SELF-SERVICE GARAGE, PITTSBURGH, PENNSYLVANIA. 1947.

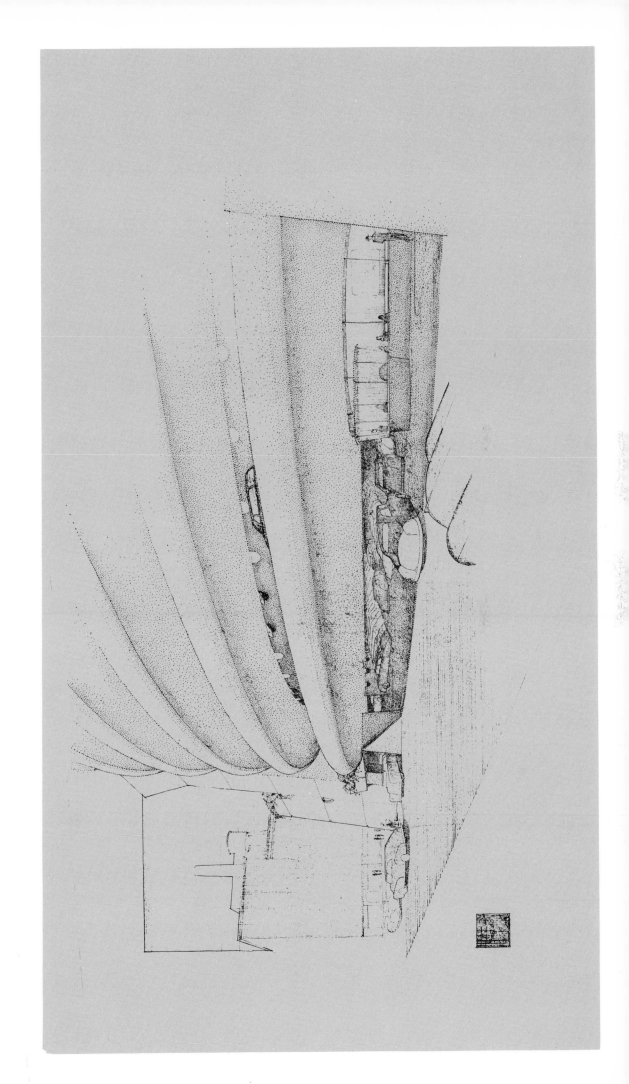

227. PROJECT: SELF-SERVICE GARAGE, PITTSBURGH, PENNSYLVANIA. 1947.

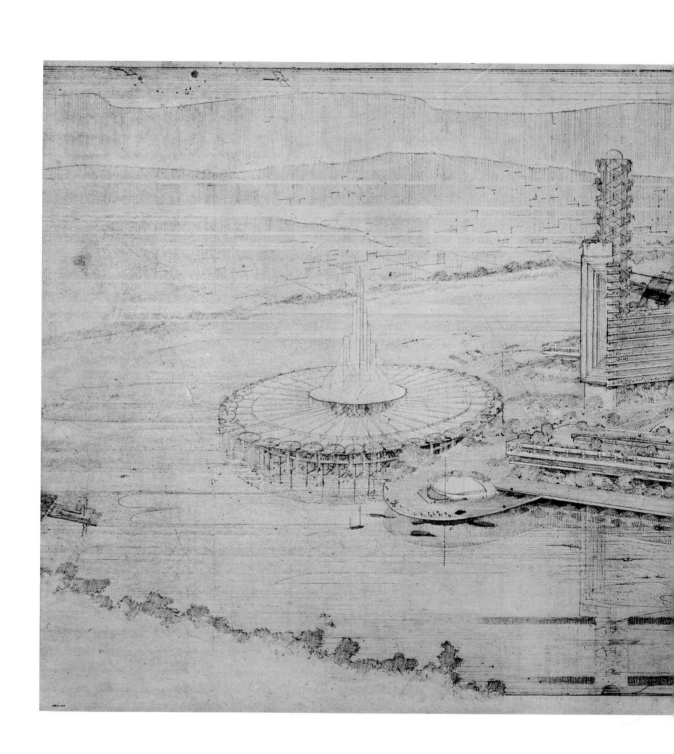

228. PROJECT: COMMUNITY CENTER, POINT PARK, PITTSBURGH, PENNSYLVANIA. 1947.

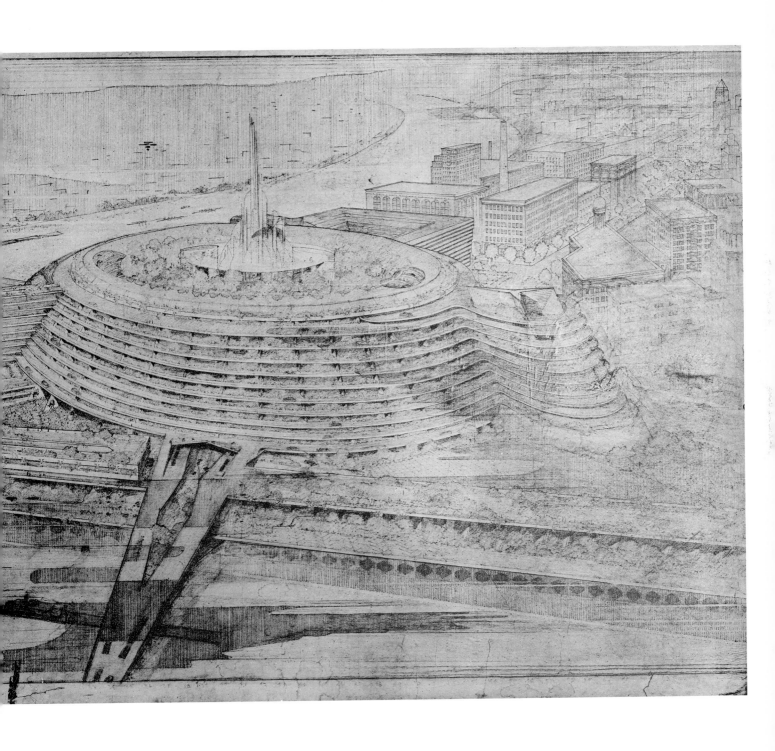

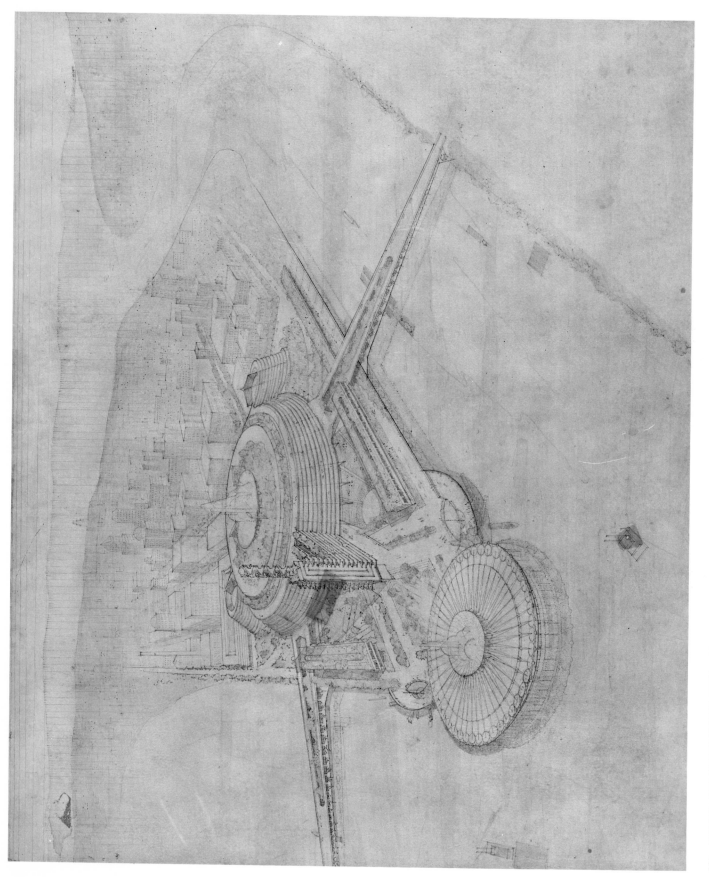

229. PROJECT: COMMUNITY CENTER, POINT PARK, PITTSBURGH, PENNSYLVANIA. 1947.

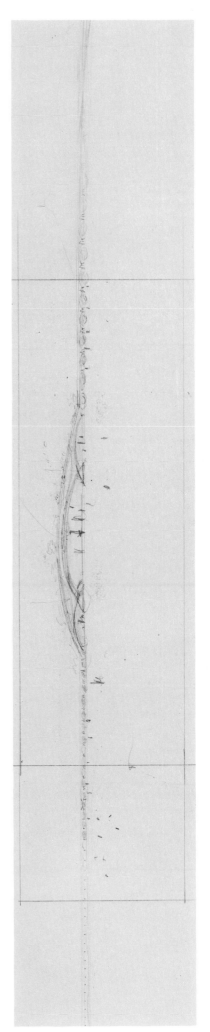

230. PROJECT: TWIN SUSPENSION BRIDGES AND COMMUNITY CENTER, POINT PARK, PITTSBURGH, PENNSYLVANIA. 1947.

231. PROJECT: CONCRETE BRIDGE, SAN FRANCISCO, CALIFORNIA. 1949.

232. PROJECT: CONCRETE "BUTTERFLY" BRIDGE, WISCONSIN RIVER NEAR SPRING GREEN, WISCONSIN. 1947.

233. PROJECT: AYN RAND HOUSE, HOLLYWOOD, CALIFORNIA. 1947.

COTTAGE STUDIO
FOR AYN RAND
FRANK LLOYD WRIGHT

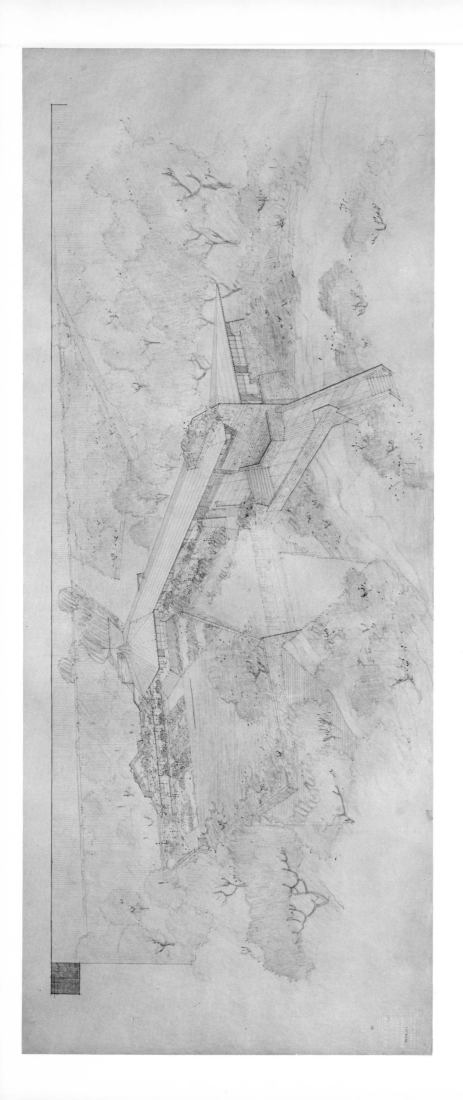

234. PROJECT: GILLEN HOUSE, DALLAS, TEXAS. 1950.

235. PROJECT: MASIERI MEMORIAL, VENICE, ITALY. 1953.

236. PROJECT: "RHODODENDRON" CHAPEL, BEAR RUN, CONNELLSVILLE, PENNSYLVANIA. 1953.

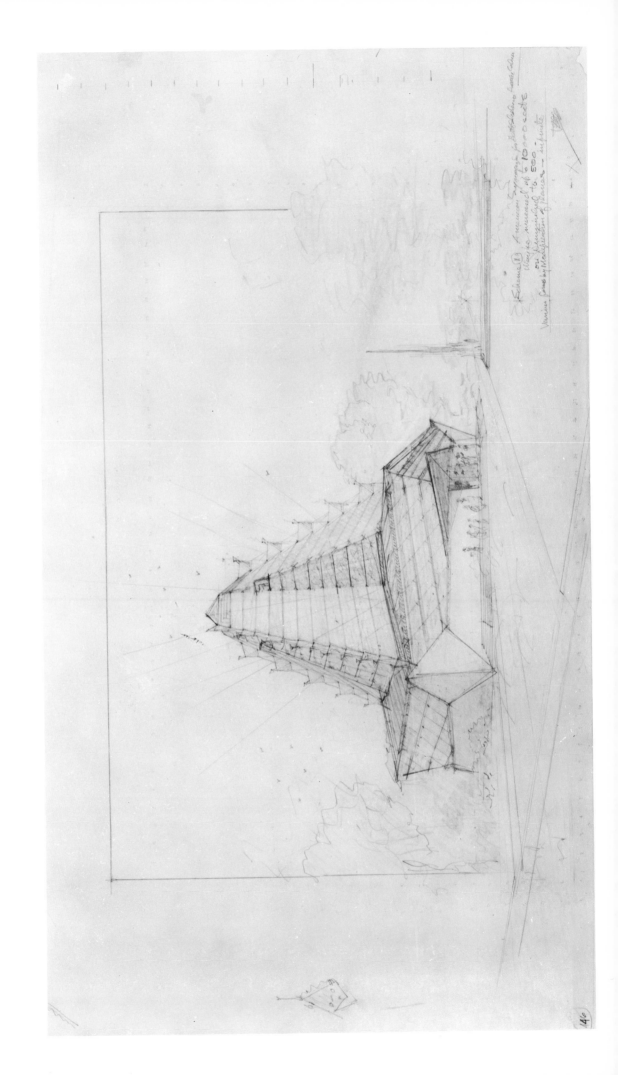

237. BETH SHOLOM SYNAGOGUE, ELKINS PARK, PHILADELPHIA, PENNSYLVANIA. 1959.

238. PROJECT: TRINITY CHAPEL, NORMAN, OKLAHOMA. 1958.

239. PILGRIM CONGREGATIONAL CHURCH, REDDING, CALIFORNIA. 1958.

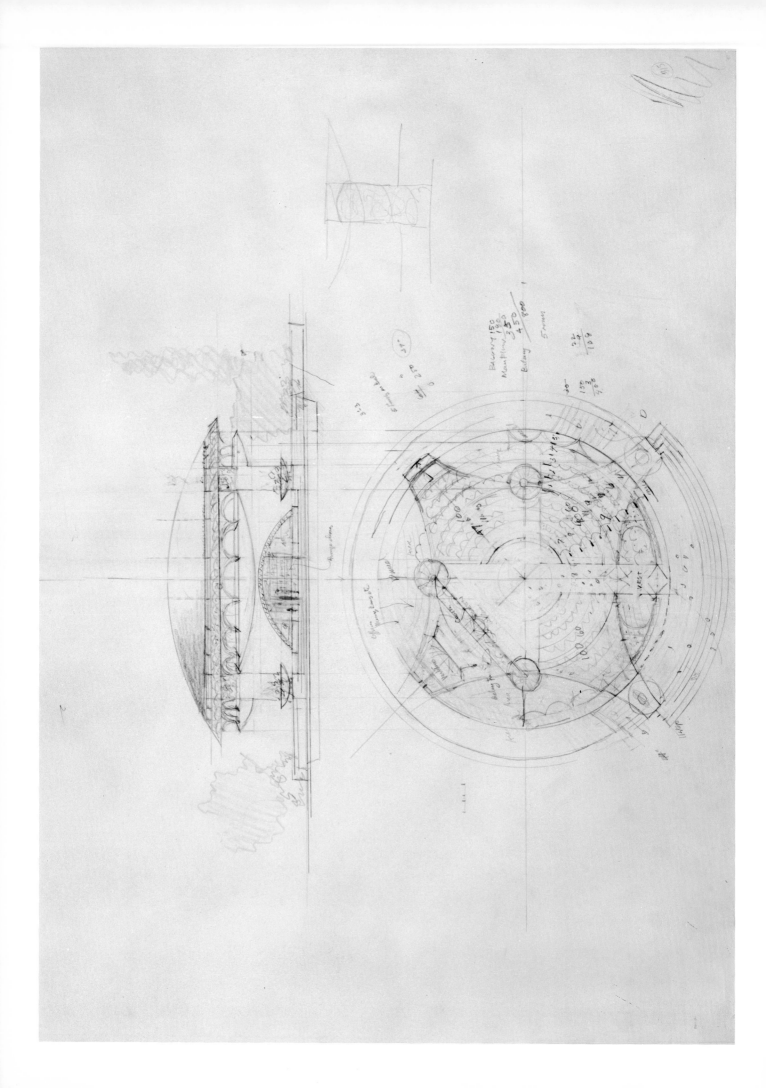

240. GREEK ORTHODOX CHURCH, WAUWATOSA, MILWAUKEE, WISCONSIN. 1956-61.

241. PROJECT: MANHATTAN SPORTS PAVILION, NEW YORK CITY, N. Y. 1959.

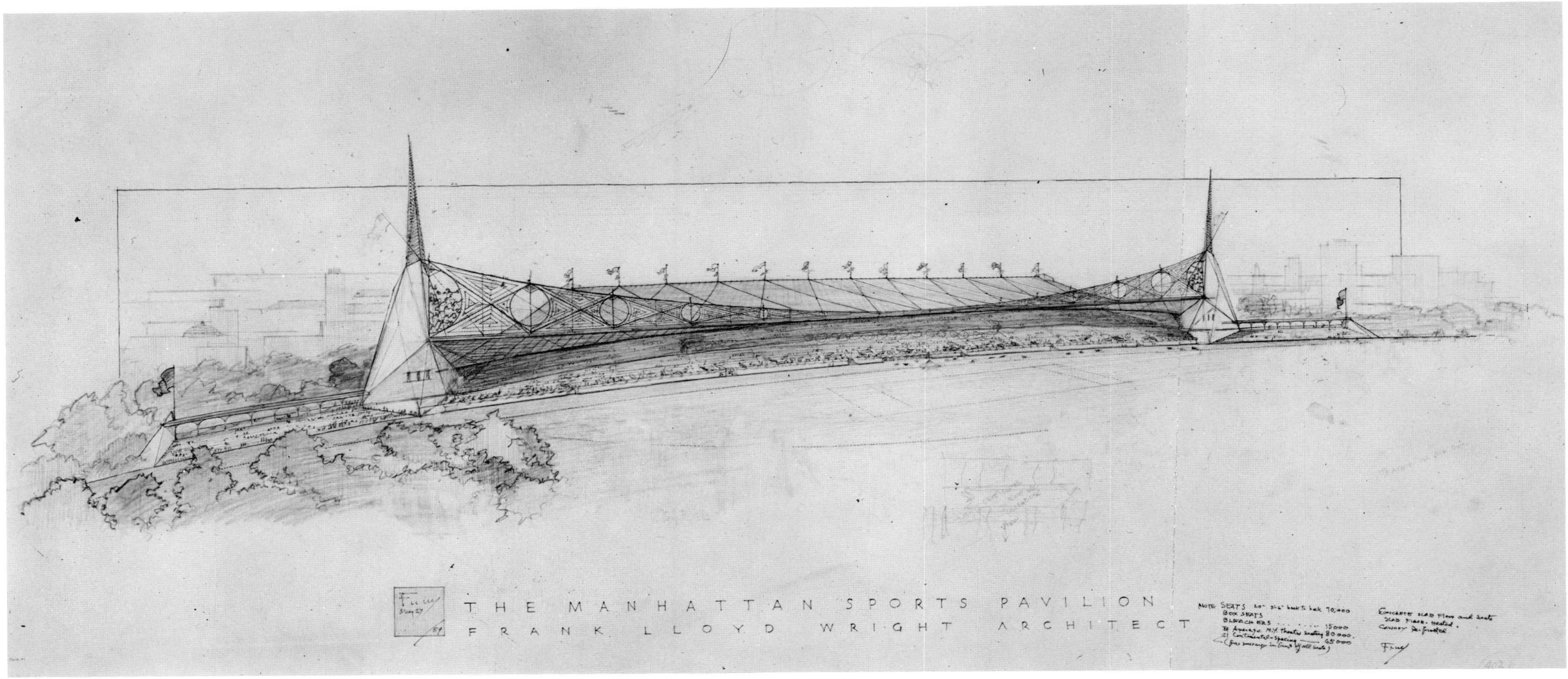

THE MANHATTAN SPORTS PAVILION

FRANK LLOYD WRIGHT ARCHITECT

242, 243. KALITA HUMPHREYS THEATRE, DALLAS, TEXAS. 1955.

244. S. C. JOHNSON AND SON, INC. RESEARCH LABORATORY TOWER, RACINE, WISCONSIN. 1947.

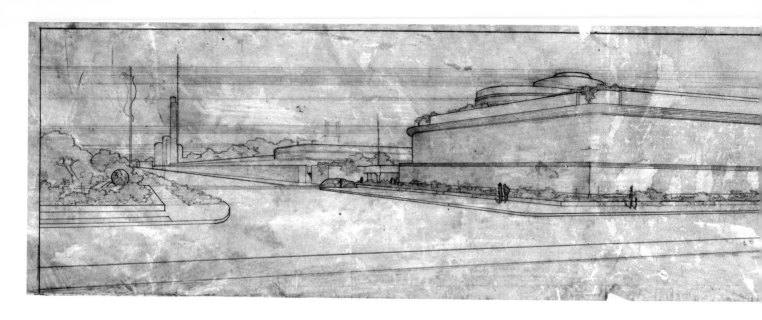

245, 246. S. C. JOHNSON AND SON, INC. ADMINISTRATION BUILDING, RACINE, WISCONSIN. 1936.

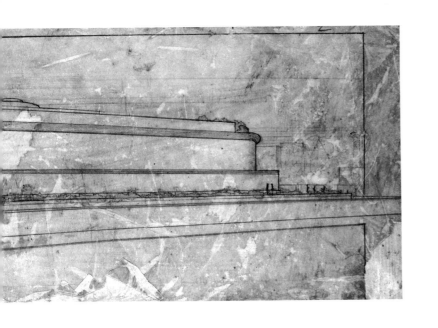

VIEW FROM NORTHWEST
POINT VIEW RESIDENCES
FOR THE EDGAR J. KAUFMANN CHARITABLE TRUST
FRANK LLOYD WRIGHT ARCHITECT SHEET

247. PROJECT: POINT VIEW APARTMENT TOWER, PITTSBURGH, PENNSYLVANIA. 1953.

VIEW FROM NORTHEAST
POINT VIEW RESIDENCES
FOR THE EDGAR J. KAUFMANN CHARITABLE TRUST
FRANK LLOYD WRIGHT ARCHITECT

248. PROJECT: POINT VIEW APARTMENT TOWER, PITTSBURGH, PENNSYLVANIA. 1953.

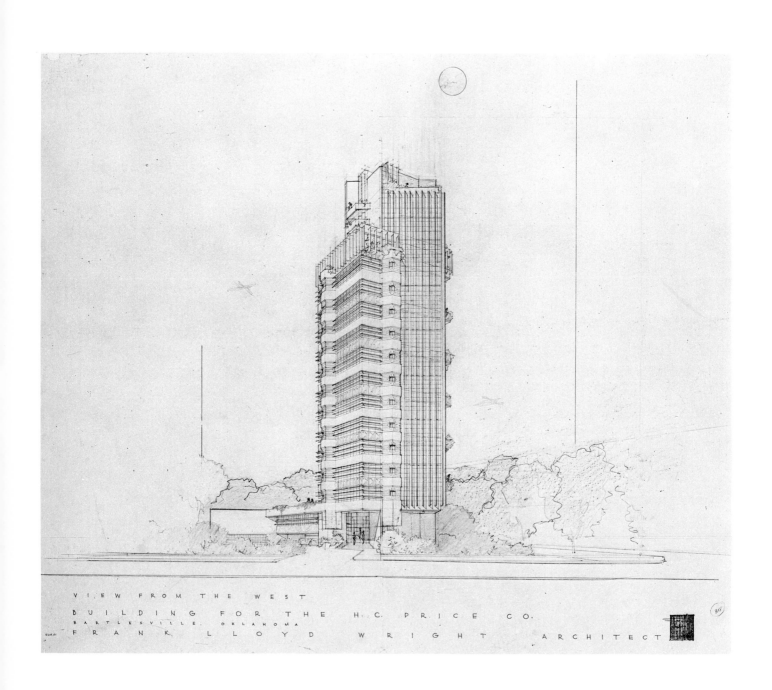

VIEW FROM THE WEST
BUILDING FOR THE H.C. PRICE CO.
BARTLESVILLE, OKLAHOMA
FRANK LLOYD WRIGHT ARCHITECT

249, 250. H. C. PRICE COMPANY TOWER, BARTLESVILLE, OKLAHOMA. 1952-56.

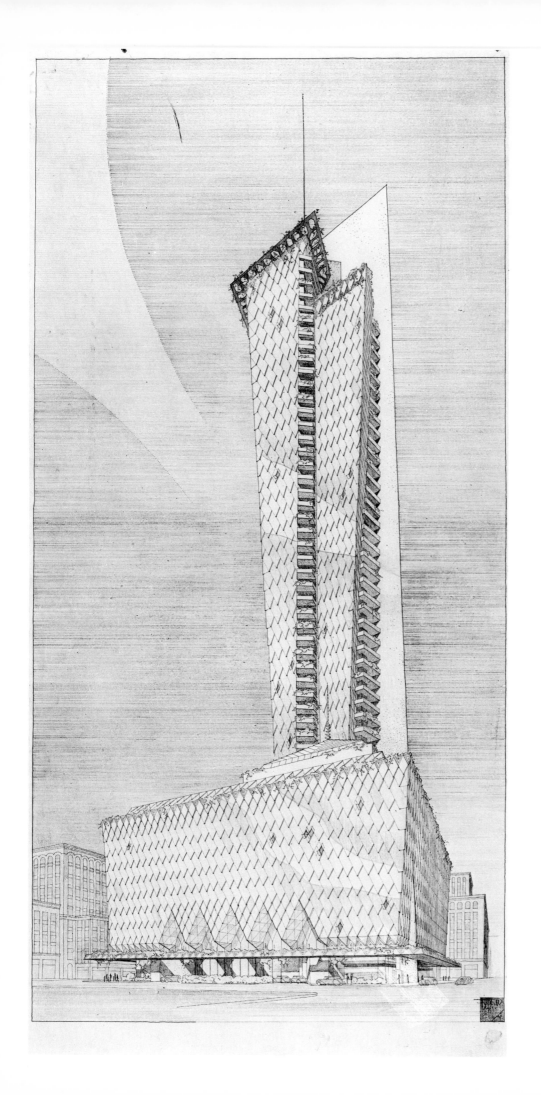

251. PROJECT: ROGERS LACY HOTEL, DALLAS, TEXAS. 1946.

252. PROJECT: SKYSCRAPER, "THE GOLDEN BEACON", CHICAGO, ILLINOIS. 1956.

THE GOLDEN BEACON
CHICAGO · ILLINOIS
FRANK LLOYD WRIGHT, ARCHITECT

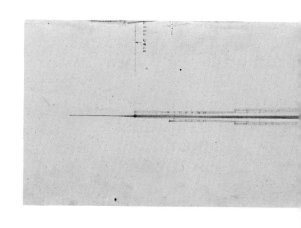

THE ILLINOIS CANTILEVER-STRUCTURE MILE HIGH
528 STORIES OR 5280 FEET, 400-FOOT AERIAL
FRANK LLOYD WRIGHT, ARCHITECT

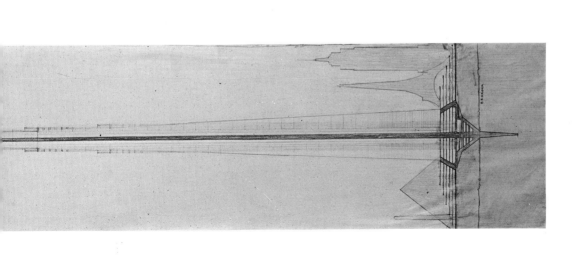

253, 254. PROJECT: MILE-HIGH SKYSCRAPER, "THE ILLINOIS", CHICAGO, ILLINOIS. 1956.

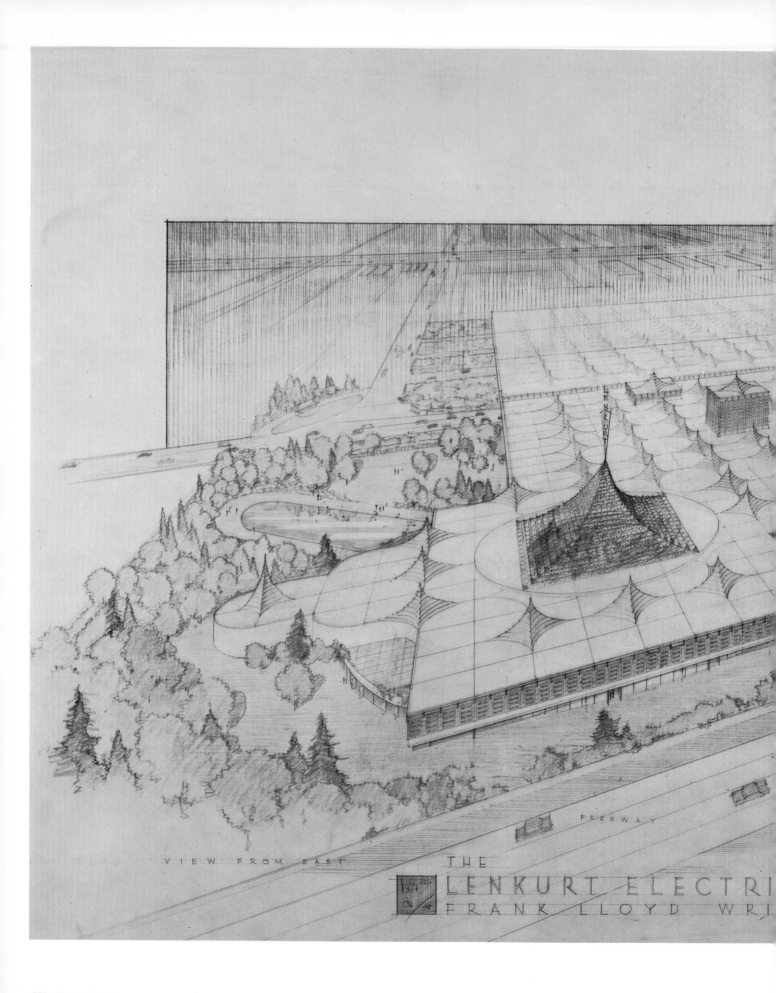

VIEW FROM EAST

THE
LENKURT ELECTRI
FRANK LLOYD WRI

FREEWAY

255. PROJECT: LENKURT ELECTRIC COMPANY BUILDING, LONG ISLAND, NEW YORK. 1955.

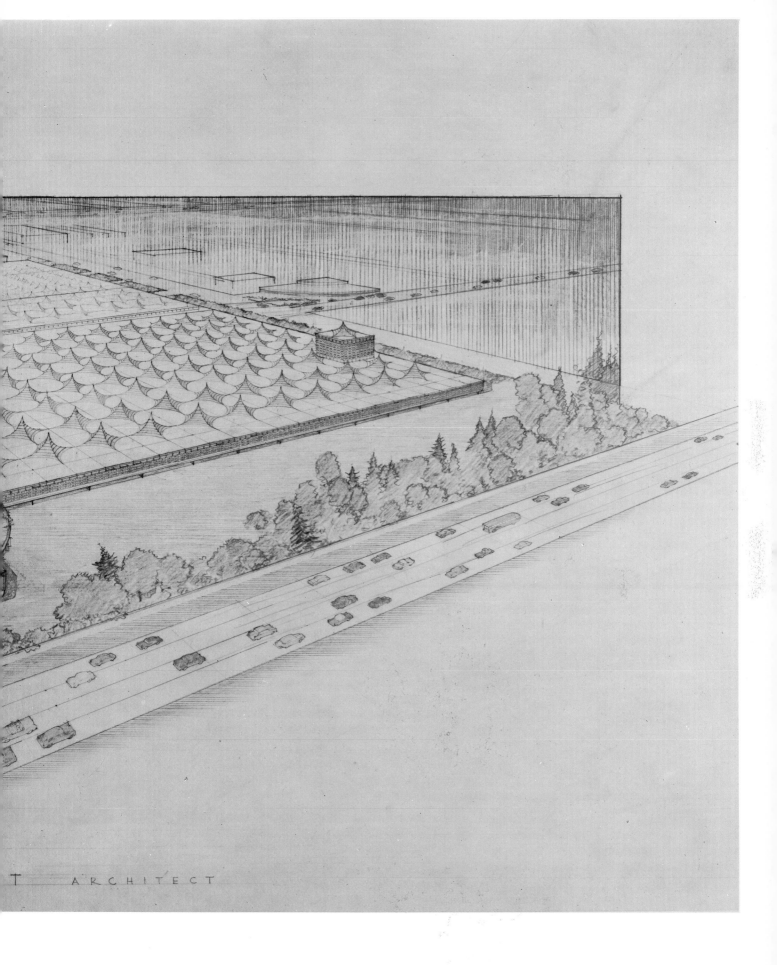

ARCHITECT

256. PROJECT: DANIEL WIELAND MOTOR HOTEL, HAGERSTOWN, MARYLAND. 1955.

257. PROJECT: WEDDING CHAPEL, CLAREMONT HOTEL, BERKELEY, CALIFORNIA. 1957.

WEDDING CHAPEL FOR CLAREMONT HOTEL
BERKELEY, CALIFORNIA
FRANK LLOYD WRIGHT ARCHITECT

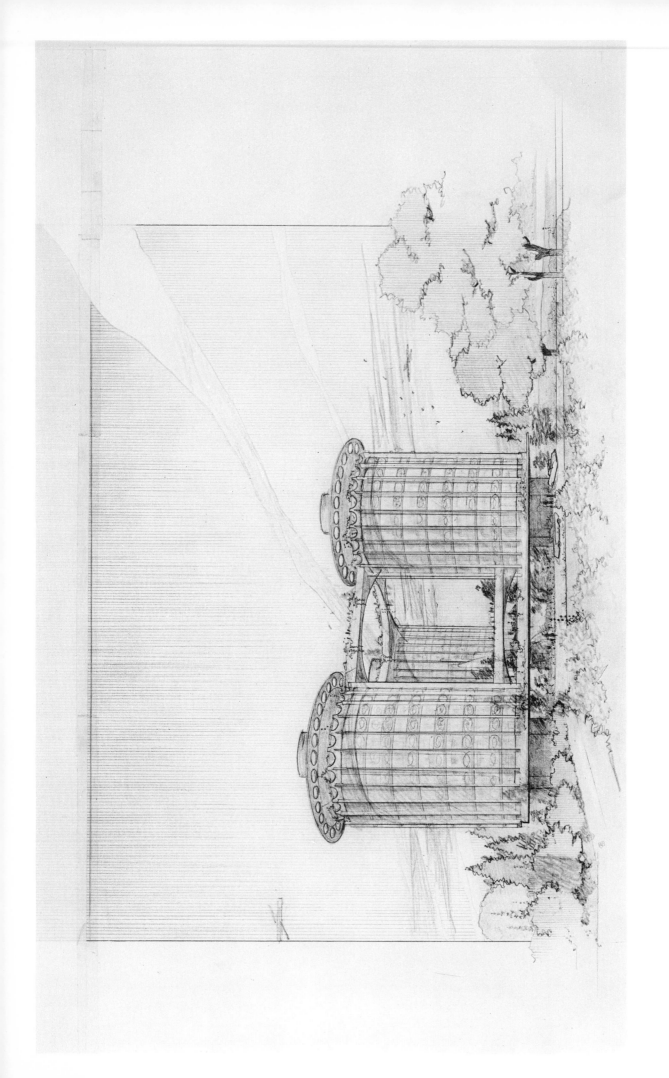

258. PROJECT: BRAMLETT MOTOR HOTEL. 1956.

259. PROJECT: ARIZONA STATE CAPITAL, "OASIS", PHOENIX, ARIZONA. 1957.

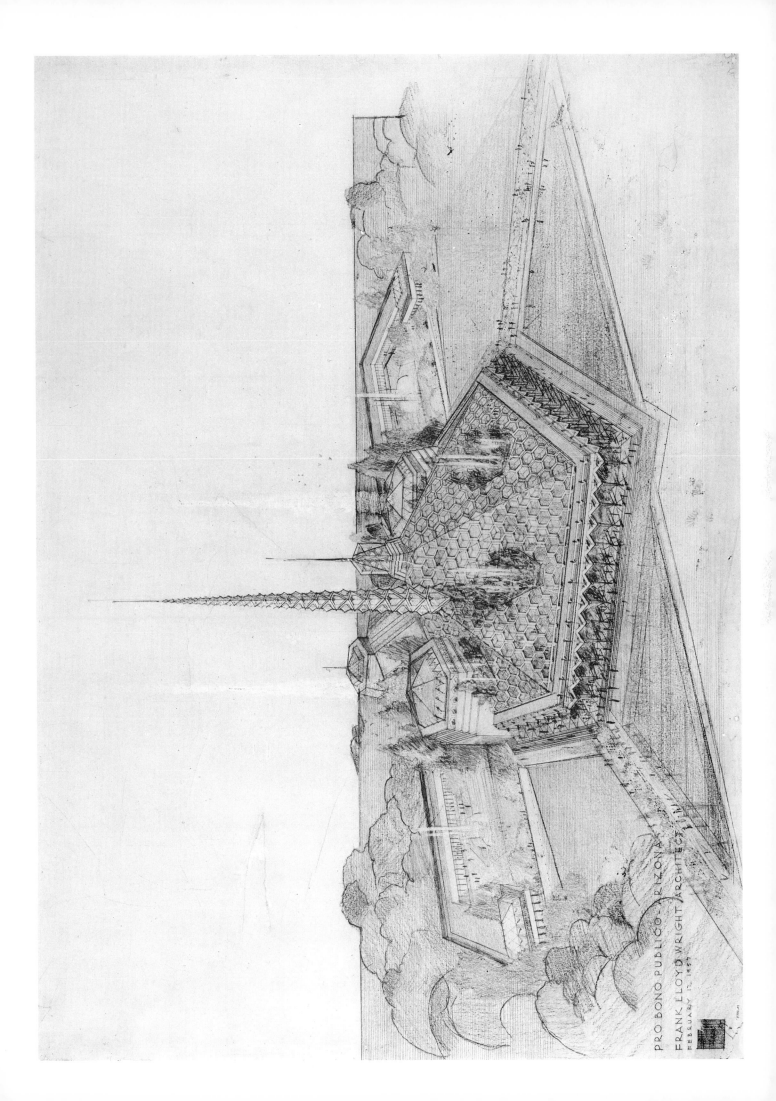

PRO BONO PUBLICO—ARIZONA

FRANK LLOYD WRIGHT ARCHITECT
FEBRUARY 17, 1957

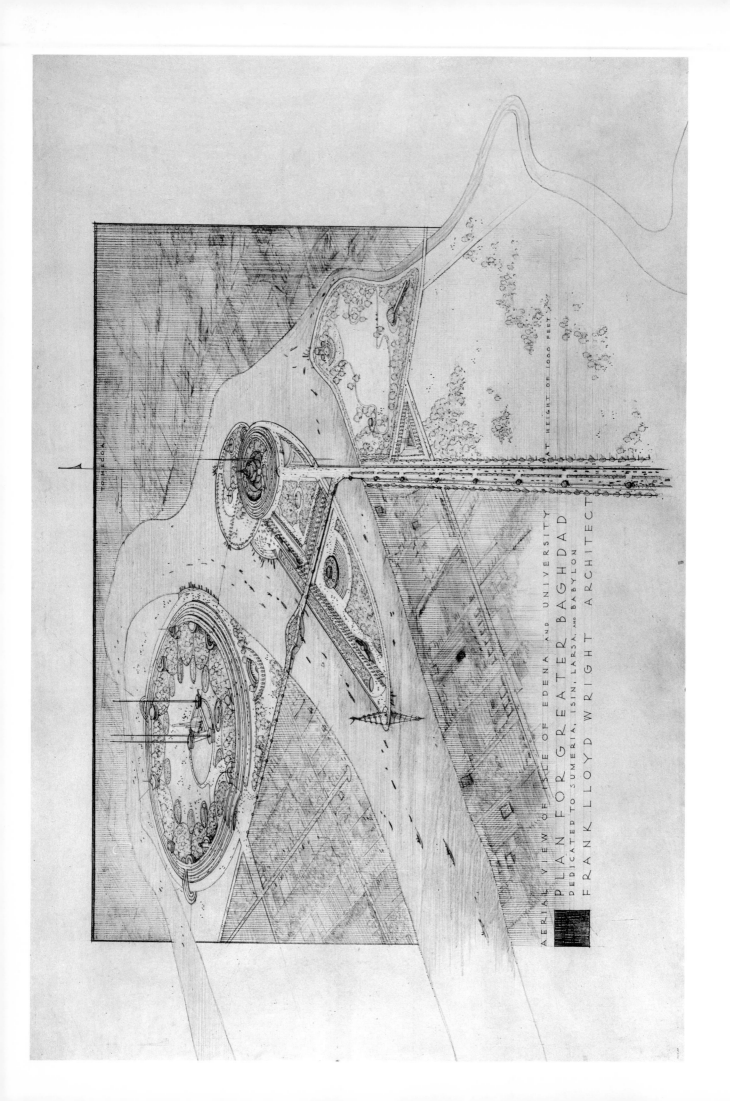

AERIAL VIEW OF ISLE OF EDENA AND UNIVERSITY
PLAN FOR GREATER BAGHDAD
DEDICATED TO SUMERIA, ISIN, LARSA, AND BABYLON
FRANK LLOYD WRIGHT ARCHITECT

AT HEIGHT OF 1000 FEET

260. PROJECT: PLAN FOR GREATER BAGHDAD, IRAQ. 1957.

261. PROJECT: OPERA HOUSE AND GARDENS, BAGHDAD, IRAQ. 1957.

CRESCENT OPERA, CIVIC AUDITORIUM. GARDEN OF E.DEN
PLAN FOR GREATER BAGHDAD
FRANK LLOYD WRIGHT ARCHITECT

AERIAL VIEW OF THE UNIVERSITY   AT HEIGHT OF 300 FEET
PLAN FOR GREATER BAGHDAD
DEDICATED TO SUMERIA, ISIN, LARSA AND BABYLON
FRANK LLOYD WRIGHT ARCHITECT

262. PROJECT: UNIVERSITY COMPLEX AND GARDENS, BAGHDAD, IRAQ. 1957.

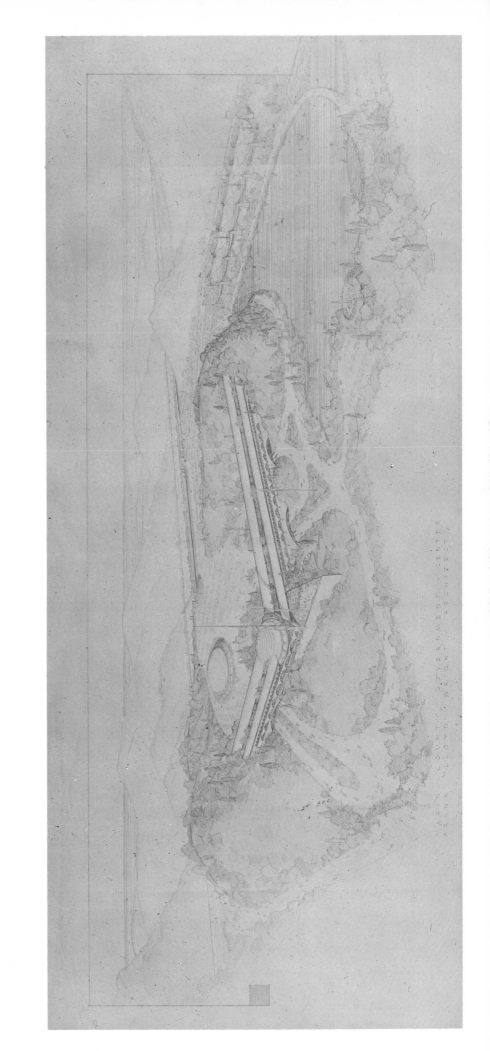

263. MARIN COUNTY CIVIC CENTER, CALIFORNIA. 1959.

264, 265. PROJECT: "BROADACRE CITY". 1934-58.

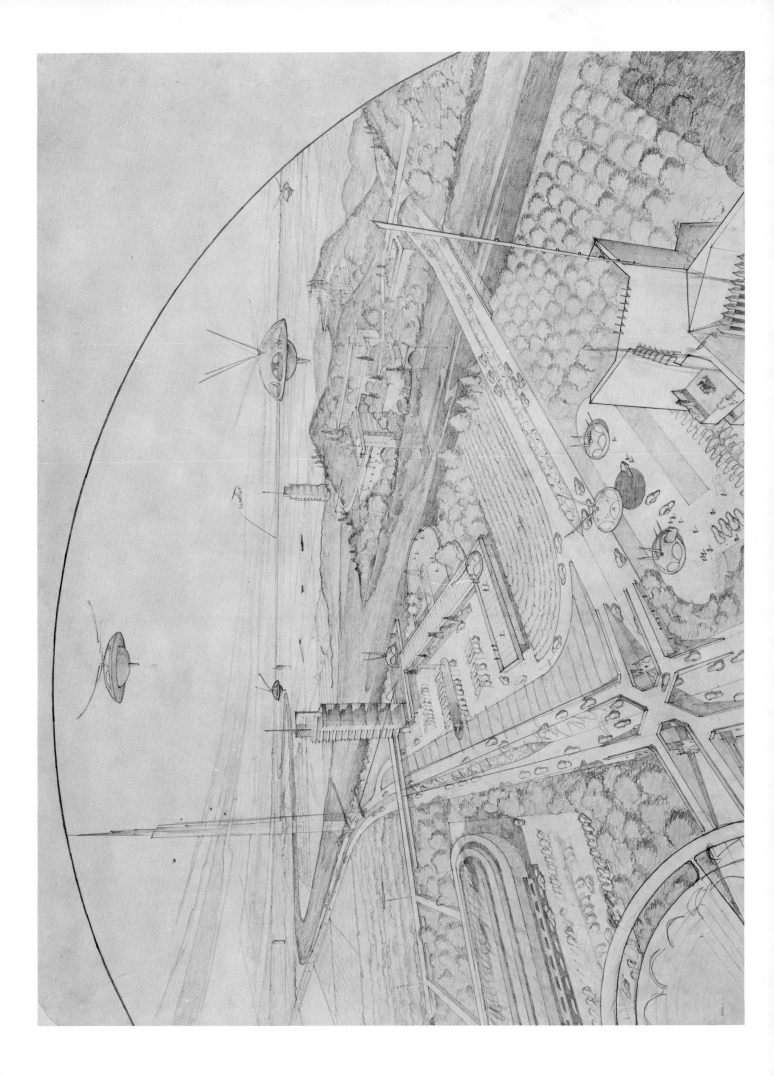

266, 267. PROJECT: "BROADACRE CITY". 1934-58.

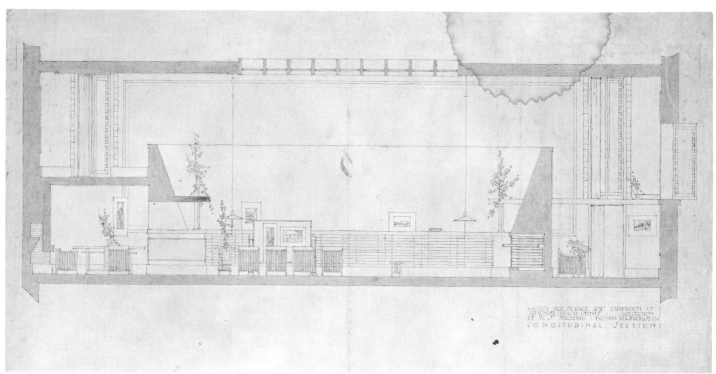

268, 269. W. S. SPAULDING PRINT GALLERY, BOSTON, MASSACHUSETTS. 1919.

270, 271, 272. PROJECT: GORDON STRONG AUTOMOBILE OBJECTIVE, SUGAR LOAF MOUNTAIN, MARYLAND. 1925.

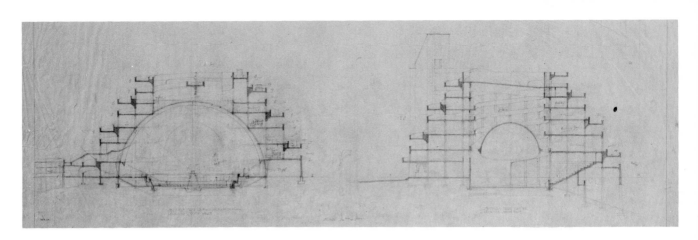

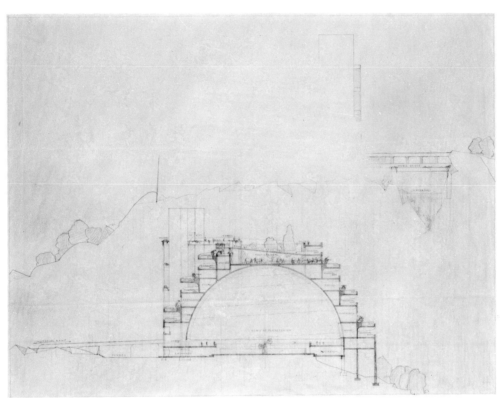

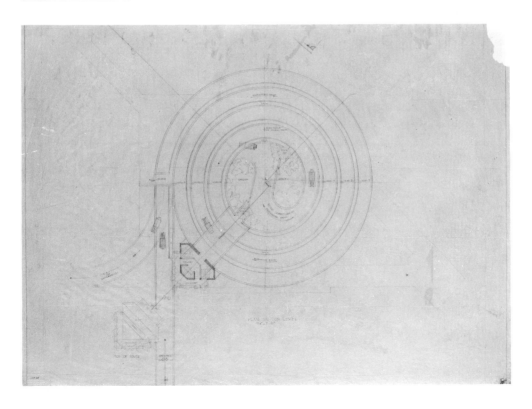

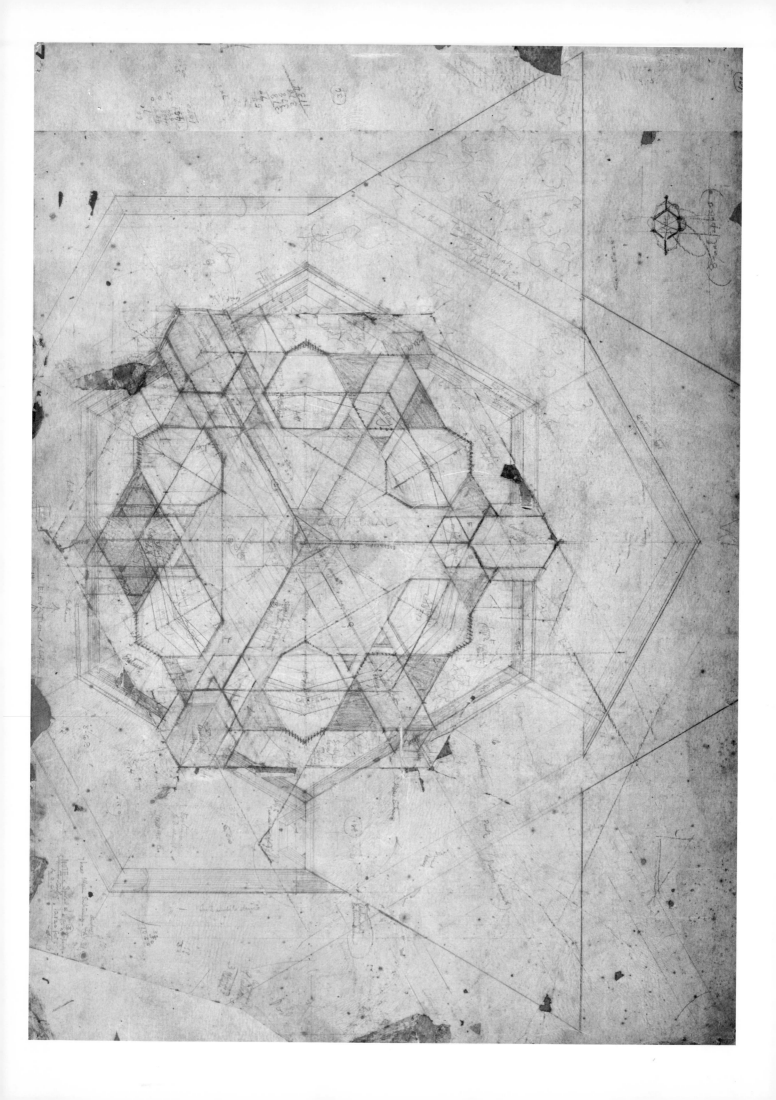

273. PROJECT: STEEL CATHEDRAL, NEW YORK CITY, N. Y. 1926.

274. CHARLES ENNIS HOUSE, LOS ANGELES, CALIFORNIA. 1924.

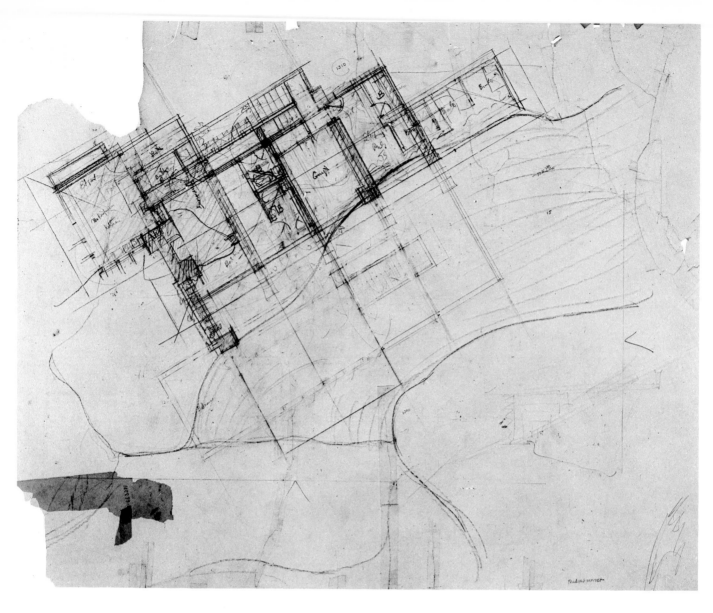

275. EDGAR J. KAUFMANN HOUSE, "FALLINGWATER", BEAR RUN, PENNSYLVANIA. 1936.

276. SOLOMON R. GUGGENHEIM MUSEUM, NEW YORK CITY, N. Y. 1943.

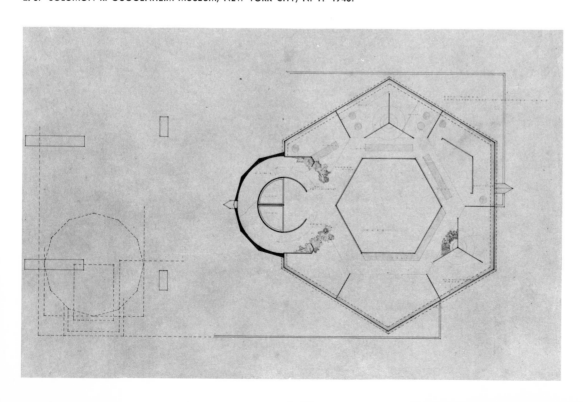

277. PROJECT: COMMUNITY CENTER, POINT PARK, PITTSBURGH, PENNSYLVANIA. 1947.

278. HUNTINGTON HARTFORD PLAY RESORT, HOLLYWOOD HILLS, CALIFORNIA. 1947.

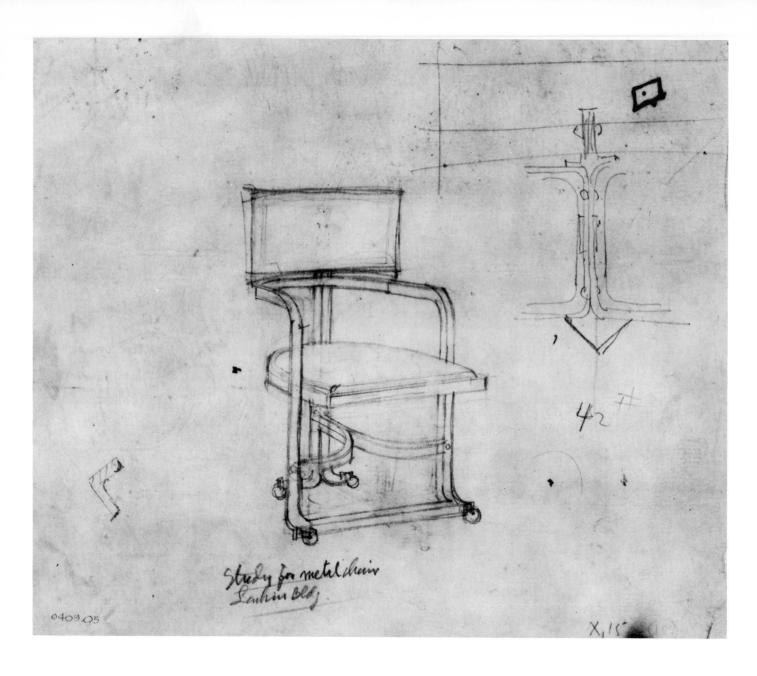

Study for metal chair
Larkin Bldg

0403.05

X,15

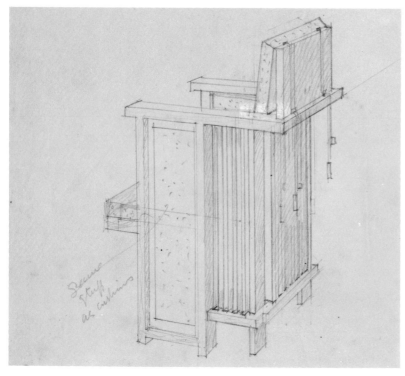

Secure
stuff
as cushions

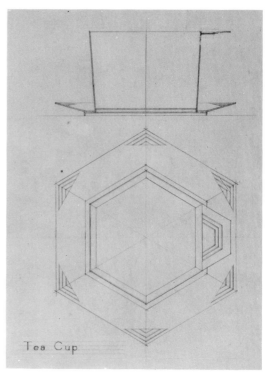

Tea Cup

279. METAL CHAIR, LARKIN BUILDING, BUFFALO, NEW YORK. 1904.

280. CHAIR. 1905.

281. PROJECT: TEA CUP AND SAUCER. 1929-30.

282. TABLE, CHAIRS AND LAMP, MIDWAY GARDENS, CHICAGO, ILLINOIS. 1914.

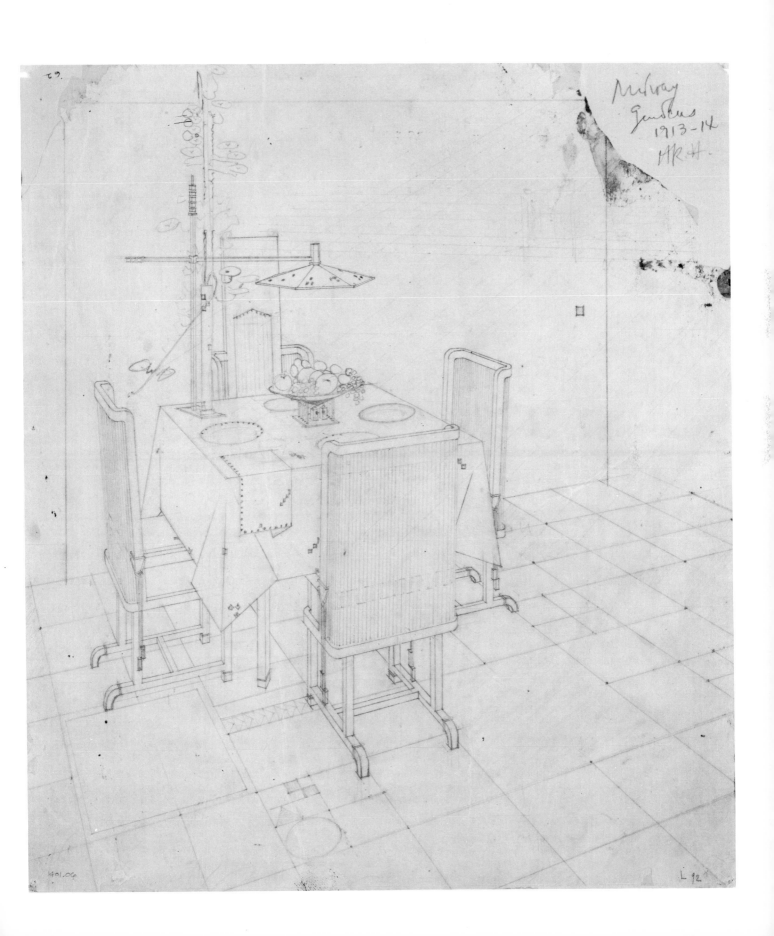

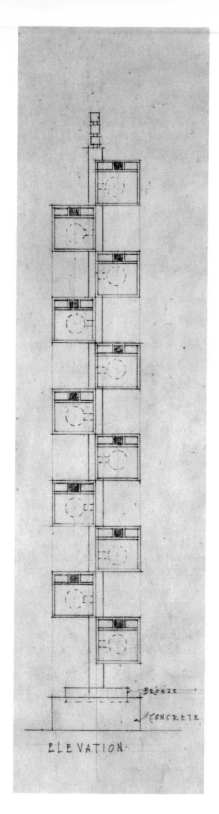

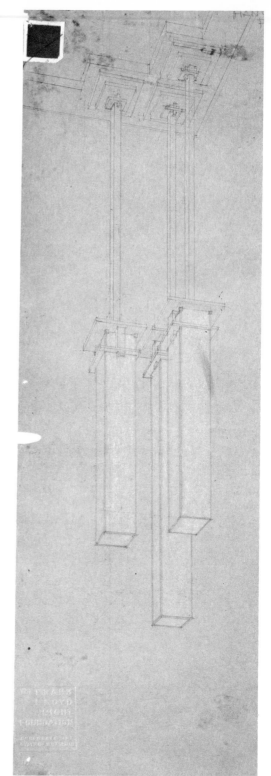

283. LIGHT FIXTURE, MIDWAY GARDENS, CHICAGO, ILLINOIS. 1914.

284. EXTERIOR LIGHT. 1915.

285. HANGING LIGHT FIXTURE, IMPERIAL HOTEL, TOKYO, JAPAN. 1915.

286. CARVED POLYCHROME DECORATION, IMPERIAL HOTEL, TOKYO, JAPAN. 1915.

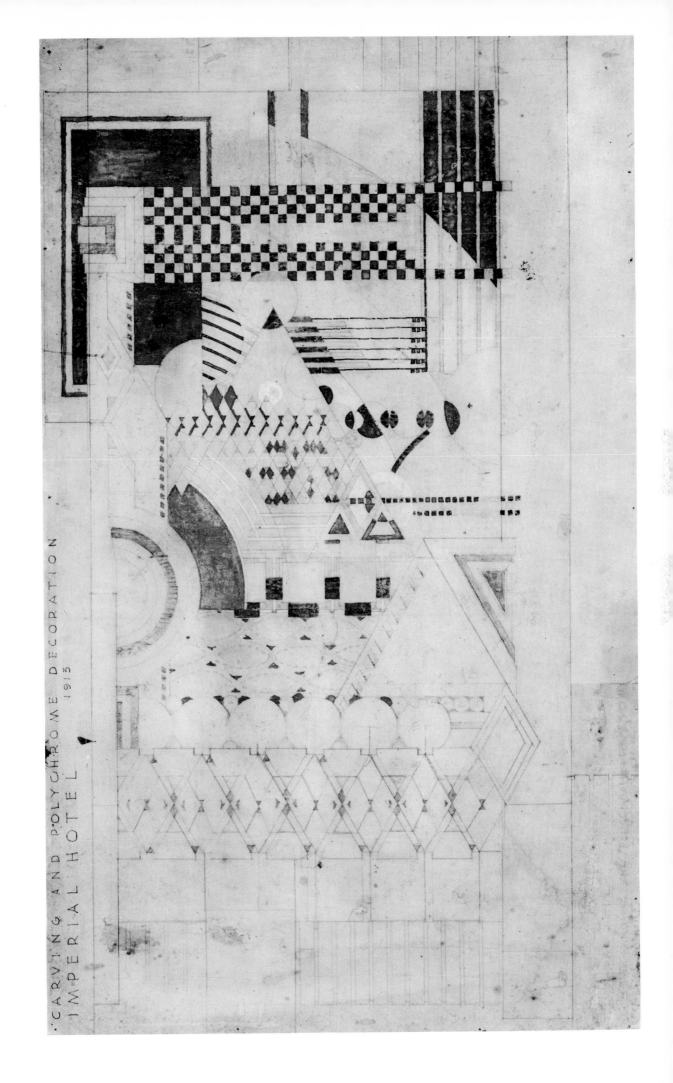

CARVING AND POLYCHROME DECORATION
IMPERIAL HOTEL
1915

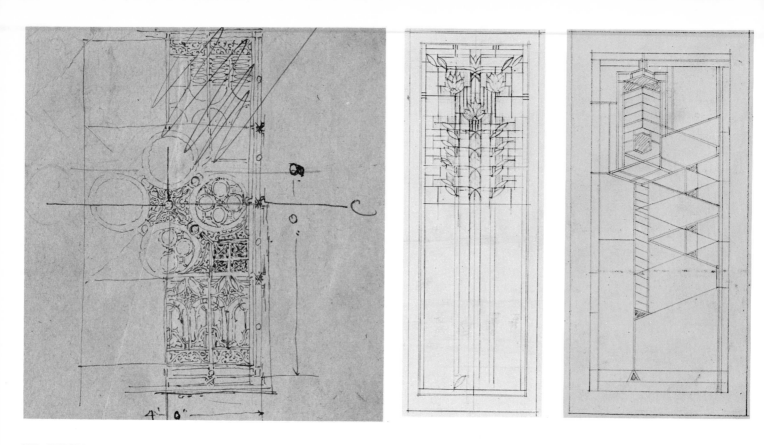

287. PERFORATED SCREEN, DINING ROOM CEILING, OAK PARK STUDIO, CHICAGO, ILLINOIS. 1889.

288. SCREEN. c. 1909.

289. DINING ROOM WINDOW, ROBIE HOUSE, CHICAGO, ILLINOIS. 1909.

290. GATE, ROBIE HOUSE, CHICAGO, ILLINOIS. 1909.

291. WINDOW, COONLEY HOUSE, RIVERSIDE, ILLINOIS. 1908.

29   ⸱⸱ CEILING LIGHT, OAK PARK STUDIO, CHICAGO, ILLINOIS. 1889.

293. DESIGN FOR RELIEF SCULPTURE, NAKOMA COUNTRY CLUB, MADISON, WISCONSIN. 1924.

294. DESIGN FOR SCULPTURE, MIDWAY GARDENS, CHICAGO, ILLINOIS. 1914.

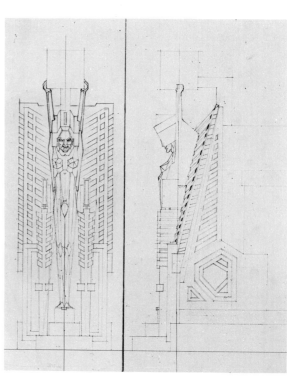

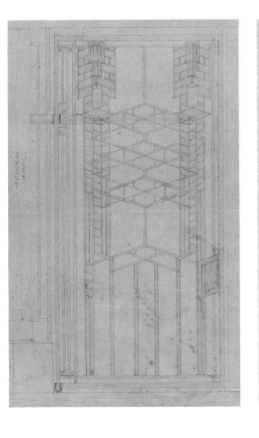

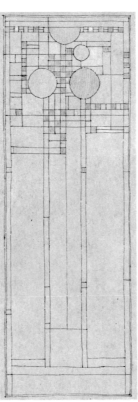

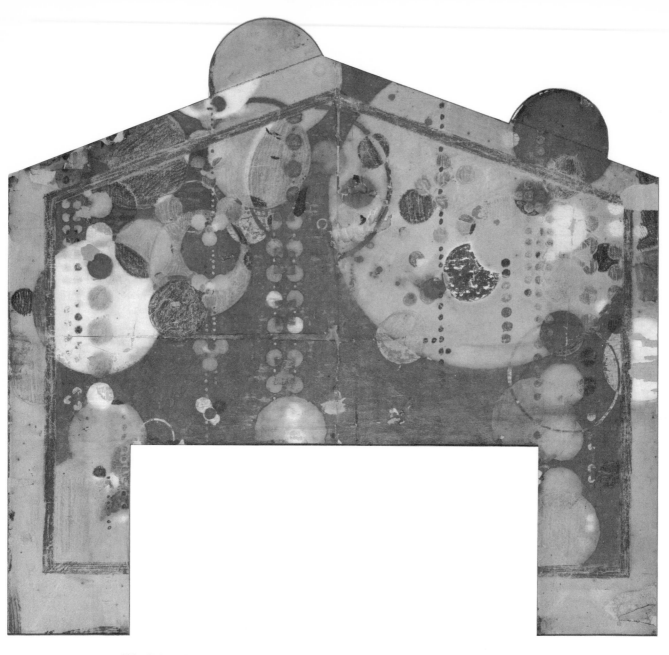

295. STUDY FOR MURAL, "CITY BY THE SEA", MIDWAY GARDENS, CHICAGO, ILLINOIS. 1914.

296. THEATRE CURTAIN, HILLSIDE THEATRE, TALIESIN, SPRING GREEN, WISCONSIN. 1933.

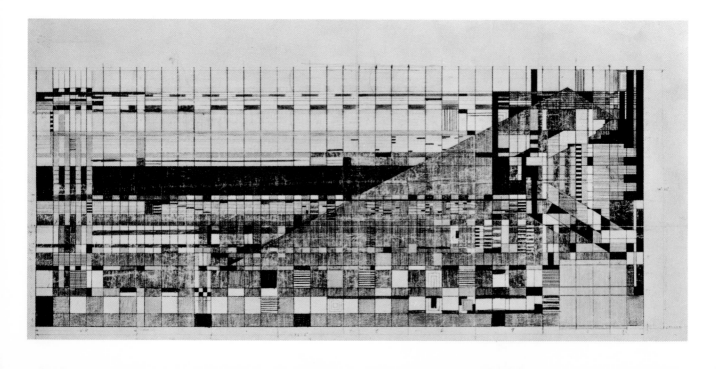

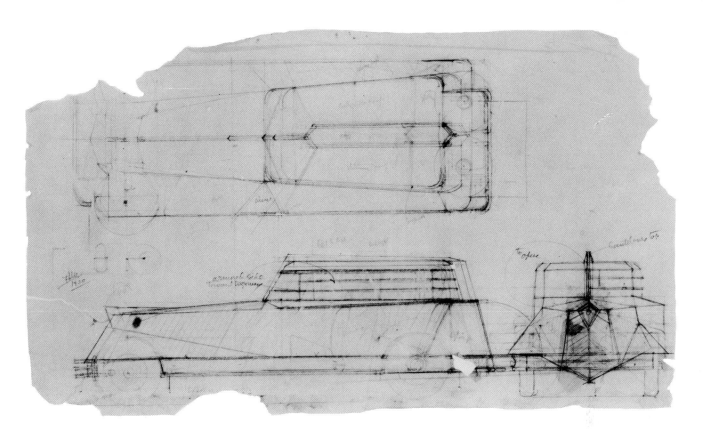

297. PROJECT: AUTOMOBILE WITH CANTILEVERED TOP. 1920.

298. PROJECT: MOTOR CAR (ROAD MACHINE). 1958.

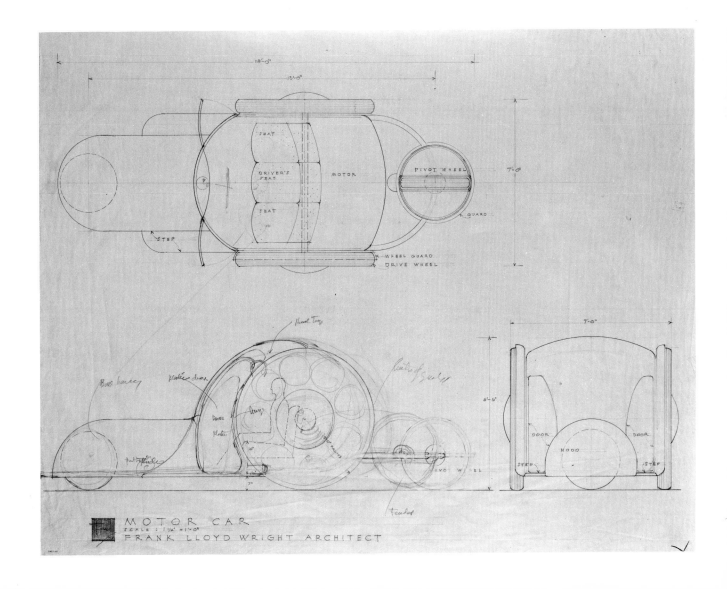

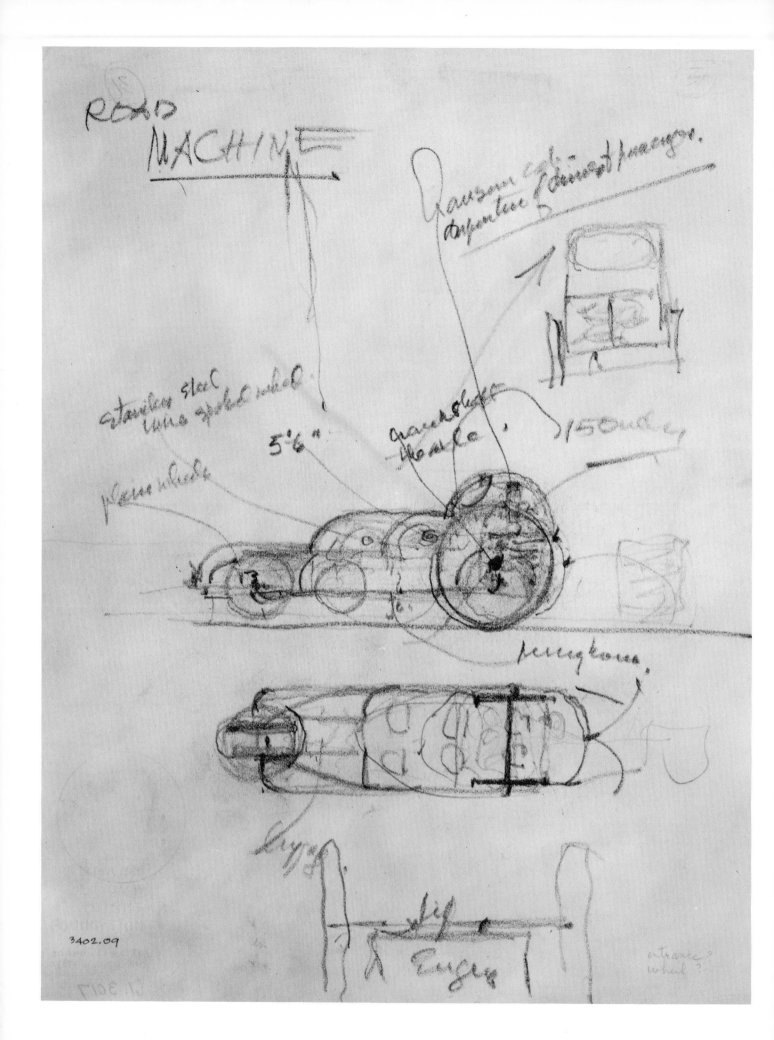

299. PROJECT: ROAD MACHINE. 1958.

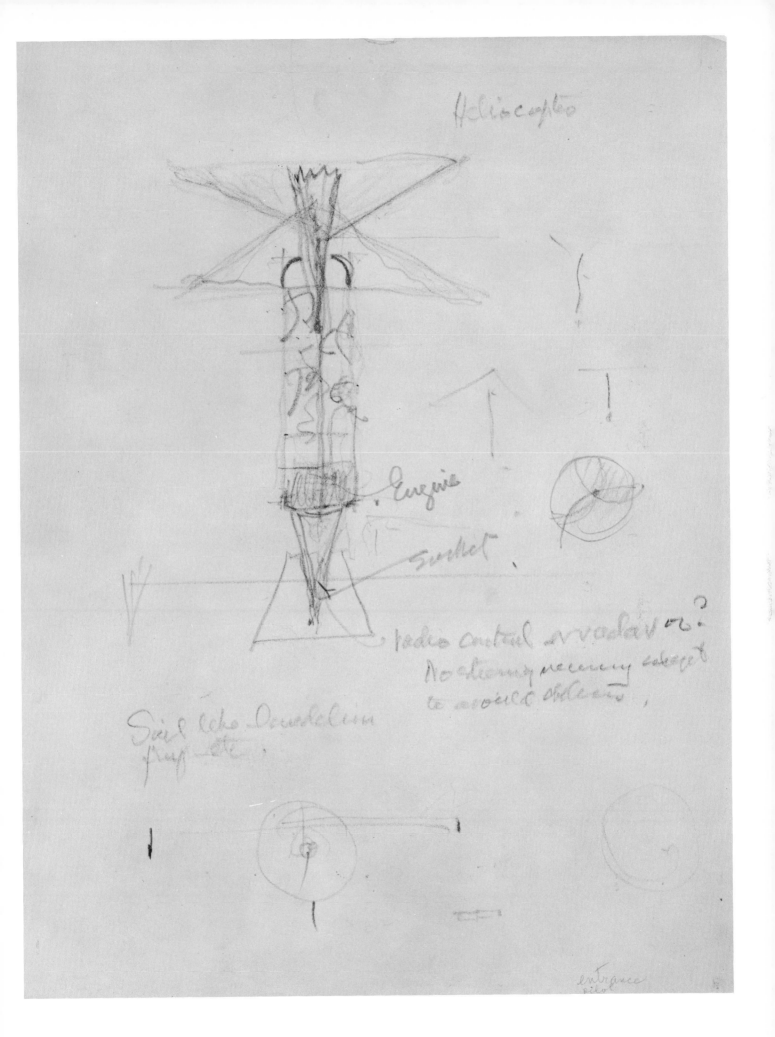

300. PROJECT: HELICOPTER. 1958.

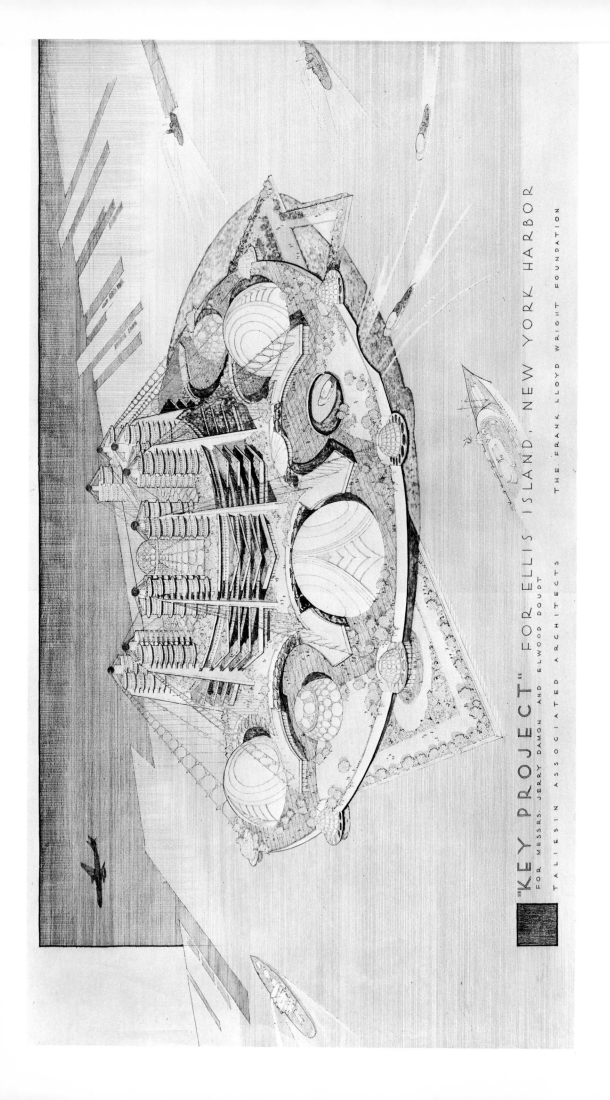

"KEY PROJECT" FOR ELLIS ISLAND, NEW YORK HARBOR

FOR MESSRS. JERRY DAMON AND ELWOOD DOUDT

TALIESIN ASSOCIATED ARCHITECTS   THE FRANK LLOYD WRIGHT FOUNDATION

301. (T.A.A.) "KEY PROJECT", APARTMENT AND HOTEL TOWERS AND GARDENS, ELLIS ISLAND, NEW YORK HARBOR. 1959-61.

302. (T.A.A.) PROJECT: HOTEL, KONA COAST OF HAWAII. 1959.

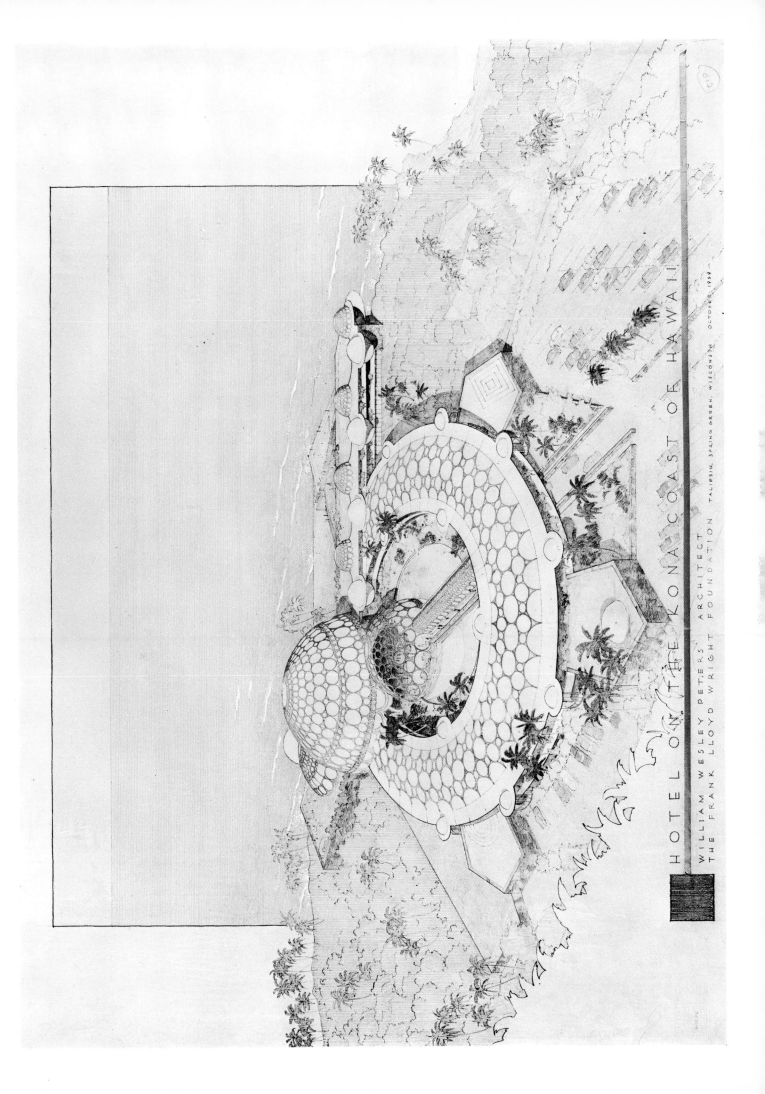

HOTEL ON THE KONA COAST OF HAWAII

WILLIAM WESLEY PETERS' ARCHITECT
THE FRANK LLOYD WRIGHT FOUNDATION TALIESIN, SPRING GREEN, WISCONSIN OCTOBER 1959

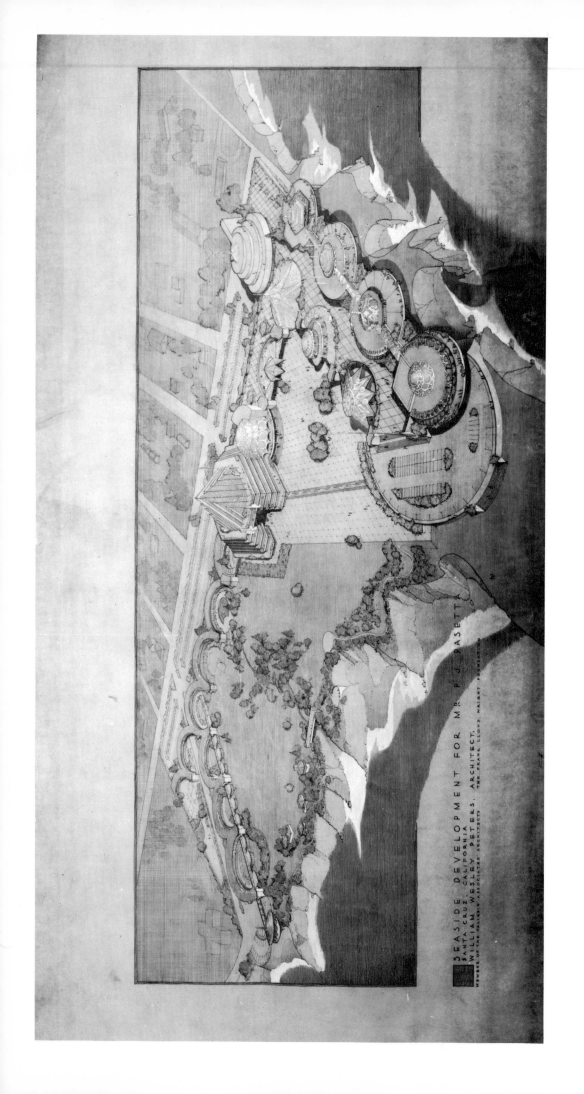

303. (T.A.A.) PROJECT: SEASIDE DEVELOPMENT, "COURT OF THE SEVEN SEAS", FOR P. J. PASETTA. SANTA CRUZ, CALIFORNIA. 1962.

NOTES TO THE PLATES

The plates in this book faithfully reproduce all details of the drawings as well as of the various kinds of paper on which they were drawn. In order to retain the quality of the often fragile originals, the greatest care has been taken to reproduce all the marks of the architect's work: his handwritten notes and erasures as well as the patches, tears and stains that resulted from the constant handling of these drawings in Frank Lloyd Wright's daily work. Because he placed each picture in a specific relation to the size and shape of the paper on which it was drawn, it was necessary to retain the background in order to preserve each composition as Wright planned it and saw it. Because some of the original sheets are of enormous size, it was desirable not to reduce too greatly the size of the drawing itself; in these cases, where large surrounding areas of blank paper were not reproduced, every effort was made to follow the proportions of the original compositions.

The plates of three hundred of the drawings were made directly from the originals. In the three cases where the original drawings were no longer in the Taliesin archives, photographs of the originals fortunately existed; for these three, plates were made from the photographs, because the inclusion of these pictures was deemed necessary both for their intrinsic importance and for a better understanding of other work.

In the notes on the following pages the dimensions given are of the untrimmed sheet. Height precedes width.

As described in the notes, many of the drawings on tracing paper are mounted to different kinds of backing. The term "board" as used in the notes refers to heavy white or grey cardboard.

Where drawings have been cataloged by The Frank Lloyd Wright Foundation, the catalog number is given at the end of each note: (F 3402.15). The first two numbers represent the year in which the design of the project is believed to have been inaugurated (not the year the project was completed); the second two numbers represent the project's place in the sequence of the year's work; the last two numbers refer to the place the drawing occupies in the sequence of studies made for a given project.

Many dates and comments were written on the drawings by Frank Lloyd Wright years after the projects were designed. The reader will observe that the dates assigned by The Frank Lloyd Wright Foundation occasionally vary from the notations made on the drawings by Frank Lloyd Wright, or from the dates assigned by various historians of Wright's work. In general the dates given for the earlier buildings follow those established by Professor Henry-Russell Hitchcock in his monograph on Wright *In the Nature of Materials.*

NOTES TO THE PLATES

1. DORMER WINDOW, CHAUNCEY L. WILLIAMS HOUSE, RIVER FOREST, ILLINOIS. 1895.
Perspective. 8¾"x4". Pencil on tracing paper.
(F 9505.01)

This early study of a dormer window offers some familiar signs of accomplished draftsmanship: rapid, light lines pointed with abrupt dots and dashes.

2. PROJECT: LUXFER PRISM COMPANY SKYSCRAPER. 1895.
Elevation and section. 28¼"x17⅝". Pencil on tracing paper. Noted at bottom right: *Study for office building facade employing Luxfer Prism-lighting 1894-5.*
(F 9509.01)

In this early study for an office building facade Wright gives nearly equal stress to verticals and horizontals. The design is related to the steel framing he was later to reject, in favor of concrete piers and cantilevered floors. Together with the study for a dormer window of the same year, this drawing suggests Wright's background and interests in 1895.

3. PROJECT: WOLF LAKE AMUSEMENT PARK, ILLINOIS. 1895.
Aerial perspective 20¼"x49¼". Black ink, watercolor and gold paint on heavy white paper mounted to linen.
(F 9510.01)

A formal "presentation" rendering, decorative rather than atmospheric in style, but conveying clearly the project's immense scale.

4. PROJECT: LEXINGTON TERRACE APARTMENTS, CHICAGO, ILLINOIS. 1901-09.
Aerial perspective. 16½"x33". Pencil, black ink and purple wash on opaque paper; foreground separately drawn and pasted on. Signed at lower left in red square: *FLlW-1898.* Noted at bottom left: *study for urban housing 1898 Lexington Terrace, Chicago for E. G. Waller FLlW.*
(F 0111.02)

5. PROJECT: LEXINGTON TERRACE APARTMENTS, CHICAGO, ILLINOIS. 1901-09.
Perspective. 8⅝"x14⅝". Pencil, black ink and thin white wash on opaque cream-colored paper. Collection Henry Russell Hitchcock.

6. PROJECT: YAHARA BOAT CLUB, MADISON, WISCONSIN. 1902.
Perspective. 6¾"x22". Brown ink on tracing paper mounted to board. Signed in red square at center right: *FLlW.* Collection Henry Russell Hitchcock.

7. PROJECT: YAHARA BOAT CLUB, MADISON, WISCONSIN. 1902.
Perspective (on left side of sheet including plan of second story). 7⅝"x22⅜". Brown ink on opaque paper mounted to board. (F 0211.01)

8. PROJECT: WALTER GERTS HOUSE, GLENCOE, ILLINOIS. 1906.
Perspective. 18½"x25½", Brown ink on opaque cream-colored paper. (F 0203.01)

9. FRANK LLOYD WRIGHT STUDIO, OAK PARK, ILLINOIS. 1895-1911.
Perspective elevation. 5"x14⅛". Pencil, black ink, and white paint on opaque cream-colored paper mounted to board. Collection Henry Russell Hitchcock.

This drawing differs from its companion version in the use of white paint and a wider range of values. The building seems to sit comfortably on the ground, and the high roofs are held more closely to the background plane of trees.

10. FRANK LLOYD WRIGHT STUDIO, OAK PARK, ILLINOIS. 1895-1911.
Perspective elevation. 6"x19½". Pencil and black ink on opaque paper. (F 8901.03)

11. SUSAN LAWRENCE DANA HOUSE, SPRINGFIELD, ILLINOIS. 1902-04.
Interior perspective. 12⅝"x19¼". Pencil on tracing paper. Inscribed at bottom right: *Sketch for Dana Studio 1900 FLlW.* (F 0302.02)

12. SUSAN LAWRENCE DANA HOUSE, SPRINGFIELD, ILLINOIS. 1902-04.
Interior perspective. 11⅜"x19". Pencil on tracing paper. (F 0302.01)

Like the preceding drawing, this is a rough layout for a color rendering, with written color notations. The vagueness of detail and the absence of a confining frame or border contribute to an illusion of space, often lost in the more highly finished interior perspectives.

13. PROJECT: VICTOR METZGER HOUSE, ONTARIO, CANADA. 1901.
Perspective. 9⅜″x38⅞″. Black ink and color wash on tracing paper mounted to board. Signed at bottom left: *FLlW/1900.* (F 0209.02)

14. GEORGE MADISON MILLARD HOUSE, HIGHLAND PARK, ILLINOIS. 1906.
Perspective. 12½″x32¼″. Pencil, brown ink, and water color on tracing paper mounted to board. (F 0606.01)

Framed by intricate groups of trees, the house is given some solidity by a deft use of shadow, particularly on the wall just beneath the eaves (but not on the roof soffits themselves).

15. PROJECT: WOOD AND PLASTER HOUSE, HIGHLAND PARK, ILLINOIS. 1904.
Perspective. 12½″x17⅛″. Pencil and brown ink on opaque paper. (F 0501.01)

16. WARD W. WILLITTS HOUSE, HIGHLAND PARK, ILLINOIS. 1902.
Perspective. 8¾″x32½″. Black and brown ink, water color, gouache and crayon on opaque paper. (F 0208.01)

This precise and formal rendering of the Willitts house combines a realistic density of surface and shadow with stylized circular trees. Graduations of tone are worked out so that no two adjacent areas are of the same value.

17. AVERY COONLEY HOUSE, RIVERSIDE, ILLINOIS. 1908-11.
Perspective. 9″x32″. Pencil on tracing paper mounted to board. Noted at lower right: *Coonley 1908-10.* (F 0803.04)

The garden elevation for this famous house is here shown before the terrace was given a triangular prow projecting into the pool.

18. E. E. BOYNTON HOUSE, ROCHESTER, NEW YORK. 1908.
Perspective. 11⅜″x33¾″. Pencil and colored pencils on tracing paper mounted to opaque paper. Signed in red square at lower right: *FLlW/1903.* (F 0801.01)

19. PROJECT: WILLIAM NORMAN GUTHRIE HOUSE, SEWANEE, TENNESSEE. 1908.
Perspective. 12⅝″x25⅞″. Pencil and brown ink on tracing paper mounted to board. (F 0819.01)

20. C. THAXTER SHAW HOUSE, MONTREAL, CANADA. 1906.
Aerial perspective. 21½″x27½″. Pencil and brown ink on opaque cream-colored paper. (F 0610.02)

The stolid exterior of this granite house conceals a complex play of space inside.

21. THOMAS P. HARDY HOUSE, RACINE, WISCONSIN. 1905.
Perspective. 8⅜″x16⅝″. Pencil, black and brown ink, grey and white wash on opaque cream-colored paper. Noted at lower right: *Marion Mahony Hardy 1905.* (F 0506.02)

Among the numerous drawings executed by Marion Mahony with flat, heavily outlined areas, this unfinished study is especially interesting as an indication of how foreground planes, often established by overlapping tree trunks, were placed to frame the building without obscuring important details. Pencil shadow lines on the walls and smudged pencil on the roof soffits; and the tentative penciled revisions to tree branches at the far left and just to the right of the house, suggest the care with which these details were studied.

22. THOMAS P. HARDY HOUSE, RACINE, WISCONSIN. 1905.
Perspective. 19″x5½″. Pencil and colored pencil, brown ink and white wash on opaque paper. (F 0506.03)

Of the several versions of this drawing the best known consists of ink lines without background tone; the version reproduced here employs delicate touches of color in the water and sky, and shadows cast on the walls by the overhanging roofs (although the soffits of the roofs themselves are left unshaded). The purely linear version includes a single spray of flowers at the bottom. In both versions, the placement of the building at the top of an almost empty sheet of paper and the great prominence given to minor details, are devices consciously borrowed from Japanese prints to make the house appear as an incident in nature.

23. LARKIN COMPANY ADMINISTRATION BUILDING, BUFFALO, NEW YORK. 1904.
Perspective and partial plan. 20⅞″x18″. Brown ink on tracing paper mounted to board. (F 0403.03)

This and similar drawings of the Larkin building, on the following pages, have most often been reproduced in solid black or brown ink without tonal gradations, as was probably intended. The original drawings, however, show considerable variation of tone within these apparently solid areas. The extreme simplification concentrates almost entirely on suggesting effects of mass through dense shadow, but a few details picked out in blue ink (perhaps added at a later date?) relieve the austerity.

24. LARKIN COMPANY ADMINISTRATION BUILDING, BUFFALO, NEW YORK. 1904.
Perspective and partial plan. 36⅜"x21⅛". Brown ink, silver paint for metal grill, on opaque cream-colored paper. Red square (unsigned) pasted on at lower right. (F 0403.02)

25. LARKIN COMPANY ADMINISTRATION BUILDING, BUFFALO, NEW YORK. 1904.
Perspective and inset detail perspective of entrance. 12¾"x24¼". Pencil and green pencil on tracing paper. (F 0403.01)

26. PROJECT: LARKIN COMPANY WORKERS' ROWHOUSES, BUFFALO, NEW YORK. 1904.
Perspective. 14⅛"x23¾". Grey ink wash on opaque paper mounted to board. (F 0706.01)

27. LARKIN COMPANY PAVILION, JAMESTOWN TERCENTENARY EXPOSITION, VIRGINIA. 1907.
Perspective. 4½"x11⅛". Pencil on tracing paper mounted to board. (F 0408.01)·

28. LARKIN COMPANY ADMINISTRATION BUILDING, BUFFALO, NEW YORK. 1904.
Perspective. 11"x6⅛". Black ink on tracing paper mounted to board. Inscribed: *Grammar of the Protestant.* (F 0403.07)

29. FREDERICK C. ROBIE HOUSE, CHICAGO, ILLINOIS. 1909.
Perspective and partial plan. 21½"x37½". Brown ink, blue ink foliage, on opaque cream-colored paper. Embossed red and white square pasted to lower right. (F 0908.03)

30. UNITY CHURCH, OAK PARK, ILLINOIS. 1906.
Perspective and partial plan. 23"x36". Brown ink, some blue ink foliage, on opaque cream-colored paper. Signed *FLlW* on embossed red and white square pasted to lower right; lettered date, *1908.* (F 0611.07)

31. UNITY CHURCH, OAK PARK, ILLINOIS. 1906.
Elevation. 20⅛"x41". Pencil on tracing paper. Inscribed at lower right: *Grammar of the Temple—Secular Section designed to match Temple Section (same temple)FLlW.* (F 0611.04)

32. UNITY CHURCH, OAK PARK, ILLINOIS. 1906.
Perspective. 12"x25⅛". Brown ink and water color wash on tracing paper mounted to board. (F 0611.03)

33. UNITY CHURCH, OAK PARK, ILLINOIS. 1906.
Interior perspective. 20¼"x27". Pencil on tracing paper. Inscribed at bottom left: *The unlimited overhead. Interior space enclosed by screen—fixtures only. Idea later used in Johnson Bldg. Racine Wis.* (F 0611.09)

34. UNITY CHURCH, OAK PARK, ILLINOIS. 1906.
Interior perspective. 15¼"x25⅜". Brown ink lines, pencil shading, on opaque cream-colored paper. Inscribed at top right: *Sense of Space—to be lived in—the REALITY of the bldg. The big vision coming through—the outside coming in.* (F 0611.02)

35. K. C. DE RHODES HOUSE, SOUTH BEND, INDIANA. 1906.
Perspective. 18⅝"x25¾". Brown ink, pencil and blue pencil on opaque cream-colored paper. Inscribed: *Drawn by Mahony—After FLlW and Hiroshige.* (F 0602.01)

The Japanese character of this drawing, executed by Marion Mahony, is acknowledged in the inscription given above.

36. RICHARD BOCK STUDIO HOUSE, MAYWOOD, ILLINOIS. 1906.
Perspective. 11¾"x22½". Pencil and brown ink on opaque paper. (F 0612.01)

37. MRS. THOMAS H. GALE HOUSE, OAK PARK, ILLINOIS. 1909.
Perspective. 13"x16¼". Brown and red-brown ink, pencil accents and white watercolor wash on opaque cream-colored paper. Signed at lower left. *FLlW.* The sky at the upper right and between the trees at the left has been cut out; the drawing is pasted over another sheet of the same paper on which are drawn additional tree branches. (F 0905.01)

Perhaps the most abstract of Wright's early houses, this study in rectilinear planes was cited by Wright, in later years, as the first of a series of compositions which culminated in the famous Fallingwater house for Edgar Kaufmann.

38. PROJECT: FRANK LLOYD WRIGHT HOUSE AND STUDIO, VIALE VERDI, FIESOLE, ITALY. 1910.
Perspective. 12½"x28". Pencil on tracing paper; pencil shading on reverse side, probably preparatory to transferring the drawing to opaque paper. Inscribed: *The Florentine Study for house for the Architect at Fiesole: 1910 To Russell Hitchcock at Taliesin 1941 FLlW*. Collection Henry Russell Hitchcock.

39. PROJECT: EDWARD SCHROEDER HOUSE, MILWAUKEE, WISCONSIN. 1912.
Perspective. 15⅜"x31". Brown ink and white water color wash on opaque cream-colored paper mounted to board. In the reproduction several inches have been trimmed from the bottom. (F 1112.01)

The blank but mottled surfaces of the building are not contrasted with details of landscape, except for the somewhat artful trees framing the low wing at the left.

40. "TALIESIN." FRANK LLOYD WRIGHT HOUSE, STUDIO, AND FARM BUILDINGS, SPRING GREEN, WISCONSIN. 1911.
Aerial perspective. 32⅛"x38¾". Black ink and grey wash on tracing cloth. (F 1104.01)

The drawing is of interest primarily as an indication of the scale and character of the first *Taliesin*, still maintained in its present (third) version. Complex intersections of hipped roofs, and courtyards formed by sheltering wings, may here be studied in detail.

41. PROJECT: CARNEGIE LIBRARY, OTTOWA, CANADA. 1913.
Perspective. 12¾"x23¼". Pencil and black ink on opaque paper.

The flat roof cantilevered at both ends recalls the Yahara Boat Club project of 1902.

42. BANFF NATIONAL PARK PAVILION, CANADA. 1911-12.
Perspective. 7⅛"x21⅛". Black ink and pencil shading on opaque paper. Inscribed at lower left: *Banff Pavilion Park in Canada for Canadian Pacific Rwy. FLlW/1911-12.* (F 1302.01)

43. PROJECT: SHERMAN M. BOOTH HOUSE, GLENCOE, ILLINOIS. 1911.
Perspective. 20⅜"x27⅞". Pencil, colored pencil, white watercolor wash with green, blue and red accents, on tracing paper mounted to board.

This project is one of Wright's most fascinating, and in this drawing it is given a deceptively quiet presentation. The house is approached by a road bridging a ravine; part of the house itself then bridges the road. Wright often used pronounced axial compositions, usually to extend or relate separate masses with a long low pergola or covered gallery. Here he has taken the road, as the most intrinsically axial of all space experiences, and incorporated it as an architectural element.

44. BRIDGE, RAVINE BLUFFS DEVELOPMENT FOR SHERMAN M. BOOTH, GLENCOE, ILLINOIS. 1915.
Perspective. 17½"x23½". Pencil, opaque and transparent watercolor wash with accents in orange, blue and green, on opaque paper mounted to board.

45. PROJECT: PRESS BUILDING *(SAN FRANCISCO CALL)* SAN FRANCISCO, CALIFORNIA. 1912.
Perspective. 38¾"x18¼". Black ink on tracing cloth mounted to board. (F 1207.01)

46. PROJECT: STATE BANK, SPRING GREEN, WISCONSIN. 1914.
Perspective. 20½"x29¾". Pencil and colored pencil on tracing cloth. (F 1405.01)

47. LAKE GENEVA INN (NOW GENEVA HOTEL), LAKE GENEVA, WISCONSIN. 1912.
Aerial perspective. 13½"x23⅜". Pencil and colored pencil on tracing paper mounted to board. (F 1202.01)

Axial composition offset by asymmetry (in the foreground element) produces a characteristically Wrightian scheme.

48. MIDWAY GARDENS, CHICAGO, ILLINOIS. 1914.
Aerial perspective. 16⅝"x40⅛". Black pencil, white and pink water color (on balloons) and blue wash (on water); on tracing cloth mounted to board. Lettered at bottom left: *FIRST SKETCH OF MIDWAY GARDEN:, 1913 FLlW.* (F 1401.07)

49. PROJECT: WOOD HOUSE, DECATUR, ILLINOIS. 1915.
Aerial perspective. 15¾"x25". Pencil and colored pencil on tracing paper mounted to board. (F 1511.01)

One of Wright's favorite themes—terraces and balconies overlooking a pool—is here given a wonderfully free and spontaneous interpretation. Well-placed trees, energetically sketched, lend depth and interest; the drawing is in fact much more intricately balanced than many of Wright's comparable studies.

50. PROJECT: AMERICAN SYSTEM READY-CUT HOUSES. 1913-15.
Perspective. 11⅝"x18". Black ink lines drawn free-hand over pencil lines, some of which are left uninked. (F 1506.01)

51. PROJECT: AMERICAN SYSTEM READY-CUT HOUSES. 1913-15
Interior perspective. 11"x8¼". (Printed reproduction from brochure.)

Some versions of these semi-prefabricated houses were built. The drawings are in a simple but sufficiently detailed style to make them readily understood by the layman. Of the original drawings most have disappeared: this and the following plate are reproduced from promotion literature, distributed in envelopes together with a description of the entire project.

52. PROJECT: AMERICAN SYSTEM READY-CUT HOUSES. 1913-15.
Perspective. 11"x8¼". (Printed reproduction from brochure.)

53. A. D. GERMAN WAREHOUSE, RICHLAND CENTER, WISCONSIN. 1915.
Perspective. 21½"x24⅜". Pencil, colored pencil, and gouache on linen-backed cream-colored paper mounted to board. (F 1504.01)

An unusually heavy, dense rendering of a heavy building, this drawing is especially interesting for such details as the treatment of the curb and the supports for flagpoles.

54. PRELIMINARY DESIGN: IMPERIAL HOTEL, TOKYO, JAPAN. 1915.
Aerial perspective. 33½"x74½". Pencil, black ink, and blue and red pencil accents on pools and lanterns, on tracing cloth. Noted at top left: *FIRST STUDY OF THE BUILDING APPROVED 1913.* (F 1509.03)

The extraordinary complexity of this vast building could only be suggested by an aerial view. In this study the disposition of extended low wings leading to a high central block at the rear is clear enough; but distortions of perspective at the bottom right corner are distracting.

55. PROJECT: FRANK LLOYD WRIGHT HOUSE, GOETHE STREET, CHICAGO, ILLINOIS. 1911.
Perspective. 25⅜"x8½". Black ink and water color wash on opaque paper mounted to board. (F 1113.04)

This project for the architect's own house and studio recalls the abstract, monumental arrangement of piers and blank walls of the Larkin and Unity Church buildings.

56. PROJECT: URBAN HOUSE. 1912-13.
Perspective. 16½"x7⅝". Black and grey ink with pencil accents on opaque cream-colored paper. Noted at bottom: *SMALL TOWN HOUSE–PLASTERED FRAME 1912-1913 wood [illegible] and mullions.* Engraver's trim marks and instructions written across bottom of drawing. (F 1506.06)

In the style of drawing and in its actual design, this house has a curiously Viennese *Jugendstil* look, recalling Josef Hoffmann's similar use of horizontal stripes on boxlike buildings. Corner windows and projecting masses, however, mark it as Wright's.

57. PROJECT: ZONED HOUSE, CITY VERSION. 1935.
Perspective and inset cross-section.

During the thirties Wright designed a series of houses whose thin, blank walls, floating roof planes, and generally light, abstract character were developments of his own earlier work in a direction already taken by younger European architects. Among these designs, which Wright called Zoned Houses, is this town house with a nearly blank facade, a roof garden, and a two and one half story high living room running from front to back of the narrow lot; bedrooms open onto it from mezzanine levels.

58. ALINE BARNSDALL "HOLLYHOCK HOUSE," OLIVE HILL, LOS ANGELES, CALIFORNIA. 1916-20.
Elevation. 6⅜"x11". Pencil on opaque paper. Noted at bottom left: *Mr. Wright's original sketch of Olive Hill.* (Above, probably noted at a later date): *For A. B.* [Aline Barnsdall] *Study—FLlW 1913.* (F 1705.01)

59. PROJECT: ALINE BARNSDALL THEATER, LOS ANGELES, CALIFORNIA. 1920.
Perspective. 4⅝"x6¾" (reproduced full size). Pencil on opaque paper. (F 2005.01)

60. PROJECT: ALINE BARNSDALL THEATER, LOS ANGELES, CALIFORNIA. 1920.
Perspective. 7⅞"x19⅝". Pencil on white tracing paper mounted to board. The drawing is a fragment cut out of a sheet and mounted to a larger board, on which the top of a tree has been added. (F 2005.02)

61. ALINE BARNSDALL "HOLLYHOCK HOUSE," OLIVE HILL, LOS ANGELES, CALIFORNIA. 1916-20.
Perspective. 11½"x38½". Pencil and grey ink wash. Noted at bottom left: *STUDY FOR BARNSDALL HOUSE 1913*. (F 1705.03)

Although badly weather-stained, the grey ink washes of this drawing still produce a lively, fresh quality, particularly in the indication of foliage.

62. PROJECT. ALINE BARNSDALL THEATER, LOS ANGELES, CALIFORNIA. 1920.
Perspective. 6¾"x23". Pencil, colored pencil and white wash on tracing paper mounted to board. (F 2005.03)

63. ALINE BARNSDALL "HOLLYHOCK HOUSE," OLIVE HILL, LOS ANGELES, CALIFORNIA. 1916-20.
Aerial perspective. 18"x18¼". Pencil and green pencil on opaque paper. Noted at top: *FIRST STUDY FOR BARNSDALL DWELLING HOLLYWOOD 1913 FLlW*. (F 1705.02)

The delicate lines and pale green tones of this drawing understate the monumental design. Shading, on the roof parapets and under the roof bridging the entrance to the patio, adds solidity and depth.

64. PROJECT: CEMENT BLOCK HOUSE, LOS ANGELES, CALIFORNIA. 1921.
Perspective and partial plan. 22¼"x28½". Pencil on tracing paper. (F 2103.01)

Details of massing and ornament recall the Barnsdall projects and anticipate the more convincingly organized compositions of individual buildings for the Doheny ranch project. (See 65-70.)

65. PROJECT: CONCRETE BLOCK HOUSE, LOS ANGELES, CALIFORNIA. 1923.
Elevation. 11⅛"x14⅛". Pencil on thin Japanese tracing paper. Dark patches made by tape. Noted at bottom right: *FLlW Los Angeles March 20th—1923*. (F 2104.01)

66. PROJECT: EDWARD H. DOHENY RANCH, SIERRA MADRE MOUNTAINS, CALIFORNIA. 1921.
Perspective and partial plan. 17"x21⅝". Pencil and colored pencils on tracing paper mounted to board. Signed in red square at lower left: *FLlW/1921*. (F 2104.06)

The design is based on a retaining wall which breaks at the center; the upper part of the wall recedes into the

hillside; the lower advances to form a terrace. Balconies and vertical moldings further enrich an already complex scheme. The preceding elevation drawing shows alternative treatments of the wall at each side of the terrace.

67. PROJECT: EDWARD H. DOHENY RANCH, SIERRA MADRE MOUNTAINS, CALIFORNIA. 1921.
Perspective. 12⅝"x29½". Pencil and colored pencil on tracing paper mounted to board. Inscribed at bottom left: *Doheny Hill Development Block Housing—Roadway built with houses as Architecture. Contours of Hills undisturbed. FLlW. Los Angeles 1921*. Signed at lower left in red square: *FLlW*. (F 2104.05)

One of Wright's great technical innovations was the development of pre-cast hollow concrete blocks. Built up a few layers at a time, the blocks themselves served as shuttering for the poured concrete with which they were filled, together with steel reinforcing rods, to make an exceptionally durable structure. An additional advantage, for Wright's purpose, was that decorative geometric patterns could be cast as an integral part of the block. The series of houses Wright built during the twenties exploited this technique brilliantly, but nowhere more than in the unexecuted Doheny Ranch project shown in this and the following drawing. The richness of texture made possible by the block system is here subordinated to a breathtaking conception of architecture as a kind of terracing of the landscape. As in the 1914 Booth house project (43) the road is treated as no less important an architectural element than the wall or roof. In the perspective looking across the valley (68) depth is indicated with a greater pictorial freedom than in other drawings of large projects, and a woman with a Japanese parasol, among other details, adds scale and interest.

68. PROJECT: EDWARD H. DOHENY RANCH, SIERRA MADRE MOUNTAINS, CALIFORNIA. 1921.
Aerial perspective. 18½"x36⅝". Pencil and colored pencils on tracing paper mounted to board. Inscribed at bottom left: *Doheny Hill Development looking down on Terraced roofs. The whole becoming a terraced "garden" suitable to the Region. FLlW/1921*. (F 2104.08)

69. PROJECT: EDWARD H. DOHENY RANCH, SIERRA MADRE MOUNTAINS, CALIFORNIA. 1921.
Perspective. 15⅝"x42¼". Pencil and colored pencils on tracing paper mounted to board. Signed in red square at lower left. Inscribed: *Doheny Hill Development Housing and Garden and garage in connection with roadway. Block construction. Los Angeles.* (F 2104.07)

70. PROJECT: EDWARD H. DOHENY RANCH, SIERRA MADRE MOUNTAINS, CALIFORNIA. 1921.
Perspective and partial plan. 16¼"x20⅞". Pencil and colored pencils on tracing paper mounted to board. (F 2104.04)

71. MRS. GEORGE MADISON MILLARD HOUSE, PASADENA, CALIFORNIA. 1923.
Perspective. 9⅞"x13⅞". Pencil and colored pencil on tracing paper mounted to board. (F 2302.01)

72. MRS. GEORGE MADISON MILLARD HOUSE, PASADENA, CALIFORNIA. 1923.
Plan, elevation, plot plan, and details. 15⅝"x21". Pencil on tracing paper mounted to board. Signed in red square at lower right: *FLlW.* (F 2302.02)

With this famous house Wright achieved a richness of texture related more to tapestry than to concrete blocks. This sheet of preliminary details suggests how completely Wright visualized a design even in its earliest stages.

73. DR. JOHN STORER HOUSE, LOS ANGELES, CALIFORNIA. 1923.
Perspective. 11¼"x21¼". Pencil and green and blue pencil on tracing paper mounted to board. Signed at lower left: *FLlW.*

74. DR. JOHN STORER HOUSE, LOS ANGELES, CALIFORNIA. 1923.
Perspective. 8⅜"x17½". Pencil and green pencil on tracing paper mounted to board. (F 2304.02)

75. DR. JOHN STORER HOUSE, LOS ANGELES, CALIFORNIA. 1923.
Elevation. 14¼"x15⅜". Pencil on thin Japanese tracing paper. Inscribed at right: *FLlW/1920-21 Los Angeles.* Inscribed on lower half of sheet: *California Block houses designed and built in Los Angeles and Pasadena the year after my return from Japan—1919 to 1921.* At bottom of sheet: *STORER ORIGINAL.* (F 2304.01)

76. CHARLES ENNIS HOUSE, LOS ANGELES, CALIFORNIA. 1924.
Elevation. 21⅜"x40⅝". Pencil on tracing paper. (F 2401.01)

77. CHARLES ENNIS HOUSE, LOS ANGELES, CALIFORNIA. 1924.
Perspective and partial plan. 17"x30⅛". Pencil and colored pencils on tracing paper mounted to board. Signed at lower left in red square: *FLlW.* (F 2401.02)

Like the Barnsdall house, this building has often been compared with Mayan temples. The inward pitch of the walls and the relative absence of windows contribute most of all to an atmosphere at once monumental and secret, and the insistent horizontal striations do not lighten the effect. This and the following drawing are among the most painstakingly executed of the concrete block houses; number 78 is of particular interest for its deep patches of shadow on the vertical masses at the center.

78. CHARLES ENNIS HOUSE, LOS ANGELES, CALIFORNIA. 1924.
Perspective and partial plan. 20⅝"x39⅝". Pencil and green and purple pencil on tracing paper mounted to board. Signed at bottom right in red square: *FLlW/1920-1.* Inscribed across trees at left: *1920-1 Perspective Drawing of ENNIS House, Hollywood, Los Angeles.* (F 2401.03)

79. SAMUEL FREEMAN HOUSE, LOS ANGELES, CALIFORNIA. 1924.
Perspective. 9⅜"x15⅞". Pencil and colored pencils on tracing paper mounted to board. (F 2402.02)

This building is simpler in composition than either the Ennis or Storer houses. Its symmetry is gently offset by a projecting mass at the lower left and by a vertical element at the right; and its use of textured block ornament is relatively restrained. The drawing is also more relaxed in the handling of trees and in the vaguely Mediterranean landscape at the bottom right; the latter passage in particular recalls the Italian drawings of Corot.

80. SAMUEL FREEMAN HOUSE, LOS ANGELES, CALIFORNIA. 1924.
Aerial perspective. 10⅞"x21⅝". Pencil and green pencil on tracing paper mounted to board. Paste used to mount the drawing has spotted the paper. (F 2402.01)

81. PROJECT: DR. ALEXANDER CHANDLER SAN MARCOS-IN-THE-DESERT WINTER RESORT, CHANDLER, ARIZONA. 1927.
Perspective. 16⅜"x55¼". Pencil and green and pink pencil accents, on tracing paper mounted to board. Signed in red triangle at bottom left: *FLlW/Ocatillo.* (F 2704.05)

This project for a resort hotel in the Arizona desert reached the working-drawing stage but was doomed by the 1929 stock market collapse. It differs from the vast Doheny project in being essentially one structure, with two or more semi-detached houses, rather than being a sequence of separate buildings connected by terraces. Another departure is the use of the 30-60° triangle, in both plan and elevation. This pencil drawing captures the project's intricacy and contrasts it with hills drawn in a broadly naturalistic style.

82. PROJECT: SAN MARCOS-IN-THE-DESERT WINTER RESORT, CHANDLER, ARIZONA. 1927.
Aerial perspective. 23"x64¾". Water color and pencil on opaque paper mounted to board. (F 2704.07)

The full size and complexity of the project is conveyed in this superb water color, probably executed by the architect's son, Lloyd Wright (see also plate 88). The background hills are freely abstracted without losing the softness of the natural forms or overpowering the small-scale geometry of the building. Although it is badly stained the drawing is still clear and fresh.

83. PROJECT: SAN MARCOS-IN-THE-DESERT WINTER RESORT, CHANDLER, ARIZONA. 1927.
Perspective. 20½"x35¾". Pencil and red pencil accents on tracing paper mounted to board. (F 2704.06)

A partial view of the main entrance to this desert hotel suggests the complexity but not the clarity of its design. The drawings of semi-detached houses (85-9) achieve this through a more varied use of line and tone.

84. ALINE BARNSDALL KINDERGARTEN, "THE LITTLE DIPPER," OLIVE HILL, LOS ANGELES, CALIFORNIA. 1923.
Aerial perspective. 15¾"x27⅛". Pencil and colored pencils on tracing paper mounted to board. Signed at lower left in red square: *FLlW/1924.* (F 2301.02)

The triangle was to be employed by Wright, in both plan and section, for concrete block houses attached to the San Marcos winter resort project of 1927 (85, 86). This 1923 design for a kindergarten anticipates the innovation in its plan, at least, and is also a remarkably cheerful building in comparison with some of the other block houses.

85. PROJECT: OWEN D. YOUNG HOUSE, SAN MARCOS-IN-THE-DESERT, ARIZONA. 1927.
Perspective. 16⅝"x27⅞". Pencil and green pencil on tracing paper mounted to board. Signed in red square at lower left: *FLlW/1927.* Inscribed: *Owen D. Young San Marcos in the Desert. (Desert camp at Ocatillo).* (F 2707.01)

The Young house was to have been a semi-detached villa at one end of the San Marcos hotel. It echoes the main building in its massing but goes beyond it with concrete blocks set at a 45 degree angle, and matching panes of glass. In this drawing triangular rocks and mountains complete the prismatic effect.

86. PROJECT: WELLINGTON AND RALPH CUDNEY HOUSE, SAN MARCOS-IN-THE-DESERT, ARIZONA. 1927.
Elevation and partial plan. 18¾"x31". Pencil with orange and blue pencil accents, on tracing paper. Inscribed at bottom right: *FLlW/Original Cudney Desert Cottage FLlW/1927-Chandler Arizona.* (F 2706.01)

With this rapid sketch Wright established the character of the Cudney house, projected, like the Young house, for the San Marcos hotel. Perspective studies follow.

87. PROJECT: WELLINGTON AND RALPH CUDNEY HOUSE, SAN MARCOS-IN-THE-DESERT, ARIZONA. 1927.
Perspective and partial plan. 26⅞"x42¼". Pencil and colored pencils on tracing paper. (F 2704.02)

Details of the design are not yet resolved in this preliminary perspective study. Compare the treatment of the terrace spanning a stream, at the left, with the two following drawings.

88. PROJECT: WELLINGTON AND RALPH CUDNEY HOUSE, SAN MARCOS-IN-THE-DESERT, ARIZONA. 1927.
Perspective. 16⅛"x26¾". Pencil, colored pencils, charcoal and pastel on tracing paper. Inscribed at bottom left: *Rough Sketch of Cudney Cottage. (Terminal of Hotel Group) Sketch by son Lloyd from drawings.* (F 2704.04)

As sketched here by Wright's son, the building seems to pour across the hillside. Strong shadows and soft edges produce a richness lost in the following, and presumably final, drawing of the series.

89. PROJECT: WELLINGTON AND RALPH CUDNEY HOUSE, SAN MARCOS-IN-THE-DESERT, ARIZONA. 1927.
Perspective. 14"x21⅞". Pencil with red, purple and green pencil accents on tracing paper mounted to board. Signed in red square at bottom right: *FLlW/June 1927.* (F 2704.05)

90. PROJECT: A. M. JOHNSON DESERT COMPOUND AND SHRINE, DEATH VALLEY, CALIFORNIA. 1922.
Aerial perspective. 12"x33½". Pencil and colored pencils on tracing paper. Inscribed at bottom left: *Irrigated Desert Compound for A. M. Johnson FLlW.* (F 2306.01)

91. PROJECT: RICHARD LLOYD JONES HOUSE, "WESTHOPE," TULSA, OKLAHOMA. 1929.
Aerial perspective. 17⅜"x47⅞". Pencil and green and blue pencil accents on tracing paper mounted to board. (F 2901.02)

The drawing shows an alternate (and unbuilt) version of the Lloyd Jones house, related to the various San Marcos projects in its use of the triangle.

92. RICHARD LLOYD JONES HOUSE, "WESTHOPE," TULSA, OKLAHOMA. 1929.
Aerial perspective. 13⅛"x29¼". Pencil and green and blue pencil on tracing paper. (F 2902.01)

Trees in this preliminary sketch have almost the quality of handwriting. Alternate heights for some of the chimneys are lightly drawn.

93. PROJECT: SINGLE BLOCK HOUSE, CHANDLER, ARIZONA. 1927.
Perspective. 11¼"x13¼". Pencil and colored pencils on heavy opaque paper. Signed at lower left in red square: *FLlW/1927.* Inscribed: *Single Block House for Chandler, Arizona.* (F 2708.01)

94. PROJECT: ROSENWALD FOUNDATION SCHOOL FOR NEGRO CHILDREN. 1929.
Aerial perspective. 13"x26". Pencil and colored pencils on tracing paper mounted to board. Signed in red square at bottom left: *FLlW/1928.* Inscribed: *"To Albert Kahn" a token of esteem and affection—this "original." Frank Lloyd Wright. N.B. (Never built not "Colonial.")*

95. PROJECT: OAK PARK PLAYGROUND ASSOCIATION PLAY HOUSES (NO. 4), OAK PARK, ILLINOIS. 1926.
Perspective. 10⅝"x14⅛". Pencil and colored pencils on tracing paper mounted to board. Signed in red square at bottom center: *FLlW/.* (F 2601.01)

96. PROJECT: DR. ALEXANDER CHANDLER SAN MARCOS WATER GARDENS TOURIST CAMP, CHANDLER, ARIZONA. 1927-8.
Perspective. 6¾"x25⅞". Pencil and yellow and gold pencil on tracing paper. (F 2705.02)

The canvas roofs of these tourist cabins resemble peaked caps or, perhaps, Indian tents. The theme preoccupied Wright for many years and its variations include the designs for children's playhouses (95), the school projected for the Rosenwald Foundation (94) and the following series of buildings for Lake Tahoe.

97. PROJECT: FLOATING CABIN, TAHOE SUMMER COLONY, LAKE TAHOE, CALIFORNIA. 1922.
Perspective. 10"x14¾". Pencil and colored pencils on tracing paper mounted to board. Inscribed: *Tahoe Cabin Barge "for two."* (F 2205.04)

This and the following drawing show designs for "house-boats" on Lake Tahoe, as part of a summer colony.

98. PROJECT: FLOATING CABIN, TAHOE SUMMER COLONY, LAKE TAHOE, CALIFORNIA. 1922.
Perspective. 6⅝"x11⅝". Pencil and colored pencils on tracing paper mounted to board. Signed at lower left: *FLlW.* Inscribed: *Floating Cabin—"Fallen Leaf"—1922.* (F 2205.02)

The reflection in the water is not reversed.

99. PROJECT: CABIN, TAHOE SUMMER COLONY, LAKE TAHOE, CALIFORNIA. 1922.
Perspective 13¾"x18½". Pencil on thin Japanese tracing paper. (F 2205.17)

This drawing is remarkable both for the design it represents and for the incisive rendition of a jagged profile made by overlapping boards. A terrace jutting out of a hillside like the prow of a ship was one of Wright's favorite themes; another version can be seen in the Doheny Ranch project (66).

100. PROJECT: CABIN, TAHOE SUMMER COLONY, LAKE TAHOE, CALIFORNIA. 1923.
Perspective and partial plan. 18¾"x15⅜". Pencil and colored pencils on tracing paper mounted to board. Signed at lower left in red square: *FLlW/1923.* Inscribed: *Tahoe Cabin "Shore Type"—white Sand Blocks, Stained Board, (copper, [illegible] and ridges).* (F 2205.03)

101. PROJECT: HUNTING LODGE, TAHOE SUMMER COLONY, LAKE TAHOE, CALIFORNIA. 1923.
Perspective. 21⅞"x15⅛". Pencil and colored pencils on tracing paper mounted to board. Signed in red square at lower left: *FLlW/*. Part of title at lower left missing; inscribed: *Hunting Lodge, Tahoe 1922-3*. (F 2205.01)

The pitched roof is an abstraction of the delicately drawn tree in the background. At the far right a lady poses behind her parasol.

102. PROJECT: CABIN, TAHOE SUMMER COLONY, LAKE TAHOE, CALIFORNIA. 1922.
Perspective. 16⅛"x15⅞". Pencil and colored pencils on tracing paper mounted to board. Signed at lower left: *FLlW*. Inscribed: *Tahoe Cabin Big Tree Type. TEPEE –WIGWAM TYPE Los Angeles—June 28, 1922*. Noted on mast at right: *totem*.

103. PROJECT: E. A. SMITH HOUSE, PIEDMONT PINES, CALIFORNIA. 1938.
Perspective. 23"x21⅝". Pencil and colored pencils on tracing paper mounted to board. Signed at bottom right: *FLlW/*.

A variation, made approximately sixteen years later, of the design shown in plate 102. The wide range of line weights and the handling of foliage in broad planes put this among Wright's most personal drawings.

104. PROJECT: NAKOMA COUNTRY CLUB AND WINNEBAGO CAMPING GROUND INDIAN MEMORIAL, MADISON, WISCONSIN. 1924.
Perspective. 15¾"x35⅝". Pencil and colored pencils on tracing paper mounted to board. Noted at lower right: *Indian Camp* [Group?] *Tepee—Nakoma*. (F 2403.02)

The pyramidal roofs of individual Tahoe projects are here combined in a linked series.

105. PROJECT: MRS. SAMUEL WILLIAM GLADNEY HOUSE, FORT WORTH, TEXAS. 1925.
Perspective. 14¼"x21¼". Pencil and colored pencils, white wash on undersides of roofs; on tracing paper mounted to board. Noted at lower left: *1st House—Concrete and boards—Gladney, Fort Worth Texas—1924.* (F 2502.01)

The massing of this somewhat bizarre design cannot be considered a success, but the reverse pitch of its upper walls prefigures much later work, and may be seen at its best in the beautiful Pauson house of 1940 (166).

106. PROJECT: GORDON STRONG AUTOMOBILE OBJECTIVE AND PLANETARIUM, SUGAR LOAF MOUNTAIN, MARYLAND. 1925.
Aerial perspective. 8"x6½" (reproduced full size). Pencil on tracing paper. Signed and noted at lower left: *FLlW/ Small scale study—(Birds eye)*. (F 2505.23)

Unaccountably omitted by Wright from any detailed publication of his work, this was one of the most elaborately studied projects of the 'twenties. The eleven drawings reproduced here (106-113; 270-272) are taken from portfolios containing at least five times that number. The building was to have housed a planetarium and to have been enclosed by double spiral ramps for ascending and descending traffic, joined at the top by a bridge over a roof garden. Pyramidal compositions were basic to Wright's work from the earliest prairie houses on, but it has not always been realized that the circle, which makes its appearance as an element of the plan around 1938, with the Jester house (162), and culminates in the spiral Guggenheim Museum of 1943-57 (190), was very much in Wright's mind as early as 1925. The Guggenheim Museum is in fact the Sugarloaf Mountain Automobile Objective turned inside out. The following drawings suggest the evolution of the idea.

107. PROJECT: GORDON STRONG AUTOMOBILE OBJECTIVE AND PLANETARIUM, SUGAR LOAF MOUNTAIN, MARYLAND. 1925.
Aerial perspective and plan. 11½"x11⅛". Pencil on tracing paper. (F 2505.58)

108. PROJECT: GORDON STRONG AUTOMOBILE OBJECTIVE AND PLANETARIUM, SUGAR LOAF MOUNTAIN, MARYLAND. 1925.
Perspective. 15⅝"x19". Pencil on tracing paper. (F 2504.-54)

In this early stage of its design the spiral is faceted into straight segments. Compare this with the plan for a preliminary version of the Guggenheim Museum (276).

109. PROJECT: GORDON STRONG AUTOMOBILE OBJECTIVE AND PLANETARIUM, SUGAR LOAF MOUNTAIN, MARYLAND. 1925.
Perspective. 17¾"x21½". Pencil; center guide line and perspective points in blue ink; on tracing paper. (F 2505.55)

110. PROJECT: GORDON STRONG AUTOMOBILE OBJECTIVE AND PLANETARIUM, SUGAR LOAF MOUNTAIN, MARYLAND. 1925.
Perspective. 24¾x32". Pencil on tracing paper. Signed in square at bottom right: *FLlW/23-4*. (F 2505.53).

A bridge over a waterfall connects the building to the adjacent hillside. The cantilevered ramp is for ascending traffic only; the wall supporting the intermediate (descending) ramp is ornamented with triangular windows and decorations.

111. PROJECT: GORDON STRONG AUTOMOBILE OBJECTIVE AND PLANETARIUM, SUGAR LOAF MOUNTAIN, MARYLAND. 1925.
Aerial perspective. 24½"x31⅞". Pencil and green pencil accents on tracing paper. Signed in square at lower right: *FLlW/23*. (F 2505.52)

112. PROJECT: GORDON STRONG AUTOMOBILE OBJECTIVE AND PLANETARIUM, SUGAR LOAF MOUNTAIN, MARYLAND. 1925.
Perspective. 19⅞"x30⅞". Pencil and colored pencils on tracing paper. Signed in red square at center right: *FLlW/24*. (F 2505.39)

The shaded mass of the building, with near-Gothic or Moorish geometric decoration delicately picked out, is in marked contrast to the free handling of trees and rocks in the foreground. Note corrections on the mast at top right. Colors used in this drawing are purple for stones and people, green for the trees, and touches of blue in the fountain; the building itself is outlined and shaded in black pencil only.

113. PROJECT: GORDON STRONG AUTOMOBILE OBJECTIVE AND PLANETARIUM, SUGAR LOAF MOUNTAIN, MARYLAND. 1925.
Perspective. 19¾"x31¼". Pencil and colored pencils on tracing paper. (F 2505.36)

This unsigned drawing, rather than the preceding one, is probably the final version of the project. The major change is a slight reduction of height for the parapets on the ramps and, more importantly, the base of the building just below the first ramp has been pushed back so that the first cantilevered ramp projects beyond it. The building itself is shaded in black pencil with much greater delicacy than in the preceding drawing, while the foliage in the foreground is drawn in green, yellow, and other colors with still greater liveliness—although it is held almost to one plane and gives the impression of a stage flat propped up before the building. With the design now completely resolved, the style in which it is drawn becomes more discreet, making the architecture seem at first sight almost an afterthought to the intense rendering of nature. The drawing, no less than the building itself, is among the most compelling images in Wright's work.

114. PROJECT: STEEL CATHEDRAL INCLUDING MINOR CATHEDRALS FOR A MILLION PEOPLE, NEW YORK CITY, N. Y. 1926.
Elevation. 26⅜"x28¾". Pencil and red and green pencil on tracing paper. Small piece of paper hinged to drawing at lower left contains alternate study of masts. At far right: architect's memoranda concerning fees. (F 2602.01)

The scale of this super-cathedral can be gauged by the dots at the bottom, representing people. (See plate 273 for the plan.) A pyramidal or tent-like roof of metal and glass was finally realized in the Beth Sholom Synagogue of 1959 (237).

115. PROJECT: SKYSCRAPER REGULATIONS, CHICAGO, ILLINOIS. 1926.
Elevation. 20¼"x34¾". Pencil on yellow tracing paper. Signed in square at lower left: *FLlW*. (F 2603.01)

Note erasures on the second building from the left, showing alternate massing; and elevated sidewalks, glass enclosed bridges, roof gardens, and cantilevered signs on top of the building at the far right.

116. PROJECT: SKYSCRAPER, CHICAGO, ILLINOIS. 1931.
Elevation. 27½"x35¾". Pencil and colored pencils on tracing paper. Noted at lower left: *2000 feet high—112 Stories—*. (F 3103.01)

117. PROJECT: SKYSCRAPER, CHICAGO, ILLINOIS. 1931.
Elevation. 26¼"x36". Pencil and colored pencils on tracing paper. (F 3103.02)

The building includes two plazas above grade and one below; a colosseum to seat 25,000; an arena for 75,000; and parking space for 20,000 cars. The massing of this building parallels the "dynamic" style of the Rockefeller Center buildings, and particularly the R.C.A. tower, in New York City.

118. PROJECT: NATIONAL LIFE INSURANCE COMPANY SKYSCRAPER, CHICAGO, ILLINOIS. 1924.
Aerial perspective. 45⅝"x30¼". Black ink and pencil on tracing paper mounted to heavy paper; upper and lower left corners missing. (F 2404.01)

The ribs and fins at the top of this stupendous set of linked office towers suggest the character of its structure. Wright early rejected the rigid "box-like" regularity of the skeleton steel frame in favor of reinforced concrete piers, like tree trunks, from which floors could be cantilevered. Relatively small pieces of glass in copper frames would make the enclosing wall a shimmering web. The drawing is a rare example in Wright's work of isometric perspective (without vanishing points). It is perhaps more impressive as a *tour de force* than as an accurate picture of what such a building would look like.

119. PROJECT: NATIONAL LIFE INSURANCE COMPANY SKYSCRAPER, CHICAGO, ILLINOIS. 1924.
Perspective. 23¾"x16⅞". Pencil on tracing paper mounted to heavy paper; upper left corner missing. (F 2404.05)

120. PROJECT: ST. MARK'S APARTMENT TOWER, ST. MARK'S-IN-THE-BOUWERIE, NEW YORK CITY, N. Y. 1929.
Aerial perspective. 19¾"x15". Pencil on tracing paper. (F 2905.04)

One eighteen story and two fourteen story residential towers are shown tightly grouped around the Church of St. Mark's-in-the-Bouwerie, New York, from which the project takes its name.

121. PROJECT: ST. MARK'S APARTMENT TOWER, ST. MARK'S-IN-THE-BOUWERIE, NEW YORK CITY, N. Y. 1929.
Perspective. 39"x23¾". Black ink and pencil on tracing paper mounted to heavy paper. (F 2905.02)

In this version spandrels on alternate floors are ornamented with stamped copper panels. Note hanging mullions above entrance level.

122. PROJECT: GROUPED APARTMENT TOWERS, CHICAGO, ILLINOIS. 1930.
Perspective. 19⅛"x28¼". Pencil on tracing paper. (F 3001.01)

Five of the St. Mark's Towers are here linked to make a faceted wall twenty-six stories high. The complex interlocking rhythms of glass curtain-walls, ornamented and unornamented spandrels, and changing perspectives produces even in this pencil sketch the effect of a shimmering fabric. No other design for a glass-walled building by Wright surpasses this magnificent scheme, and no executed glass-walled skyscraper in the United States or elsewhere exploits the possibilities of the material so imaginatively.

123. PROJECT: ST. MARK'S APARTMENT TOWER, ST. MARK'S-IN-THE-BOUWERIE, NEW YORK CITY, N. Y. 1929.
Perspective. 28¼"x10⅛". Pencil and colored pencils on tracing paper. Signed in red square at bottom left: *FLlW*, and noted: *original sketch St. Mark's-in-the-Bouwerie, 1925.* (F 2905.06)

This is a more freely drawn version of 121, with stamped copper spandrels omitted.

124. PROJECT: ELIZABETH NOBLE APARTMENT HOUSE, LOS ANGELES, CALIFORNIA. 1929.
Elevation; detail of parapet and glass wall. 11½"x25¼". Pencil and pink pencil on tracing paper. (F 2903.01)

125. PROJECT: ELIZABETH NOBLE APARTMENT HOUSE, LOS ANGELES, CALIFORNIA. 1929.
Perspective. 15⅜"x26¼". Black ink and pencil shading on tracing paper. (F 2903.02)

126. PROJECT: "HOUSE ON THE MESA", DENVER, COLORADO. 1931.
Aerial perspective. 20⅝"x36⅛". Pencil on tracing paper. (F 3102.07)

127. PROJECT: "HOUSE ON THE MESA", DENVER, COLORADO. 1931.
Interior perspective. 18⅜"x36". Pencil and green and blue pencil accents on tracing paper. (F 3102.19)

128. PROJECT: "HOUSE ON THE MESA", DENVER, COLORADO. 1931.
Perspective. 17⅝"x36". Pencil on tracing paper. (F 3102.17)

This is one of a series of drawings in which the details of a large, sprawling house are studied and refined. The upper part of the main room is formed by glass, cantilevered in tiers; some modifications to it can be seen, sketched freehand, in the following drawings.

129. PROJECT: "HOUSE ON THE MESA", DENVER, COLORADO. 1931.
Perspective: 18½"x35⅞". Pencil on tracing paper. (F 3102.18)

130. PROJECT: "HOUSE ON THE MESA", DENVER, COLORADO. 1931.
Perspective. 18¾"x36". Pencil and tracing paper. (F 3102.06)

131. PROJECT: "HOUSE ON THE MESA", DENVER, COLORADO. 1931.
Perspective. 10¼"x36". Pencil on tracing paper. (F 3102.15)

132. PROJECT: DEAN MALCOLM M. WILLEY HOUSE, MINNEAPOLIS, MINNESOTA. 1934.
Perspective. 18½"x35½". Black ink (for house only), and pencil lines and shading, on tracing paper. (F 3204.01)

133. HILLSIDE BUILDINGS, TALIESIN FELLOWSHIP, SPRING GREEN, WISCONSIN. 1933.
Aerial perspective. 17¼"x20½". Pencil and colored pencil on tracing paper. Signed at bottom left: *FLlW/1933.* (F 3301.04)

This is a study of projected buildings to have been added to the original Hillside School group, at center right. Note "Romeo and Juliet" tower at upper left.

134. PROJECT: NEW THEATRE. 1932.
Perspective. 6¼"x6½" (reproduced full size). Pencil on tracing paper. (F 3203.02)

135. PROJECT: NEW THEATRE. 1932.
Perspective. 3¾"x11¾". Pencil and pink pencil (on building) on tracing paper. (F 3203.03)

136. PROJECT: NEW THEATRE. 1932.
Aerial perspective. 4⅛"x11⅞". Pencil and pink pencil (on building) on tracing paper. (F 3203.01)

137. EDGAR J. KAUFMANN HOUSE, "FALLINGWATER," BEAR RUN, PENNSYLVANIA. 1936.
Aerial perspective. 18½"x29⅝". Pencil and colored pencils on tracing paper mounted to heavy paper. (F 3602.01)

This and the following two rough sketches, previously unpublished, give a livelier impression of *Fallingwater* than does the well-known formal color rendering. Among Wright's masterpieces this house is perhaps the most famous example of his attitude toward architecture and its place in nature.

138. EDGAR J. KAUFMANN HOUSE "FALLINGWATER," BEAR RUN, PENNSYLVANIA. 1936.
Aerial perspective. 14⅜"x31½". Pencil and colored pencils on tracing paper mounted to heavy paper. Left side of drawing missing. (F 3602.02)

139. EDGAR J. KAUFMANN HOUSE "FALLINGWATER," BEAR RUN, PENNSYLVANIA. 1936.
Perspective. 14⅜"x31½". Pencil and colored pencils on tracing paper mounted to heavy paper. (F 3602.03)

140. EDGAR J. KAUFMANN HOUSE "FALLINGWATER," BEAR RUN, PENNSYLVANIA. 1936.
Perspective. 17"x33". Pencil and colored pencils on tracing paper mounted to board. Signed in red square at center right: *FLlW/Arizona/36.* (F 3602.04)

141. PROJECT: "ALL STEEL" HOUSES DEVELOPMENT, LOS ANGELES, CALIFORNIA. 1937.
Section, plan, and perspective. 23¼"x25". Pencil and red pencil on tracing paper. Inscribed: *Original—Steel House Studies 1937/FLlW/.* (F 3705.02)

The structural steel skeleton held little interest for Wright, and his project is characteristically concerned with interwoven walls made of panel sections. The project is related to similar houses in Los Angeles by Richard Neutra.

142. PROJECT: "ALL STEEL" HOUSES DEVELOPMENT, LOS ANGELES, CALIFORNIA. 1937.
Plans and aerial perspective. 28⅜"x36¼". Pencil and red ink (on plans) on tracing paper. Signed in red square at lower right: *FLlW/*; and noted: *Study—"All Steel Houses" Los Angeles.* (F 3705.05)

143. PROJECT: "ALL STEEL" HOUSES DEVELOPMENT, LOS ANGELES, CALIFORNIA. 1937.
Perspective. 23½"x36". Pencil on tracing paper. (F 3705.03)

144. PROJECT: "ALL STEEL" HOUSES DEVELOPMENT, LOS ANGELES, CALIFORNIA. 1937.
Aerial perspective. 24⅛"x36⅛". Pencil on tracing paper.

Signed in red square at bottom left: *OK FLlW/1937;* and noted: *Study for "All Steel House" Taliesin May 1937.* (F 3705.06)

145. PROJECT: LEO BRAMSON DRESS SHOP, OAK PARK, ILLINOIS. 1937.
Perspective. 14⅜"x15¾". Pencil, colored pencils, and black ink on opaque white paper circle, cut out and pasted to orange paper; mounted to board. Signed at lower right in red square: *FLlW/.* (F 3706.01)

146. PROJECT: LITTLE SAN MARCOS, CHANDLER, ARIZONA. 1936. Sketch plan. 14"x19⅛". (Top half of sheet combining this and the following drawing, pasted together.) Red ink contour lines and pencil on tracing paper mounted to heavy paper. (F 3606.02)

147. PROJECT: LITTLE SAN MARCOS, CHANDLER, ARIZONA. 1936. Elevation. 14"x19⅛". (Bottom half of sheet combining this and above drawing, pasted together.) Pencil on tracing paper mounted to heavy paper. Signed at bottom left: *FLlW/Little San Marcos in the Desert.* (F 3606.03)

148. PROJECT: LITTLE SAN MARCOS, CHANDLER, ARIZONA. 1936 Elevation. 14¾"x29½". Pencil and colored pencils on tracing paper mounted to heavy opaque paper. (F 3606.01)

149. TALIESIN WEST, FRANK LLOYD WRIGHT WINTER RESIDENCE AND STUDIO, PARADISE VALLEY, ARIZONA. 1938. Aerial perspective. 23½"x105⅜". (Three sheets pasted together.) Pencil and colored pencils on tracing paper mounted to opaque paper. (F 3803.03)

An early study of the famous desert camp, much revised and expanded throughout the years.

150. FLORIDA SOUTHERN COLLEGE, LAKELAND, FLORIDA. 1938. Aerial perspective. 22¼"x46¾". Pencil, brown pencil and brown ink on tracing paper. (F 3805.01)

Although Wright formulated no comprehensive approach to city planning, some of his largest projects are designed as small communities. This scheme for a college campus presents individual buildings connected by lateral roads and paths, many of them sheltered by cantilevered arcades. Several of the buildings have been completed.

151. HERBERT F. JOHNSON, JR. HOUSE, "WINGSPREAD," WINDY POINT, WISCONSIN. 1937. Perspective. 16⅞"x40". Pencil and colored pencils on tracing paper mounted to board. Signed in red square at right. *FLlW/37.* (F 3808.01)

152. HERBERT F. JOHNSON, JR. HOUSE, "WINGSPREAD," WINDY POINT, WISCONSIN. 1937. Aerial perspective. 33¼"x42⅛". Pencil and colored pencils on tracing paper. Signed in red square at lower right: *FLlW/Feb 37.* (F 3703.01)

153. PROJECT: ROBERT D. LUSK HOUSE, HURON, S. DAKOTA. 1936. Aerial perspective. 24"x36¼". Pencil on tracing paper. Signed in red square at bottom right: *FLlW/1936;* and noted: *Lusk S. Dakota.* (F 3605.01)

Unusual details in Wright's architecture are the tall, thin chimneys flanking the living room of this house.

154. HERBERT JACOBS HOUSE, MADISON, WISCONSIN. 1937. Perspective. 21¾"x32⅜" (two drawings on one sheet). Pencil, sepia pencil, and brown ink on tracing paper mounted to board. Signed in square at bottom right: *FLlW/38.* (F 3702.02)

Wright called his conception of the ideal house for the United States "Usonian," a name meant to suggest a certain rugged American idealism. Among the finest of his many Usonian houses is this early one in Wisconsin: an L shaped plan, a top-lighted kitchen with a small basement for utilities just below it, radiant heat incorporated in the concrete slab floor, and a cantilevered roof making a "carport" at the entrance. The two drawings reproduced here fully convey its long, low lines and its comfortable relation to the ground.

155. HERBERT JACOBS HOUSE, MADISON, WISCONSIN. 1937. Aerial perspective. (See above).

156. PAUL R. HANNA HOUSE, PALO ALTO, CALIFORNIA. 1937. Aerial perspective. 22"x36¼". Pencil and black ink on tracing paper mounted to board. Signed in white square pasted to drawing at bottom left: *FLlW/Feb 19.* (F 3701.01)

An extremely elegant drawing of a complex house planned on a hexagonal module.

157. PAUL R. HANNA HOUSE, PALO ALTO, CALIFORNIA. 1937. Aerial perspective. 9¾"x29". Pencil and colored pencils on tracing paper mounted to board. (F3701.02)

158. CARL WALL HOUSE, PLYMOUTH, MICHIGAN. 1939. Perspective. 20"x33⅜". Pencil and colored pencils on tracing paper mounted to board. Signed in red square at bottom left: *FLlW/July 1/39.* (F 3908.01)

159. EDGAR J. KAUFMANN GUEST HOUSE, BEAR RUN, PENNSYLVANIA. 1939. Aerial perspective. 17"x35¾". Pencil and colored pencils on tracing paper. (F 3812.01)

160. PROJECT: "HOUSE FOR A FAMILY OF $5,000-$6,000 INCOME," FOR *LIFE* MAGAZINE. 1938.
Perspective. 24"x36". Sepia pencil, light brown crayon, and brown ink on tracing paper. Signed in red square at lower right: *FLlW/Aug 15/38;* and inscribed: *to Howard M[yers] From FLlW/.* (F 3806.01)

Like the Jacobs house (154) this design was intended to demonstrate how well an American family of small income might live. The house is L shaped in plan, with a two story high, top-lighted kitchen at the convergence of the two wings. The living room walls are of heavy stone piers, with glass doors opening onto a pergola-covered terrace and a narrow swimming pool. A seating alcove, not readily visible in these drawings, terminates the living room. The conception is completely and carefully worked out to the last detail; and the drawing is suitably crisp and emphatic. This combination of elements was to be given one more major variation, shown in plates 162 and 163.

161. BERNARD SCHWARTZ HOUSE, STILL BEND, WISCONSIN. 1939.
Aerial perspective. 14"x35¾". Pencil, sepia pencil and brown ink accents on tracing paper mounted to board. Signed in red square at lower right: *FLlW/Aug 15/38.* (F 3904.01)

This executed house is almost identical to the *Life* magazine project described above.

162. PROJECT: RALPH JESTER HOUSE, PALOS VERDES, CALIFORNIA. 1938.
Plan and elevation. 14"x21¼". Pencil and colored pencils on tracing paper mounted to board. Inscribed at top: *Original Sketch, FLlW/;* and at bottom right: *For Ralph Jester Palos Verde Cal FLlW/July 24.* (F 3707.02)

One of Wright's most brilliant ideas for a house is this variation of the project described above (160). In this version, intended for a warm climate, individual elements such as a seating alcove, a dining area, and bedrooms are placed in separate plywood cylinders. Each element has glass doors opening onto a terrace, covered by a flat roof broad enough to encompass all of the circular units. In addition, the narrow pool of the *Life* house is here turned into a great bowl, its retaining wall projecting out of the hillside site (163). Unbuilt, this conception remains one of Wright's major achievements in house design.

163. PROJECT: RALPH JESTER HOUSE, PALOS VERDES, CALIFORNIA. 1938.
Perspective. 34¾"x32½". Brown ink and colored pencils on tracing paper mounted to opaque paper. Signed in red square at lower right of perspective: *FLlW/;* inscribed at upper left of perspective: *The Plywood house—plywood back to back [. . .] and [. . .] applied to each other to form outside walls. The whole an open [. . .] room beside a pool. Hollywood Hills or Hawaiian Mountains FLlW/.* (F 3807.03)

164. GEORGE D. STURGES HOUSE, BRENTWOOD HEIGHTS, CALIFORNIA. 1939.
Perspective. 22¼"x36". Pencil and red and green pencil on tracing paper signed in red square at top right: *FLlW.* (F 3905.01)

Note revisions to the bracket supporting the cantilevered terrace, and to the trellis at the upper left.

165. GEORGE D. STURGES HOUSE, BRENTWOOD HEIGHTS, CALIFORNIA. 1939.
Perspective. 22"x36⅜". Pencil and colored pencils on tracing paper mounted to board. Signed in red square at bottom right: *FLlW/Sept 1/39.* (F 3905.02)

166. ROSE PAUSON HOUSE, PHOENIX, ARIZONA. 1940.
Perspective. 24⅛"x36". Pencil on tracing paper. Signed in red square at left: *FLlW/.* (F 4011.01)

167. ROSE PAUSON HOUSE, PHOENIX, ARIZONA. 1940.
Perspective. 14¼"x28⅝". Pencil and colored pencils on tracing paper mounted to board. Signed in red square at center left: *FLlW/;* noted at bottom left: *A desert home just completed for the Pauson sisters Phoenix Arizona cost $7500.00 complete.* (F 4011.02)

This superb stone and wood house rides its site like a ship riding a wave. Completely destroyed by fire when it was rented one season, its stone ruin still testifies to Wright's mastery of siting. This and the preceding drawing show small but interesting modifications of detail as the house was in process of design.

168. LLOYD LEWIS HOUSE, LIBERTYVILLE, ILLINOIS. 1940.
Aerial perspective. 23¼"x36". Pencil and colored pencils on tracing paper mounted to board. Signed in red square at center right: *FLlW/.* (F 4008.02)

169. JOHN C. PEW HOUSE, SHOREWOOD HILLS, MADISON, WISCONSIN. 1940.
Perspective. 22"x36". Pencil and colored pencils on tracing paper mounted to board. Signed in red square at center right: *FLlW/May, 40.* (F 4012.02)

The drawing combines a high degree of finish in the treatment of the building with varying degrees of detail in the treatment of landscape.

170. PROJECT: ARCH OBOLER HOUSE, "EAGLE FEATHER," CALIFORNIA. 1940.
Perspective. 21¼"x36⅝". Pencil and blue pencil (for sky) on tracing paper mounted to board. Signed in red square at lower left: *FLlW/Aug 20/40.* F 4018.02)

171. PROJECT: ARCH OBOLER HOUSE, "EAGLE FEATHER," CALIFORNIA. 1940.
Perspective. 21⅛"x36⅝". Pencil and blue pencil (for sky only) on tracing paper mounted to board. Signed in red square at lower left: *FLlW/Aug 20/40.* (F 4018.03)

172. S. C. JOHNSON & SON, INC. ADMINISTRATION BUILDING, RACINE, WISCONSIN. 1936-39.
Aerial perspective. 29"x39⅜". (One of two drawings on single sheet; see also plate 246). Pencil and black ink on tracing paper mounted to board. (F 3601.03)

173. PROJECT: MADISON CIVIC CENTER, LAKE MONONA, MADISON, WISCONSIN. 1938.
Perspective. 11½"x40". Pencil, colored pencils and black ink on tracing paper mounted to board. Signed in red square at upper left: *FLlW/53.* (F 3909.01)

Work on this project began in 1938; this drawing is either a later revision or a fresh tracing signed in 1953. The project has encountered much opposition and its fate is still being debated by Madison's municipal government.

174. PROJECT: MADISON CIVIC CENTER, LAKE MONONA, MADISON, WISCONSIN. 1938.
Aerial perspective. 17¼"x40¼". Pencil, colored pencils and black ink on tracing paper mounted to board. The drawing is a cut-out mounted to a background on which water and fragments of architectural detail are drawn. Signed in red square at bottom left: *FLlW/.* (F 3909.02)

Legible at the bottom of the drawing is an inscription describing the project in the architect's inimitable style.

175. PROJECT: CRYSTAL HEIGHTS HOTEL TOWERS, WASHINGTON, D. C. 1940.
Elevation. 10⅜"x33½". Pencil and green and blue pencil on tracing paper. Noted at top left: *Total 2362 apartments.* [remainder illegible] (F 4016.02)

This project for an urban hotel complex, with shopping facilities and parking terraces, continues the development of the 1930 study for grouped apartment towers (122). Here they are hooked around the base of a triangular site, and variations in height contribute further to an effect of richness and intricacy, strongly contrasted with the horizontal bands made by the parapets of cantilevered terraces. Drawings 177 and 178, although in line and solid areas of dark brown ink, convey this contrast in scale and texture very well; the project is among Wright's most grandiose, and illustrates his ability to create an architectural enclave even in the most difficult conditions.

176. PROJECT: CRYSTAL HEIGHTS HOTEL TOWERS, WASHINGTON, D. C. 1940.
Elevation. 13⅝"x30¼". Pencil and green and blue pencil on tracing paper. (F 4016.03)

177. PROJECT: CRYSTAL HEIGHTS HOTEL TOWERS, WASHINGTON, D. C. 1940.
Perspective. 31½"x35". Brown ink on tracing paper. Signed in red square at upper left: *FLlW/Dec/39.* (F 4016.04)

178. PROJECT: CRYSTAL HEIGHTS HOTEL TOWERS, WASHINGTON, D. C. 1940.
Aerial perspective. 24"x34¾". Brown ink on tracing paper. Signed in red square at lower left: *FLlW/38.* (F 4016.01)

179. PROJECT: COOPERATIVE HOMESTEADS. 1942.
Perspective. 27⅜"x34½". Pencil, colored pencils and brown ink outline on tracing paper. Signed at lower left in red square pierced by ornamental stem of flowers: *OK FLlW/Feb 15/42.* (F 4201.01)

180. QUADRUPLE HOUSE, "SUNTOP HOMES," ARDMORE, PENNSYLVANIA. 1939.
Perspective. 24¼"x36¼". Pencil, colored pencils and brown ink on tracing paper. (F 4203.01)

181. QUADRUPLE HOUSE, "SUNTOP HOMES," ARDMORE, PENN-SYLVANIA. 1939.
Aerial perspective. 26"x36". Pencil, colored pencils and brown ink outline on tracing paper. Sky above horizon line on attached piece of paper. (F 4203.02)

182. PROJECT: LUDD M. SPIVEY HOUSE, FORT LAUDERDALE, FLORIDA. 1939.
Perspective. 13¼"x35". Pencil and colored pencils on tracing paper mounted to board. (F 3911.01)

183. PROJECT: BURLINGHAM HOUSE. 1940.
Aerial perspective. 20"x40⅞". Pencil, colored pencils and brown ink on tracing paper. Signed on red square at bottom left: *FLlW/Oct 10 1940*. (F 4202.01)

184. PROJECT: V. C. MORRIS HOUSE, CALIFORNIA. 1943.
Perspective. 21¾"x35". Pencil and colored pencils on tracing paper. Signed in red square at bottom left: *FLlW/May 30/43*. (F 4303.03)

The main part of the house is a circular living room cantilevered from the cliff on a cylindrical support shaped somewhat like the golf tee columns used in the Johnson's Wax Company office building. Behind this element rises an elevator shaft and retaining walls, the masses of which fade into the hill itself. The composition is echoed by the whiplash curves of waves breaking on the shoreline, and is further animated by the lively style of the drawing.

185. PROJECT: V. C. MORRIS HOUSE, CALIFORNIA. 1946.
Perspective. 39⅝"x42⅛". Colored pencils and brown ink on tracing paper. Signed in red square at bottom right *FLlW/Nov 15/46*. (F 4303.02)

186. PROJECT: V. C. MORRIS HOUSE, CALIFORNIA. 1946.
Perspective 39⅞"x42". Colored pencils and brown ink on tracing paper. Signed in red square at bottom right: *FLlW/Nov 15/46*. (F 4303.04)

187. PROJECT: V. C. MORRIS HOUSE, CALIFORNIA. 1946.
Aerial perspective. 23½"x44". Pencil, brown ink and colored pencils on tracing paper. Signed in red square at bottom right: *FLlW/Nov 15/46*. (F 4304.01)

188. PROJECT: JOHN NESBITT HOUSE, CARMEL BAY, CALIFORNIA. 1940.
Elevation. 18"x49". Pencils and colored pencils on tracing paper. (F 4017.D2)

189. PROJECT: JOHN NESBITT HOUSE, CARMEL BAY, CALIFORNIA. 1940.
Perspective. 21"x48". Pencil and colored pencils on tracing paper. Signed at top right in red square: *FLlW/Oct/40*. (F 4017.03)

190. SOLOMON R. GUGGENHEIM MUSEUM, NEW YORK CITY, N.Y. 1943.
Elevation. 20"x24¼". Pencils and colored pencils on opaque cream-colored paper. (F 4305.04)

In 1943 Wright presented to Solomon Guggenheim a set of preliminary drawings showing his ideas for the Guggenheim Museum. Among them are four elevation studies (190-93) and one plan (276) which are especially interesting today. In all of these studies the building is shown higher than it was actually built, and in each of them a low wing at the left is crowned by a balconied apartment for the director of the Museum, this feature being omitted in the executed design.

191. SOLOMON R. GUGGENHEIM MUSEUM, NEW YORK CITY, N.Y. 1943.
Elevation. 20"x24¼". Pencil and colored pencils on opaque cream-colored paper. (F 4305.05)

This version differs from the preceding study in showing seven turns of the ramp rather than six, accomplished within the same over-all height by reducing the ceiling height for each gallery level.

192. SOLOMON R. GUGGENHEIM MUSEUM, NEW YORK CITY, N.Y. 1943.
Elevation. 20¼"x24½". Pencil and colored pencils on opaque cream-colored paper. Noted at top: *SCHEME "B"*. (F 4305.07)

The arrangement of elements is essentially the same as in the previous study, but the ramp now narrows as it rises, and is terminated by a glass enclosed bridge to the elevator tower rather than by a dome.

193. SOLOMON R. GUGGENHEIM MUSEUM, NEW YORK CITY, N.Y. 1943.
Elevation. 20⅛" x 24¼". Pencil and colored pencils on opaque buff paper. Noted at top: *SCHEME "C"*. (F 4305.06)

This is by far the most surprising of the preliminary versions of the Guggenheim Museum. The building as shown here and in the plan (276) is neither spiral nor cylindrical: it is composed of normal, flat floors and the bulk of the gallery section is faceted into a hexagon (echoed in the fence) and recalling a study for the Sugar Loaf Mountain observatory of 1925. A ramp is used, however, to connect the separate gallery floors, and the whole composition is surmounted by a glass-enclosed gallery or bridge. The design has an unpleasantly Paris 1925, or *moderne*, quality Wright may unconsciously have associated with urban sophistication: it is a quality that appears also in the early studies for urban houses (56, 57).

194. SOLOMON R. GUGGENHEIM MUSEUM, NEW YORK CITY, N.Y. 1943-59.
Elevation and section. 26¾"x30¾". Pencil and colored pencils on tracing paper. C.1943, (F 4305.14)

195. SOLOMON R. GUGGENHEIM MUSEUM, NEW YORK CITY, N.Y. 1943-59.
Perspective. 20⅛"x29⅞". Pencil, sepia ink and blue ink accents on dome; on tracing paper mounted to board. Signed in square at bottom right: *FLlW/Aug 15/48.* (F 4305.15)

196. SOLOMON R. GUGGENHEIM MUSEUM, NEW YORK CITY, N.Y. 1943-59.
Perspective. 20"x30". Pencil, sepia ink and blue ink accents for dome; on tracing paper mounted to board. Signed in square at bottom right: *FLlW/Aug 15/48.* (F 4305.16)

In this version, prepared before the entire site had been acquired, the gallery is placed at the north in order to stand free of adjoining buildings.

197. SOLOMON R. GUGGENHEIM MUSEUM, NEW YORK CITY, N.Y. 1943-59.
Perspective. 27"x40⅛". Black and brown ink, brown and blue colored pencils on tracing paper mounted to board. Signed in red square at bottom right: *FLlW/Aug 5/51.* (F 4305.17)

The Museum is shown with a new fifteen story apartment house and office building; the lower floors of this structure would have served, according to Wright's proposal, to house additional rectilinear storage space, offices, and perhaps a gallery.

198. SOLOMON R. GUGGENHEIM MUSEUM, NEW YORK CITY, N.Y. 1943-59.
Perspective. 36"x49¾". Pencil and black ink on tracing paper. (F 4305.09)

Note the addition of a round projection to the second floor band at the far right (tentatively indicated on the plans as an "architecture archives" room by Wright but actually used by the Museum as a work or storage space); tentative modifications of the parapet angle on the office block at the left; and a penciled indication of the service shaft at the rear.

199. SOLOMON R. GUGGENHEIM MUSEUM, NEW YORK CITY, N.Y. 1943-59.
Interior perspective. 35⅛"x40¾". Pencil on tracing paper. Signed in square at lower left: *FLlW/55.* (F 4305.13)

This and the following three drawings were prepared by Wright (though not executed by him) to illustrate the manner in which paintings of various sizes would be placed against the outer wall of the ramp and on free standing partitions. Titles and dimensions are legible in the plates.

200. SOLOMON R. GUGGENHEIM MUSEUM, NEW YORK CITY, N.Y. 1943-59.
Interior perspective. 35⅛"x40½". Pencil and colored pencils on tracing paper. Signed in red square at bottom left: *FLlW/.* (F 4305.11)

201. SOLOMON R. GUGGENHEIM MUSEUM, NEW YORK CITY, N.Y. 1943-59.
Interior perspective. 35⅛"x40½". Pencil and colored pencils on tracing paper. Signed in square at bottom left *FLlW/.* (F 4305.12)

202. SOLOMON R. GUGGENHEIM MUSEUM, NEW YORK CITY, N.Y. 1943-59.
Interior perspective. 35"x40⅝". Pencil and colored pencils on tracing paper. Signed in red square at bottom left: *FLlW/.* (F 4305.10)

203. PROJECT: ELIZABETH ARDEN RESORT HOTEL, "SUNLIGHT", PHOENIX, ARIZONA. 1945.
Elevation. 22⅛"x36¼". Pencil and colored pencils on tracing paper. Signed at bottom right in red square: *FLlW.* (F 4506.01)

204. PROJECT: ELIZABETH ARDEN RESORT HOTEL, "SUNLIGHT", PHOENIX, ARIZONA. 1945.
Perspective. 18½"x37". Brown ink, pencil and colored pencils on tracing paper. Signed at lower left in red

square: *FLlW/Apr 11/45;* surrounded by berry ornaments made from ink blots. (F 4506.02)

The project resembles earlier studies for a desert resort hotel, but is softened by the use of circular elements.

205. PROJECT: CALICO MILLS OFFICE BUILDING, AHMEDABAD, INDIA. 1946.
Perspective. 23¾"x35⅜". Brown ink, pencil and colored pencils on tracing paper. Signed at lower left in red square: *FLlW/June 18/46.* (F 4508.01)

206. PROJECT: CALICO MILLS OFFICE BUILDING, AHMEDABAD, INDIA. 1946.
Same drawing as above, but shown with hinged flaps at upper right and lower left. In this additional study may be seen a variation of the treatment of cantilevered roof gardens and trellises, and a reduction in the length of the canopy cantilevered over the sidewalk and street in the original version.

207. PROJECT: BENJAMIN ADELMAN LAUNDRY, MILWAUKEE, WISCONSIN. 1946.
Aerial perspective. 23½"x31¼". Brown ink on tracing paper.

208. E. L. MARTING HOUSE, AKRON, OHIO. 1947.
Perspective. 21¼"x42¼". Brown ink and colored pencils on tracing paper. Signed at lower right in red square: *FLlW/Aug 31/47.* (F 4713.01)

209. ROBERT LLEWELLYN WRIGHT HOUSE. 1953.
Perspective. 15⅞"x27⅛". Brown ink and colored pencils on tracing paper mounted to board. Signed at bottom right in red square: *FLlW/53.* (F 5312.01)

Taken out of the context of Wright's work, these cantilevered circular terraces pointing in all directions seem unnecessarily animated; but the design is a logical development, in terms of a multistory house, of earlier compositions based on intersecting circles (183), and the drawing is suitably brisk.

210. PROJECT: A. K. CHAHROUDI HOUSE, PETRA ISLAND, LAKE MAHOPAC, NEW YORK. 1950.
Perspective. 14¾"x35⅞". Pencil and blue pencil (on water only) on tracing paper mounted to board. Signed at lower left in red square: *FLlW/Jan 15/50.* (F 5018.01)

Both the design and the drawing are among the most personal and completely resolved of Wright's later projects. The heavy stone masses gradually thin out, toward the water at the right, and are terminated by an excep-

tionally bold cantilever—itself terminated by a triangular projection which gives to the entire terrace the shape and direction of an arrow about to spring from a stone bow. The drawing, as in so much of Wright's best work, is modest, quiet, and thoughtful.

211. PROJECT: JOSEPH H. BREWER HOUSE, EAST FISHKILL, NEW YORK. 1953.
Perspective. 22⅝"x31⅜". Pencil and colored pencils on tracing paper mounted to board. Signed in red square at bottom right: *FLlW/1953.* (F 5309.02)

The cantilevered terraces of this design recall features of the Chahroudi house (210).

212. LOWELL WALTER HOUSE, QUASQUETON, IOWA. 1945.
Perspective. 22⅛"x35⅞". Pencil and colored pencils on tracing paper. Signed in red square at bottom left: *OK— FLlW/Nov 30/45.* (F 4505.01)

The drawing is unexceptional, but the main room of the house, with its glass walls and clerestory window, represents perhaps the most extensive use of glass in Wright's residential work.

213. HAROLD C. PRICE HOUSE, PHOENIX, ARIZONA. 1955.
Perspective. 19⅝"x50⅝". Pencil and colored pencils on tracing paper mounted to board. Signed at bottom left: *FLlW/54.*

214. PROJECT: HUNTINGTON HARTFORD PLAY RESORT, HOLLYWOOD HILLS, CALIFORNIA. 1947.
Elevation. 21¾"x20". Pencil and colored pencils on tracing paper. (F 4721.14)

This project for a private club or resort was worked out on a scale comparable to that of the 1921 Doheny Ranch (67, 68). Unlike that design, however, it is dominated by a single unique structure: a triangular stone mass from which concrete bowls are cantilevered. These elements contain various guest rooms, lounges, and other facilities, and in one case a swimming pool. (The following perspective drawings show them in detail.) Projects of this sort, in Wright's later work, sometimes have the sensationalism of the *tour de force,* more interesting for their structural gymnastics than for any apparent logic. And yet, the drama of these concrete discs looming over the hills has a mystery, and a grandeur, that makes one wonder if the design is unconvincing because it is not big enough: perhaps the structural and plastic theme deserved a larger and more serious program.

215. PROJECT: HUNTINGTON HARTFORD PLAY RESORT, HOLLY-WOOD HILLS, CALIFORNIA. 1947.
Perspective. 37⅞"x45¾". Brown ink, pencil and colored pencils on tracing paper mounted to board. Signed at bottom left in red square: *FLlW/Feb 24/47*. (F 4721.21)

216. PROJECT: HUNTINGTON HARTFORD PLAY RESORT, HOLLY-WOOD HILLS, CALFORNIA. 1947.
Perspective. 36"x52⅝". Brown ink, pencil and colored pencils on tracing paper mounted to board. Signed at center left in red square: *FLlW/Feb 24/47*. (F 4721.26)

217. PROJECT: HUNTINGTON HARTFORD PLAY RESORT, HOLLY-WOOD HILLS, CALIFORNIA. 1947.
Aerial perspective. 33¾"x58". Brown ink, pencil and colored pencils on tracing paper mounted to board. Signed at upper left in red square: *FLlW/Feb 24/47*. (F 4721.15)

218. PROJECT: COTTAGE GROUP CENTER, HUNTINGTON HART-FORD PLAY RESORT, HOLLYWOOD HILLS, CALIFORNIA. 1947.
Perspective. 18¾"x36". Brown ink and colored pencils on tracing paper mounted to board. Signed at bottom right in red square: *FLlW/Jan 30*. (F 4721.19).

Among the buildings projected for this resort estate were semi-detached cottages grouped around a club house; the entrance to this section is shown here. The drawing also includes a distant view of the "play" center, with its cantilevered terraces and pool, on a hilltop at the left.

219. PROJECT: COTTAGE GROUP CENTER, HUNTINGTON HART-FORD PLAY RESORT, HOLLYWOOD HILLS, CALIFORNIA. 1947.
Perspective. 20½"x62½". Brown ink, pencil and colored pencils on tracing paper mounted to board. Signed at lower right in red square: *FLlW/Jan 30/48*. (F 4721.16)

220. PROJECT: HUNTINGTON HARTFORD HOUSE, HOLLYWOOD HILLS, CALIFORNIA. 1947.
Perspective. 21⅞"x36⅛". Pencil on tracing paper. (F 4724.06)

The Hartford estate was also to have included a house for the owner. Its design is a variation of the Jester project (163), the chief difference being the addition of a glass dome to the round living room. The drawing shown here is a preparatory sketch for a more elaborate color rendering.

221. PROJECT: ARNOLD FRIEDMAN HOUSE, "THE FIR TREE," PECOS, NEW MEXICO. 1945.
Aerial perspective. 26¾"x36". Pencil and colored pencils on tracing paper. Signed in square at bottom left: *FLlW/*.

The sketchy style of this drawing, considering that it was intended as a formal "presentation," is particularly interesting. The background panel of landscape is unusually small and the details are vague; the fir trees in the foreground, and the shadows they cast, are more convincing. Architecturally the design is a variation of the Lake Tahoe projects, with the addition of a patio to afford shelter from the spacious landscape. In this detail the plan anticipates another project for a similar but more spectacular site (223).

222. PROJECT: BURTON TREMAINE OBSERVATORY, METEOR CRA-TER, METEOR, ARIZONA. 1948.
Perspective. 26⅞"x34½". Pencil and colored pencils on tracing paper mounted to board. Signed at bottom right in red square: *FLlW/May 17/48*. (F 4822.01)

223. PROJECT: BURTON TREMAINE OBSERVATORY, METEOR CRA-TER, METEOR, ARIZONA. 1948.
Aerial perspective. 20¾"x36". Brown ink, pencil and colored pencils on tracing paper mounted to board. Signed at bottom right in red square: *FLlW/May 17/48*. (F 4822.02)

The building was intended as an observatory, with a restaurant and parking space, overlooking a privately owned meteor crater almost one mile wide and 600 feet deep. As in the Friedman house project (221) a high stone mass is backed up by a completely enclosed patio; but here the low roofs and a leaning tower of stone are unified in a coherent abstract composition.

224. PROJECT: NICHOLAS P. DAPHNE FUNERAL CHAPELS, SAN FRANCISCO, CALIFORNIA. 1948.
Aerial perspective. 32"x36¼". Pencil, brown pencil and brown ink on tracing paper. Signed in square at bottom right: *FLlW/*.

225. PROJECT: Y.W.C.A., RACINE, WISCONSIN. 1949.
Perspective. 25½"x41". Brown ink, pencil and colored pencils on tracing paper. Signed at lower right in red square: *FLlW/Aug 1/49*. (F 4920.02)

The glass roof shelters a swimming pool on the top floor.

226. PROJECT: SELF SERVICE GARAGE, PITTSBURGH, PENNSYL-VANIA. 1947.
Perspective. Ink on tracing paper.

The original drawings for this and the following plate are no longer available: the plates were made from negatives previously taken directly from the originals. The project is included here not only because the drawings, in ink line and dots, are exceptionally handsome, but because it is among the most important of Wright's several variations on the spiral, beginning with the 1925 project for Gordon Strong (106-13) and culminating with the Guggenheim Museum (190-202). Here the spiral is again used as an automobile road. Supporting piers are omitted and the road is largely carried by cables from a central concrete mast. The sloping walls of vertical elements produce a more convincing composition than do the straight walls of comparable parts of the Guggenheim Museum.

227. PROJECT: SELF SERVICE GARAGE, PITTSBURGH, PENNSYL-VANIA. 1947.
Perspective. Ink on tracing paper.

228. PROJECT: COMMUNITY CENTER, POINT PARK, PITTSBURGH, PENNSYLVANIA. 1947.
Aerial perspective. 33⅛"x74⅝". Brown ink, pencil and colored pencils on tracing paper mounted to board. (F 4821.03).

The project was to have combined theaters, restaurants, a planetarium, an aquarium, etc., in domed spaces surrounded and enclosed by a great spiral road carried on leaning piers. At the top and along the road are gardens and fountains. A subsidiary ramp (at the right in this drawing) provides a more rapid (and steeper) ascent. Parking facilities around and under the "building" are designated for each of the attractions inside. Although such details as the tower (at center left) hark back to stylish irrelevancies of the 'thirties, they should not be allowed to obscure the significance of this brilliant project. As in the study for a garage (226) Wright has again used an automobile road to make architecture: but the architecture here is no longer on the scale of the individual building; it is instead a community, and we may begin to see the real implications of a principle Wright first noted in 1921 (67).

229. PROJECT: COMMUNITY CENTER, POINT PARK, PITTSBURGH, PENNSYLVANIA. 1947.
Aerial perspective. 31¾"x36¾". Pencil and brown ink on tracing paper mounted to board. (F 4821.04)

230. PROJECT: TWIN SUSPENSION BRIDGES AND COMMUNITY CENTER, POINT PARK, PITTSBURGH, PENNSYLVANIA. 1947.
Perspective. 29½"x44¼". Brown ink, colored pencils and gold paint on tracing paper mounted to board. (F 4821.02)

A second project for the same Pittsburgh site, this design substitutes decorative fancies for rational engineering, and represents an aspect of Wright's work that has made it difficult for younger architects to evaluate his more original achievements. That Wright could design a beautiful bridge, within the limitations of rational structure, is amply demonstrated by the two following projects.

231. PROJECT: CONCRETE BRIDGE, SAN FRANCISCO, CALIFORNIA. 1949.
Perspective. 13½"x35¾". Pencil on tracing paper. (F 4921.01)

Here is an extraordinarily sensitive drawing of a beautiful bridge. Long, and low on the water, the roads divide and rise to allow for passing boats. The supporting piers may be studied in plate 232 in a related project.

232. PROJECT: CONCRETE "BUTTERFLY" BRIDGE, WISCONSIN RIVER NEAR SPRING GREEN, WISCONSIN. 1947.
Perspective. 23¼"x37". Pencil and colored pencils on tracing paper mounted to board. Signed at bottom left: *FLlW Sept 5/47*. (F 4723.02)

233. PROJECT: AYN RAND HOUSE, HOLLYWOOD, CALIFORNIA. 1947.
Perspective. 24¼"x36¼". Brown ink, pencil and colored pencils on tracing paper. (F 4717.01)

This "cottage" for the novelist Ayn Rand recalls the 1929 project for Elizabeth Noble (125).

234. JOHN A. GILLEN HOUSE, DALLAS, TEXAS. 1950.
Aerial perspective. 17"x36". Brown ink, pencil and colored pencils on tracing paper. Signed at upper left in red square: *FLlW/Dec 29/50*. (F 5034.01)

235. PROJECT: MASIERI MEMORIAL, VENICE, ITALY. 1953.
Perspective. 26⅛"x17". Brown ink, pencil and colored pencils on tracing paper mounted to board. Signed at lower left in red square: *FLlW/Jan 20/53*. Noted on back: *final drawing by FLlW*. (F 5306.01)

The building would have contained a library for architecture students and some dwelling facilities. The project, in such a setting, greatly appealed to Wright.

236. PROJECT: "RHODODENDRON" CHAPEL, BEAR RUN, PENNSYLVANIA. 1953.
Perspective. 18⅛"x33⅛". Pencil and green pencil (on roof slab) on tracing paper. (F 5308.01)

The exuberant trees in this sketch are a superb example of Wright's "handwriting."

237. BETH SHOLOM SYNAGOGUE, ELKINS PARK, PHILADELPHIA, PENNSYLVANIA. 1959.
Perspective. 18"x29". Pencil and colored pencils on tracing paper. Noted at bottom right: *Scheme 1 American Synagogue for Beth Sholom Rabbi Cohen*
May be increased up to 10,000 seats or Diminished to 500. Various forms by Modification of planes—infinite FLlW/. (F 5420.01)

With this executed building Wright finally achieved an approximation of the glass pyramid (or tent) first proposed for the Steel Cathedral of 1926 (114).

238. PROJECT: TRINITY CHAPEL, NORMAN, OKLAHOMA. 1958.
Perspective. 35⅝"x49". Pencil and colored pencils on tracing paper mounted to board. Signed at bottom left in red square: *FLlW/58*. Noted at bottom center: *To Nature The Sectless Chapel*. (F 5810.01)

239. PILGRIM CONGREGATIONAL CHURCH, REDDING, CALIFORNIA. 1958.
Perspective. 22⅛"x35⅛". Brown ink, pencil and colored pencils on tracing paper mounted to board. Signed at bottom left in red square: *FLlW/Sept 1/58*. Noted: *LOCAL BOULDERS RED-WOOD THROUGHOUT. Pole & Boulder Gothic. FLlW/*. (F 5818.01)

240. GREEK ORTHODOX CHURCH, WAUWATOSA, MILWAUKEE, WISCONSIN. 1956-61.
Elevation and sketch plan. 29¾"x36¼". Pencil and blue and orange pencils on tracing paper. (F 5611.01)

This is Wright's initial study for the project. The building was completed in 1961.

241. PROJECT: MANHATTAN SPORTS PAVILION, NEW YORK CITY, N. Y. 1959.
Aerial perspective. 26"x57½". Brown ink, pencil and colored pencils on tracing paper. Signed at bottom left in red square: *FLlW/Aug 27/59* (F 5616.01)

Note pencil corrections on massing of towers. Notes on seating capacity and other arrangements are legible at bottom right of plate.

242. KALITA HUMPHREYS THEATER, DALLAS, TEXAS. 1955.
Perspective. 36"x53⅜". Pencil on tracing paper. Signed at bottom right in square: *FLlW/*. (F 5514.01)

243. KALITA HUMPHREYS THEATER, DALLAS, TEXAS. 1955.
Perspective. 36⅝"x42⅛". Pencil on tracing paper. (F 5514.02).

This and the preceding drawing may be compared with the 1932 sketches for a new theater (134-6); the Dallas drawings are indeed subtitled *THE NEW THEATER* and are a development of that project not only in the handling of the stage and auditorium but in the exterior expression of the various elements.

244. S. C. JOHNSON AND SON, INC. RESEARCH LABORATORY TOWER, RACINE, WISCONSIN. 1947.
Perspective. 31¼"x36". Brown ink, pencil and sepia pencil on tracing paper. (F 3601.01)

Of the two towers Wright built, this one is perhaps the more beautiful and is also, unexpectedly, without precedent in his earlier projects for similar buildings. The chief innovation in terms of Wright's characteristic approach to the problem is the use of a simple, unbroken mass, with rounded corners, rather than pointed projections and intersections. Structurally, however, the design exemplifies his preference for piers rather than columns: a central concrete core containing utilities and stairs supports floors alternately square and round in plan. Duplex laboratory suites are thus formed, and they are enclosed by walls of translucent glass tubing. As shown in the drawing, the floors were to have been made larger toward the top of the tower, but this detail was not incorporated in the executed design.

245. S. C. JOHNSON AND SON, INC. ADMINISTRATION BUILD-ING, RACINE, WISCONSIN. 1936.
Perspective. 21½"x38½" (one of two drawings on same sheet as plate 172). Brown ink on tracing paper. (F 3601.02)

The administration building as shown here was begun in 1936; the laboratory tower (244, 246) was added in 1947.

246. S. C. JOHNSON AND SON, INC. RESEARCH LABORATORY TOWER, RACINE, WISCONSIN. 1947.
Perspective. 36"x54". Brown ink on tracing paper. (F 3601.02)

247. PROJECT: POINT VIEW APARTMENT TOWER, PITTSBURGH, PENNSYLVANIA. 1953.
Perspective. 34¾"x36⅛". Brown ink, pencil and colored pencils on tracing paper. Signed at lower right in red square: *FLlW/Apr 11/53*. (F 5310.01)

248. PROJECT: POINT VIEW APARTMENT TOWER, PITTSBURGH, PENNSYLVANIA. 1953.
Perspective. 36¼"x30¼". Pencil and colored pencils on tracing paper. Signed at lower right in red square: *FLlW/June/53*. (F 5310.02)

The design may be compared with the Elizabeth Noble and Ayn Rand projects. The alternative study (247), for a fifteen story tower, makes use of three different treatments for the balconies and also employs awning-like canopies over some of the windows.

249. H. C. PRICE COMPANY TOWER, BARTLESVILLE, OKLAHOMA. 1952-56.
Perspective. 28½"x34½". Pencil on tracing paper. Signed at lower right in red square: *FLlW/Sept 30/52*. (F 5215.01)

250. H. C. PRICE COMPANY TOWER, BARTLESVILLE, OKLAHOMA. 1952-56.
Perspective. 47⅞"x33⅞". Brown ink and colored pencils on tracing paper mounted to board. (F 5215.03)

By persuading the client to include duplex suites in one section of this tower, Wright was able to double the scale with cantilevered balconies, on alternate floors, inter-weaving with the other floors in a detail reminiscent of the 1929 St. Mark's apartment towers. Here, however, the heavy vertical and horizontal fins which shade the glass conceal, rather than emphasize, the boldness of the underlying concrete structural core.

251. PROJECT: ROGERS LACY HOTEL, DALLAS, TEXAS. 1946.
Perspective. 53⅛"x24¼". Black and brown ink and colored pencils on tracing paper mounted to board. Signed at bottom right in red square: *FLlW/Aug 1/47*. (F 4606.01)

252. PROJECT: SKYSCRAPER, "THE GOLDEN BEACON," CHICAGO, ILLINOIS. 1956.
Perspective. 42⅜"x23". Pencil, colored pencil and gold paint on tracing paper. Signed at lower left in red square: *FLlW/Feb/56*. (F 5615.01)

253. PROJECT: MILE-HIGH SKYSCRAPER, "THE ILLINOIS," CHICAGO, ILLINOIS. 1956.
Elevation with pyramid of Cheops, Eiffel Tower, Empire State Building. 96"x12". Pencil and colored pencils on tracing paper mounted to plywood panel.

254. PROJECT: MILE-HIGH SKYSCRAPER, "THE ILLINOIS," CHICAGO, ILLINOIS. 1956.
Perspective. 96"x24". Pencil, colored pencils, and gold paint on tracing paper mounted to plywood panel.

The last of Wright's variations on the skyscraper theme is this startling project for a 528 story tower, one mile high. Its floors are cantilevered 16 feet from a concrete core like a tripod. Sunk deep into the ground, this structural core and the floors it carries diminish in width as they rise; the manner in which this is done for each segment of the form produces a strangely faceted, blade-like tower, and may be compared with a simpler version for the Rogers Lacy Hotel (251). The entire surface was to have been of glass and gold-colored metal. Elevators, like vertical railroad cars, would discharge passengers simultaneously on five floors. Architecturally the most interesting aspect of this design is not the tower itself but the terraces around it.

255. PROJECT: LENKURT ELECTRIC COMPANY BUILDING, LONG ISLAND, NEW YORK. 1955.
Aerial perspective. 36¼"x63½". Pencil and colored pencils on tracing paper. Signed at lower left: *FLlW/Oct/55*. (F 5520.03)

The pyramidal glass skylights are a variation on the 1936 design for the Johnson's Wax Company administration building (172).

256. PROJECT: DANIEL WIELAND MOTOR HOTEL, HAGERSTOWN, MARYLAND. 1955.
Aerial perspective. 17¼"x36". Pencil, brown ink and colored pencils on tracing paper. (F 5521.02)

257. PROJECT: WEDDING CHAPEL, CLAREMONT HOTEL, BERKELEY, CALIFORNIA. 1957.
Perspective. 25½"x35¼". Pencil and colored pencils on tracing paper. Signed at bottom left in red square: *FLlW/57*. (F 5743.01)

258. PROJECT: BRAMLETT MOTOR HOTEL. 1956.
Perspective. 28⅞"x36". Pencil and colored pencils on tracing paper. Signed at bottom left in red square: *FLlW/56.*

259. PROJECT: ARIZONA STATE CAPITAL, "OASIS," PHOENIX, ARIZONA. 1957.
Aerial perspective. 36"x46". Pencil and colored pencils on tracing paper. Signed at bottom left in red square: *FLlW/Feb 27/57*. (F 5732.01)

Spires, on two flanking elements at the rear of the glass shell, have been painted out.

260. PROJECT: PLAN FOR GREATER BAGHDAD, IRAQ. 1957.
Aerial perspective; Isle of Edena and University from height of 1000 feet. 35⅝"x52½". Blue ink, pencil and colored pencils on tracing paper mounted to board. Signed at bottom left in red square: *FLlW/June 20*. (F 5733.08)

An opera house complex is on the island; the university is in the giant circular enclosure at the upper left. This vast project is a further development of the road as architecture: here, and in one more design (263) Wright enlarges scale to such an extent that architecture becomes geography. The Isle of Edena is given a new contour to accommodate the opera house and its gardens (261), and the university (262) is a giant park walled by a spiral road in three tiers; individual buildings are hooked onto the inner side of the road. The use of the road-terrace as a base for a large building is also seen in the Mile High Illinois skyscraper (253).

261. PROJECT: OPERA HOUSE AND GARDENS, BAGHDAD, IRAQ. 1957.
Aerial perspective. 32⅞"x54½". Brown ink, pencil and colored pencils, gold paint, on tracing paper mounted to board. Signed at bottom left in red square: *FLlW/57*. (F 5733.07)

262. PROJECT: UNIVERSITY COMPLEX AND GARDENS, BAGHDAD, IRAQ. 1957.
Aerial perspective. 30½"x65½". Pencil, colored pencils and gold paint on tracing paper mounted to board. Signed at bottom left in red square: *FLlW/ June 20/57*. (F 5733.06)

263. MARIN COUNTY CIVIC CENTER, CALIFORNIA. 1959.
Aerial perspective. 36"x74½". Brown ink, pencil and colored pencils on tracing paper. Signed at center left in red square: *FLlW/Dec 24/57*. (F 5736.01)

Perhaps the most surprising aspect of this design, in the context of Wright's work, is that the two long buildings emerge directly from the hillsides; Wright long ago enjoined architects to "take care of the terminals" and in his own work terminal masses are often among the most interesting features. Here, however, the theme of the building as a bridge is also made to suggest a tunnel. Construction is underway.

264. PROJECT: "BROADACRE CITY." 1934-58.
Aerial perspective. 25"x34⅞". Pencil on tracing paper. (F 3402.12)

In his late years Wright returned to his 1934 design for Broadacre City, a plan interesting chiefly for its recapitulation of nineteenth century agrarian visions. This and the next three drawings fill out the scheme by populating it with buildings designed during the course of a very long career: at least one example of every building type Wright designed is to be found among fields, hills, and highways. Wright also developed two delightful ideas for transportation: helicopters shaped like spinning tops or like thick-stemmed parasols (or dandelions?), and a "road machine" with enormous filigreed wheels, resembling in its over-all shape certain farm tractors.

265. PROJECT: "BROADACRE CITY." 1934-58.
Aerial perspective. 27"x36". Pencil on tracing paper. (F 3402.11)

A transparent and unfinished profile of the Mile High Illinois skyscraper is seen at the left; variations of the Price Tower are at the center and foreground; some of the buildings across the river recall the terracing of the Doheny Ranch project.

266. PROJECT: "BROADACRE CITY." 1934-58.
Aerial perspective. 35¼"x42¼". Brown ink and brown pencil on tracing paper. Signed at bottom right in square: *FLlW/*. (F 3402.03)

The folded blades of the helicopter are given an ornamental serrated edge.

267. PROJECT: "BROADACRE CITY." 1934-58.
Aerial perspective. 36"x42½". Pencil on tracing paper. (F 3402.14)

Buildings shown in this drawing include, left to right: Pittsburgh Community Center (first and second projects), Huntington Hartford Country Club (on hill in background), Beth Sholom Synagogue, Marin County Government Center (at bottom of hill), Rogers Lacy hotel tower, Sugar Loaf Mountain Automobile Objective and Planetarium, Self-service Garage, Golden Beacon skyscraper; in background on hills, various projects resembling Doheny Ranch and California block houses; at left, foreground, Butterfly Bridge and four "atomic" powered barges.

That Wright could well have furnished the countryside with some of the most dazzling buildings ever seen is hardly to be doubted, and these drawings are a touching summation of the work of a lifetime.

268. W. S. SPAULDING PRINT GALLERY, BOSTON, MASSACHUSETTS. 1919.
Cross-section and perspective. 16"x21¾". Black ink and pencil shading on opaque cream paper. (F 1902.03)

Wright's own interest in painting was largely directed towards oriental art, and in this design for a print gallery he devised an arrangement suitable to the small size and intimate character of Japanese prints. The sloping wall of this 1919 project reappears in the Guggenheim Museum, where it is made to accommodate paintings of very different character and much greater size.

269. W. S. SPAULDING PRINT GALLERY, BOSTON, MASSACHUSETTS. 1919.
Longitudinal section. 20"x32½". Brown ink and brown pencil on opaque cream paper. Titled at bottom right:

GALLERY AND SECTION FOR EXHIBITION OF JAPANESE COLOR PRINTS. COLLECTION OF W.S.SPAULDING/BOSTON MASSACHUSETTS. (F 1902.04)

270. PROJECT: GORDON STRONG AUTOMOBILE OBJECTIVE, SUGAR LOAF MOUNTAIN, MARYLAND. 1925.
Sections. 18"x41⅞". Pencil on tracing paper. (F 2505.34)

271. PROJECT: GORDON STRONG AUTOMOBILE OBJECTIVE, SUGAR LOAF MOUNTAIN, MARYLAND. 1925.
Section. 26"x36". Pencil and colored pencils on tracing paper. (F 2505.57)

272. PROJECT: GORDON STRONG AUTOMOBILE OBJECTIVE, SUGAR LOAF MOUNTAIN, MARYLAND. 1925.
Plan at top level. 24⅝"x31¾". Pencil on tracing paper. Signed at lower right in red square: *FLlW/23.* (F 2505.40)

273. PROJECT: STEEL CATHEDRAL, NEW YORK CITY, N. Y. 1926.
Plan. 23⅝"x31½". Pencil and colored pencils on tracing paper mounted to board. Main section of plan cut out and pasted over plan of steps. (F 2602.02)

274. CHARLES ENNIS HOUSE, LOS ANGELES, CALIFORNIA. 1924.
Perspective studies of concrete blocks. 24¼"x41". Pencil on tracing paper. Inscribed at bottom: *STUDY FOR CONCRETE BLOCKS OF ENNIS HOUSE LOS A. 1914* [sic]. (F 2401.04)

275. EDGAR J. KAUFMANN HOUSE, "FALLINGWATER," BEAR RUN, PENNSYLVANIA. 1936.
Plan. 27½"x31¼". Pencil and colored pencils on tracing paper.
This is the architect's first study; the final design follows the general arrangement quite closely.

276. SOLOMON R. GUGGENHEIM MUSEUM, NEW YORK CITY, N. Y. 1943.
Plan, scheme "C". 20⅛"x24¼". Brown ink and colored pencils on opaque cream-colored paper. (F 4305.03)

277. PROJECT: COMMUNITY CENTER, POINT PARK, PITTSBURGH, PENNSYLVANIA. 1947.
Section. 30"x81⅜". Brown ink, pencil, gold and colored pencils on tracing paper mounted to board. (F 4821.05)

278.　HUNTINGTON HARTFORD PLAY RESORT, HOLLYWOOD HILLS, CALIFORNIA. 1947.
Section. 23¾"x38⅝". Brown ink, gold and colored pencils on tracing paper mounted to board. Signed at bottom left in red square: *FLlW/Feb 24/47.* (F 4721.18)

In Wright's work the cross section is frequently the most informative drawing, in that his conception of structure and space is fully revealed.

279.　METAL CHAIR, LARKIN BUILDING, BUFFALO, NEW YORK. 1904.
Perspective. 8"x9⅝". Pencil on tracing paper mounted to board. Inscribed: *Study for metal chair Larkin Bldg.* (F 0403.05)

280.　CHAIR. 1905.
Perspective. 14½"x10½". Pencil on tracing paper. Noted: *same stuff as cushions* [refers to fabric-covered side panels]. (F 0509.01)

281.　PROJECT: TEA CUP AND SAUCER. 1929-30.
Plan and section. 10½"x14". Ink on opaque paper. (F 3003.07)

This design for a cup and saucer is from a group of nine designs for tableware. Like Wright's lighting fixtures, furniture, and ornaments, the cup is intended to be part of the architecture, however unwieldy it may be. The plan of the hexagonal cup, with its projecting handle, should be compared with the preliminary plan for the Guggenheim Museum (276).

282.　TABLE, CHAIRS AND LAMP, MIDWAY GARDENS, CHICAGO, ILLINOIS. 1914.
Perspective.　14¾"x13⅛".　Pencil　on　tracing　paper mounted to board. (F 1401.06)

283.　LIGHT FIXTURE, MIDWAY GARDENS, CHICAGO, ILLINOIS. 1914.
Elevation. 15⅝"x7⅝". Pencil on tracing paper mounted to board. (F 1401.01)

284.　EXTERIOR LIGHT. 1915.
Perspective. 12¼"x3⅞". Black ink, gold, red and white paint on opaque cream-colored paper. (F 1502.02)

285.　HANGING LIGHT FIXTURE, IMPERIAL HOTEL, TOKYO, JAPAN. 1915.
Perspective 15¾"x7¾". Pencil, white chalk and light green pencil on opaque tan paper. Signed at upper left in red and white embossed square pasted to drawing: *FLlW/.* Noted at upper right: *hanging fixture—1904* [sic]. (F 1509.01)

These designs for light fixtures resemble earlier designs for the 1904 Unity Temple, which may account for their having subsequently been re-dated by Wright.

286.　CARVED POLYCHROME DECORATION, IMPERIAL HOTEL, TOKYO, JAPAN. 1915.
Elevation. 22¼"x35¾". Pencil, colored pencils, and gold paint on tracing paper mounted to board. (F 1509.05)

287.　PERFORATED SCREEN, DINING ROOM CEILING, OAK PARK STUDIO, CHICAGO, ILLINOIS. 1889.
8¾"x5⅝". Black ink on opaque cream-colored paper. (F 8901.02)

288.　SCREEN. c. 1909.
Elevation. 17¼"x13⅜". Pencil on tracing paper.

289.　DINING ROOM WINDOW, ROBIE HOUSE, CHICAGO, ILLINOIS. 1909.
14"x12", one of two drawings on sheet. Pencil on tracing paper. (F 0908.04)

290.　GATE, ROBIE HOUSE, CHICAGO, ILLINOIS. 1909.
Elevation.　18⅝"x21⅛".　Pencil　on　tracing　paper. (F 0908.01)

291.　WINDOW, COONLEY HOUSE, RIVERSIDE, ILLINOIS. 1908.
14"x14", one of three drawings on sheet. Pencil on tracing paper. Signed at lower left: *FLlW/1909.* (F 0803.01)

292.　GLASS CEILING LIGHT, OAK PARK STUDIO, CHICAGO, ILLINOIS. 1889.
6"x12¼". Pencil and white, green and orange crayon pencils on cream-colored paper. (F 8901.05)

293.　DESIGN FOR RELIEF SCULPTURE, NAKOMA COUNTRY CLUB, MADISON, WISCONSIN. 1924.
17⅛"x23¼". Pencil on opaque cream-colored paper. Signed in red square at bottom left: *FLlW/1926.* (F 2404.03)

294.　DESIGN FOR SCULPTURE, MIDWAY GARDENS, CHICAGO, ILLINOIS. 1914.
15¼"x18⅛". Pencil on tracing paper. (F 1401.12)

295. STUDY FOR MURAL "CITY BY THE SEA," MIDWAY GARDENS, CHICAGO, ILLINOIS. 1914.
18⅞"x20¾". Crayon and water color wash, predominantly brown and green, on white tracing paper mounted to board. Signed at lower right: *FLlW/1913*. Inscribed at bottom: *This type of abstract* [. . .] *occupied me from 1893 to the present time, FLlW/*. (F 1401.08)

296. THEATER CURTAIN, HILLSIDE THEATER, TALIESIN, SPRING GREEN, WISCONSIN. 1933.
30¾"x58½". Colored pencils and gold and white paint on tracing paper. (F 3301.01)

297. PROJECT: AUTOMOBILE WITH CANTILEVERED TOP. 1920.
Plan and elevations. 15"x26⅝". Pencil and colored pencil on tracing paper. Signed at center left: *FLlW/1920*.

298. PROJECT: MOTOR CAR (ROAD MACHINE). 1958.
Plan, side and front elevations. 36⅛"x42¾". Pencil on tracing paper. Signed at lower left in red square: *FLlW/59*. (F 3402.07)

299. PROJECT: ROAD MACHINE. 1958.
Section and plan. 11"x8½". Reproduced actual size. Blue pencil on white note paper. (F 3402.09)

300. PROJECT: HELICOPTER. 1958.
Elevation. 11"x8½". Reproduced actual size. Blue pencil on note paper.

This and the preceding drawing are Wright's first notations of an idea.

301. (TALIESIN ASSOCIATED ARCHITECTS) "KEY PROJECT," APARTMENT AND HOTEL TOWERS AND GARDENS, ELLIS ISLAND, NEW YORK HARBOR. 1959-61.
Aerial perspective. 33⅞"x51⅛". Pencil and colored pencils, ink, and gold paint on tracing paper. Courtesy Jerry Damon and Elwood Doudt.

Since the death of Frank Lloyd Wright on April 9, 1959, his former students and colleagues have been continuing the practice of architecture according to the principles he established. This project for Ellis Island is based on sketches Wright made just before his death. A semicircular terrace is superimposed on the existing rectangular island; apartment and hotel towers rise at the back, and domed theaters and shops are set into the terrace-park.

302. (TALIESIN ASSOCIATED ARCHITECTS) PROJECT: HOTEL, KONA COAST OF HAWAII. 1959.
Aerial perspective. 33¼"x41¾". Pencil, colored pencils, ink, and gold paint on tracing paper. (F 5923.01)

This project for a hotel in Hawaii, designed by William Wesley Peters, uses a dome similar in design to others developed by Wright, but in a manner not previously seen in Wright's work.

303. (TALIESIN ASSOCIATED ARCHITECTS) PROJECT: SEASIDE DEVELOPMENT, "COURT OF THE SEVEN SEAS", FOR P. J. PASETTA. SANTA CRUZ, CALIFORNIA. 1962. WILLIAM WESLEY PETERS, ARCHITECT.
Aerial Perspective. 36"x72". Brown ink, colored pencils, opaque and transparent water colors and gold paint on grey paper.

The several buildings of this project will occupy a forty acre site. A hotel, motor hotel, convention halls and restaurants provide facilities for visitors to the series of buildings designed for shops, international exhibitions, concerts and festivals.

INDEX TO THE PLATES